THE PHILADELPHIA
MUSEUM OF ART PRESENTS

The Fine Art of Cooking

Merry Christmas – 1998
to
Rose

The Women's Committee
Philadelphia Museum of Art
Philadelphia, Pennsylvania

Cover: Camille Pissarro (French, 1830-1903), *The Fair at Dieppe on a Sunny Afternoon*, 1901, oil on canvas, 29 x 36½". Bequest of Lisa Norris Elkins

Back Cover: East Facade of the Philadelphia Museum of Art.

Published by
The Women's Committee
Philadelphia Museum of Art
P.O. Box 7646
Philadelphia, PA 19101-7646

Designed by
James A. Scott
Publications, Philadelphia Museum of Art

Printed by
Wimmer Brothers
Memphis   Dallas

For over a century, The Women's Committee of the Philadelphia Museum of Art has worked to encourage, support, and increase public interest in the Museum and its collection. All the works of art depicted in this cookbook are part of that collection, which is open to the public at 26th Street and Benjamin Franklin Parkway in Philadelphia. The proceeds from the sale of this cookbook will benefit the Philadelphia Museum of Art.

Library of Congress Catalog Card Number 89-50956

ISBN 0-87633-078-2

Order Form on last page

Arjuna and His Charioteer Lord Kṛṣṇa Confront Karṇa, India, Garhwal school, c. 1820, opaque water-color on paper, 60 x 120". Purchased: Edith H. Bell Fund

The ancient Indian epic the *Mahābhārata* tells of the great civil war between the Pāṇḍavas and the Kauravas. Both factions sought the help of Lord Kṛṣṇa, the eighth incarnation of the Hindu god Viṣṇu. This large work shows the carnage of the battle in which the Pāṇḍava prince Arjuna, with Kṛṣṇa as his charioteer (left), confronts Karṇa, commander of the Kauravas. The mosaic-like arrangement of the figures on the opaque ground creates a complex scene of variety and richness.

3

$\mathcal{F}$OREWORD

The fine arts and the culinary arts have much in common and have many relationships. The art of a society and the cuisine of a society both derive from and reflect the civilization. Both have long art historical traditions, studied and taken seriously, and both nourish. Presumably, both developed at the same times, and we can speculate that the fires which illuminated caves for the first cave paintings cooked the painters' meat, if not yet their *truffe-sous-cendre*. The ancient tombs contain not only the dead but also their art, their food, and vessels with which to cook and store it, sometimes among the finest remaining art of a civilization. Religion, the fine arts, and the culinary arts combine. Major religious events are noted by feasting and fasting; religious structures incorporate the fine arts for devotional and celebratory purposes; the fine arts depict religious topics and depict culinary topics; culinary artists seek the beautiful or challenging; all seek to inspire.

This splendid cookbook, with its recipes provided by people involved in the Museum's life and its illustrations from the Museum's collections, brings together the fine and culinary arts, in a decorative and nourishing way. Members of the Women's Committee have lovingly and carefully selected and tested a collection of outstanding recipes. They have combined these with reproductions of outstanding works from the Museum's collection of art.

One purpose of the book is to present recipes and menus. These have been chosen with an eye for use in the home because, traditionally, much of Philadelphians' eating and entertaining has been done in the home.

A second purpose is to present a tasting of the Museum's extraordinary, varied collections, with the hope that the reader will come to the Museum to feast further.

A third purpose is to raise money for the Museum from the proceeds of the sale of the book. Since its founding in 1875, the Women's Committee has been one of the most generous and consistent sources of support for the Museum, and this project is an aid of that laudable objective. It is interesting to note that the first cookbook in America to raise funds for a charitable cause was published in Philadelphia in 1864: *A Poetical Cook Book* by Maria J. Moss to benefit the "Great Central Fair for the United States Sanitary Commission". This is the Women's Committee's first cookbook, which is almost surprising since they have devised so many other ingenious and successful ways to help the Museum over the years.

The Museum is grateful indeed to the Women's Committee and to that Committee's Cookbook Steering Committee, chaired by Elizabeth T. Harbison and Beverly M. McLarnon. They gathered together a formidable number of recipes. They examined them, cooked them, tasted the results, edited and compiled them with menus for our use and delectation. To the question as to whether any recipe can be followed, the editors can answer with a confident affirmative from personal experience. We are also grateful to the many members of the Museum family who submitted recipes to the Committee in spite of the fear that the submission would be found wanting, impossible or inedible.

In classical Greek mythology, not one of the nine Muses was assigned to inspiring either the fine arts or the culinary arts: There was a muse for astronomy, but not for gastronomy. This delightful volume does much to correct Zeus's oversight.

Anne d'Harnoncourt
The George D. Widener
Director

Robert Montgomery Scott
President

$\mathcal{T}$ABLE OF CONTENTS

• *On Menu title pages, bullets (•) indicate that recipes follow.*

• *Suggestions for presentation and accompaniments follow many recipes. Where capitalized, the recipes may be found in The Fine Art of Cooking.*

Henri Matisse (French, 1869–1954), *Lady in Blue*, 1937, oil on canvas, 36 1/2 x 29". Gift of Mrs. John Wintersteen

Matisse, well known for his exuberant use of color, has painted the *Lady in Blue* in a reflective pose that is reinforced by the image with head in hand behind her. The color areas are bold and flat, without any suggestion of modeling in light and shade, and the sofa arms have been reduced to two flat S shapes. The asymmetrical contours that encircle the figure are repeated throughout the painting.

Cocktail Buffet for Twenty-Four

- Ice-Breaker Punch
- Rosemary Walnuts • Cheese Wafers
- Curry Dip in Savoy Cabbage Bowl with Assorted Crudités
- Paté en Gelée with Apple Slices and Wedges of Pumpernickel
- Pickled Shrimp or Cold Steamed Shrimp with Cocktail Sauce and • Lamaze Sauce
- Hot Herbed Cheese Canapés
- Chinese Dumplings with Soy Dipping Sauce
- Mushroom Pinwheels • Sun-Dried Tomato Tartlets
- Thinly Sliced Brisket Bourguignon on Miniature EggTwist and Sourdough Rolls
  Dill Pickle Fingers
- Lemon Rum Soufflé • Almond Raspberry Torte
  Bowl of Fresh Strawberries with • Grand Marnier Sauce

Champagne   Fumé Blanc   Valpolicello   Zinfandel
German Sweet Wine
Coffee

Marc Chagall (French, born Russia, 1887-1985), *Half-Past Three (The Poet)*, 1911, oil on canvas, 77 1/8 x 57". The Louise and Walter Arensberg Collection

Chagall's neighbor, the poet Mazin, is the subject of this painting in which the artist joins a cubist perspective with his own narrative fantasy and brilliant sense of color. *Half-Past Three* ignores the laws of gravity and perspective: A bottle hovers precariously at the poet's elbow, the flowers appear to spill over into space, and the poet's head, which is upside down, floats above his shoulders.

Ice-Breaker Punch

This festive punch will get any party off to a lively start.

- **Serves 8**
  Ice block
  2 cups light rum
  ½ cup amber rum
  ¼ cup dark rum
  ⅔ cup fresh lime juice
  ½ cup rock candy syrup
  ½ cup brandy
  2 tablespoons applejack

- Prepare ice block by freezing water in a one-quart mold overnight.

- Mix rums with lime juice, syrup, brandy and apple-jack and chill.

- Prior to serving, unmold ice block into a punch bowl. Pour rum mixture over ice and ladle into cups or old-fashioned glasses.

Note: Syrup is available in "Cocktail" sections of supermarkets or liquor stores.

Variation: Fill a large pitcher with ice cubes and pour in rum mixture. Stir well and pour into stemmed glasses.

Rosemary Walnuts

Double or triple the recipe for gift-giving.

- **Makes 1 pound**
  4 tablespoons (2 ounces) unsalted butter
  1 tablespoon dried rosemary
  ¾ tablespoon salt
  ½ teaspoon cayenne pepper
  1 pound walnut halves

- Preheat oven to 325 degrees.

- Spread walnuts on cookie sheet.

- Mix dry ingredients together and sprinkle on nuts.

- Melt butter and pour over nuts. Toss well until all nuts are coated.

- Roast for 15 minutes until well-toasted. Store in air-tight containers.

Variation: Other herbs like dill, garlic or thyme could be substituted.

Cheese Wafers

Light, crunchy and cheesy "crackers" are spicy crowd-pleasers.

- **Makes 50 to 60**
  1 pound extra sharp Cheddar cheese, grated
  1 cup (8 ounces) unsalted butter, softened
  2 cups all-purpose flour
  1 teaspoon cayenne pepper

1 tablespoon salt

4 cups rice crisps cereal

- Preheat oven to 325 degrees.

- Blend cheese and butter in electric mixer.

- Add flour, cayenne pepper and salt and mix until well blended.

- Using your hands, gently fold in rice crisps.

- Roll batter into teaspoon-size balls. Place on ungreased cookie sheet and flatten with fork.

- Bake for 25 minutes. Serve warm or at room-temperature.

Paté en Gelée

Smooth, rich and unusually seasoned

- Serves 12

Aspic

2 tablespoons port wine or brandy

1 envelope plus 1 teaspoon of unflavored gelatin

2 cups premium canned beef bouillon

Paté

1 pound chicken livers, trimmed and cleaned

Milk to soak livers

½ cup (4 ounces) unsalted butter

1 pound Spanish onions, sliced

8-ounce package cream cheese, softened

2 tablespoons port wine or brandy

1 tablespoon fresh lemon juice

2 teaspoons Dijon-style mustard

2 teaspoons salt

Dash hot pepper sauce

Freshly ground pepper

Freshly grated nutmeg

- To make aspic, soften gelatin in ½ cup warm beef bouillon. Transfer to mixing bowl and stir in remaining bouillon, substituting 2 tablespoons of port or brandy for 2 tablespoons of bouillon.

- Spoon half the aspic mixture into a greased 6-cup mold and chill until set, about ½ hour.

- To make paté, put livers into a small bowl and pour milk over to cover, soaking the livers for ½ hour.

- While livers soak, melt butter in large frying pan and sauté sliced onions over low heat until very soft, about ½ hour.

- Drain livers, discarding milk and add to frying pan, cooking over medium heat, stirring constantly until livers are no longer pink, about 10 minutes.

- Combine contents of frying pan with cream cheese, additional port, lemon juice, mustard, salt, pepper sauce, pepper and nutmeg into a food processor and blend until smooth.

- Pour into mold and chill for ½ hour and then add last layer of aspic. Chill at least 4 hours, but flavor improves if made 1 day in advance.

- To unmold, loosen paté with knife or spatula. Place hot, damp dish towel around the upside-down mold and shake both mold and platter to loosen.

Curry Dip

For a spicier dip, increase the curry and hot sauce.

- Makes 2½ cups
  1 pint Homemade Food-Processor Mayonnaise
  1½ teaspoons mild curry powder
  3 teaspoons catsup
  3 teaspoons honey
  3 teaspoons grated onion
  1¼ teaspoons lemon juice
  7 to 9 drops hot pepper sauce

- Mix all ingredients together and refrigerate overnight. Serve with raw vegetables such as broccoli, cauliflower, cucumber spears, celery, carrots, pepper strips and snow pea pods.

Pickled Shrimp

A refreshing change from plain boiled shrimp

- Serves 8
  2½ pounds cooked, peeled and deveined shrimp
  2 large onions, sliced into thin rings
  1½ cups salad oil
  1 cup white vinegar
  2½ teaspoons celery seeds
  1 tablespoon capers and juice
  4 to 5 bay leaves
  Several dashes hot pepper sauce
- Layer shrimp and onion rings in a crystal bowl.

- Combine remaining ingredients and pour over shrimp and onions.

- Cover and refrigerate at least 24 hours or up to 2 days.

- To serve, drain marinade from shrimp and serve with toothpicks.

Lamaze Sauce

A Philadelphia classic with seafood

- Makes 1 quart
  1 pint mayonnaise, chilled
  ½ cup India relish, chilled
  1 pint chili sauce, chilled
  1 tablespoon prepared mustard
  1 teaspoon chopped chives
  1 hard boiled egg, chopped
  Salt
  Pepper
  Steak sauce (garnish)

- Mix ingredients in order listed above in a chilled bowl. Add salt and pepper to taste. Refrigerate.

- Excellent served with chilled, cooked shrimp, lobster, crabmeat, cold fish salads and cold eggs. Add a dash of steak sauce over dressing when serving.

Hot Herbed Cheese Canapés

Also makes a splendid dip for crudités

- Serves 20
  8 ounces extra sharp cheese, grated
  ¾ cup Homemade Food-Processor Mayonnaise
  ⅓ cup minced onion
  ½ teaspoon salt
  ¼ teaspoon freshly ground pepper
  1 teaspoon dried sage
  1 teaspoon dried tarragon
  1 teaspoon dried thyme
  1 teaspoon dried chervil
  Toasted pita, Melba rounds or pumpernickel party bread

- Mix all ingredients together, blending thoroughly.

- Spread a teaspoonful on bread or cracker and broil until bubbly. Serve at once. (Prepared spread can be refrigerated for 1 to 2 weeks.)

Chinese Dumplings

Chinese Dumplings have become popular appetizers.

- Serves 15
  ½ pound ground veal or chicken
  ¼ pound shrimp, chopped
  3 to 4 water chestnuts, finely chopped
  2 tablespoons scallions, finely chopped
  1 tablespoon soy sauce
  1½ tablespoons cornstarch
  ½ teaspoon sesame oil
  ⅛ teaspoon dried or 1 slice fresh ginger, finely chopped
  Won-ton wrappers (available in most supermarkets or oriental markets)
  1 grated carrot
  Soy sauce

- Mix together meat, shrimp, water chestnuts and scallions.

- Add soy sauce, cornstarch, sesame oil and ginger. Add a touch of water if necessary to make mixture the consistency of meatballs.

- Fill won-ton wrapper with 1 teaspoon of mixture and press sides up to enclose. (The top will be open.)

- Dip in grated carrot.

- Steam in a wok for 20 to 25 minutes and serve warm with extra soy sauce in a small bowl for dipping.

Mushroom Pinwheels

- **Serves 40 to 50**

  1 large onion, chopped

  ¾ pound mushrooms

  2 teaspoons unsalted butter

  ¼ teaspoon salt

  ⅛ teaspoon pepper

  ¾ pound cream cheese, softened

  ½ teaspoon minced garlic

  1 loaf soft white bread, thinly sliced, crusts removed

- Chop onions and mushrooms separately in food processor.

- Brown onions in butter. Add mushrooms and brown. Pour off excess juice.

- Pour onion mixture into food processor and add salt, pepper, cream cheese and garlic and blend until smooth. Cool.

- Roll each slice of bread with a rolling pin until flat. Spread each piece of bread with cream cheese-mushroom mixture.

- Roll up each slice and wrap in waxed paper. May be prepared to this point and frozen. Defrost before continuing with recipe.

- To serve, unwrap, cut into 4 or 5 pieces, dip in melted butter. Place on cookie sheet and broil until lightly browned, 5 to 6 minutes.

Variation: Spread mixture on sliced bread, cut into 4 squares or triangles, and bake in preheated 450 degree oven for 10 minutes or until browned.

Sun-Dried Tomato Tartlets

The filling and shells can be made separately and frozen.

- **Makes 24**

  Filling

  ¼ cup vegetable oil

  2½ cups onions, thinly sliced

  1 garlic clove, minced

  12 oil-cured, sun-dried tomatoes, drained and thinly sliced

  12 oil-cured olives, pitted and finely chopped

  ¼ cup pine nuts, lightly toasted

  ½ teaspoon dried oregano

  ½ teaspoon dried basil

  Pinch of cayenne pepper

  Freshly ground pepper

  Freshly grated Parmesan cheese

- Preheat oven to 300 degrees.

- In a heavy large frying pan, heat oil over medium-low heat. Sauté onion and garlic slowly for 40 minutes. Add tomatoes, olives, pine nuts, oregano, basil, cayenne and 5 grinds of pepper. Mix thoroughly and set aside. May be made ahead to this point and refrigerated. Bring to room temperature before baking.

  Tartlet shells

  2 cups all-purpose flour

  1 teaspoon salt

  ¼ cup cold water

  ⅔ cup vegetable shortening

- Preheat oven to 400 degrees.

- In a large bowl, sift flour with salt. Take ⅓ cup of this mixture and place in a small bowl. Stir water into it to form a paste.

- Cut the shortening into the dry flour mixture until it is the size of small peas. Stir the flour paste into the dough. Work with your hands until dough can be gathered into a ball. It may be frozen and defrosted in refrigerator before rolling.

- Roll on floured board. Using a 2-inch fluted cookie cutter, cut out rounds. Transfer to tartlet tins measuring 1-inch across base. Pierce bottoms with fork. Bake for 12 to 15 minutes. This also makes a fine pie crust, baked filled or unfilled.

- Fill each tartlet shell with 1 teaspoon filling. Sprinkle with Parmesan cheese.

- Bake for 5 minutes. Serve at once.

Variation: Cut out 4-inch rounds of pastry and transfer to 3-inch tart pans and bake as above. This makes 12 tarts that are elegant luncheon entrées.

Brisket Bourguignon

- **Serves 8**
  3½ to 4 pound first-cut brisket of beef
  2 to 3 tablespoons cooking oil
  3 to 4 large onions, thinly sliced
  2 cloves of garlic, finely chopped
  1½ cups catsup
  1½ cups dry red wine
  2 bay leaves
  Freshly ground pepper
  1 teaspoon paprika

- Heat a large heavy casserole or Dutch oven until very hot. Quickly sear beef on both sides and set aside. Reduce heat and when cooled to medium, add oil, onions and garlic.

- Return beef to pan. Mix wine with catsup and pour over meat. Add bay leaves, pepper and paprika. Bring to boil; turn down to simmer. Cover and cook slowly, turning 2 or 3 times, for 2½ hours. Remove bay leaves. May be prepared 1 to 2 days in advance and heated slowly at serving time.

- To serve hot: Slice meat thinly on the diagonal, spoon on some of the gravy and pass remainder. Accompany with cooked noodles, and sweet and sour red cabbage or sauerkraut.

- To serve cold: Slice meat thinly on the diagonal and bring to room temperature. Accompany with horse-radish, pickles, coarse-grained mustard and rye bread. Meat can also be sliced and heated in gravy for hot sandwiches.

Lemon Rum Soufflé

- **Serves 8 to 10**
  10 eggs, separated
  2 cups granulated sugar
  1 cup fresh lemon juice
  Grated peel of 4 lemons
  ¼ teaspoon salt
  2 envelopes unflavored gelatin
  ½ cup light rum (or water)
  3 cups heavy cream
  Candied lemon peel (garnish)
  Candied violets (garnish)
  ½ cup ground almonds (optional)

- Fold a length of waxed paper in half lengthwise, brush inside edge with vegetable oil, and tie it around top of 8-cup soufflé dish so it extends 4 to 5 inches above it. Set aside.

- In a large bowl, beat egg yolks until fluffy. Add 1 cup of sugar, beating until thick and mixture falls from beater like a ribbon. Add lemon juice, lemon peel and salt. Pour mixture into a heavy, non-aluminum pan and stir over low heat, constantly, until thick enough to coat back of spoon. Do not let mixture curdle.

- Dissolve gelatin in rum and stir into lemon mixture. Stir until dissolved. Remove mixture from heat and cool, stirring occasionally.

- Beat egg whites until foamy. Add remaining sugar slowly, and continue beating until mixture is marshmallow-like and smooth to the touch.

- Beat 1 cup heavy cream until thick but not stiff. With a large rubber spatula, carefully fold egg-white mixture into egg-lemon mixture. Then fold in whipped cream. Make sure everything is thoroughly incorporated. Pour into prepared dish and refrigerate at least 3 hours or overnight.

- Before serving, whip remaining cup of cream and pipe decoratively on top of soufflé. Garnish with candied lemon peel and/or candied violets. Carefully remove paper collar and press almonds around the sides of soufflé extending above dish. Chill until serving time.

Variation: For a frozen daiquiri soufflé, substitute ½ cup lime juice for half of lemon juice and zest of 2 limes for 2 of lemons.

Almond Raspberry Torte

The layers of this cake freeze well and assembling the torte takes only minutes before presentation.

- **Serves 10 to 12**
  6 eggs, separated
  2 cups granulated sugar
  ½ cup sifted all-purpose flour
  ¼ teaspoon baking powder
  2 cups blanched, ground almonds
  1 12-ounce jar raspberry jam
  1 pint heavy cream
  ½ cup crushed almonds
  Fresh raspberries (optional)

- Preheat oven to 325 degrees.

- In a large bowl, beat egg yolks slightly. Add sugar, flour, baking powder and almonds, mixing well.

- Whisk egg whites until stiff but not dry. Fold carefully and completely into batter.

- Line 2 9-inch cake pans with greased brown paper or baking parchment. Pour batter into prepared pans and bake 40 minutes.

- Cool and wrap in several layers of plastic wrap, if freezing. To serve, spread cake layers with raspberry jam. Whip cream and swirl over tops and sides of cake. Refrigerate at least 1 hour. Garnish with crushed almonds and raspberries.

Grand Marnier Sauce

A richly rewarding topping for fresh fruit or pound cake

- **8 servings**
  5 egg yolks
  ½ cup granulated sugar
  ½ cup orange liqueur
  1 cup heavy cream, whipped until thick

- In a non-aluminum saucepan, mix together the egg yolks and sugar until smooth. Whisk over low heat until mixture thickens and coats a spoon. Chill immediately over ice water. Stir in orange liqueur.

- Carefully fold in whipped cream until fully incorporated. Refrigerate until serving time.

*C*hristening Brunch for Twelve

- Celebration Champagne Punch
- Salmon Caviar Cheesecake
  Rye and Pumpernickel Melba Toasts
- Fabulous French Toasted Croissants
  Baked Ham with • Cranberry Apricot Sauce
  Mixed Green Salad dressed with Raspberry Vinegar and
  Walnut Oil, Garnished with Toasted Walnuts
  Seasonal Fresh Fruit Compote
- Sugar and Spice Muffins or • Glazed Blueberry Muffins
  Coffee

Nicolas Poussin (French, 1594–1665), *The Birth of Venus*, 1635–36, oil on canvas, 38 1/4 x 42 1/2". Purchased for the George W. Elkins Collection

Poussin's interpretation of this classical scene shows Venus as she is born from the sea, delivered by her entourage of putti, dolphins, and handmaidens. Trumpet-blaring Tritons herald the pageant as the god Neptune arrives at the left of this intricately woven composition. Commissioned by Cardinal Richelieu and later acquired by Catherine the Great of Russia, this painting was purchased by the Museum from the Soviet government in 1932.

Celebration Champagne Punch

- **Serves 15 to 20**
  Ice block (see below)
  2 cups assorted fresh berries
  1 bottle (750ml) dry white wine
  1 8-ounce can frozen lemonade concentrate, thawed but chilled
  1 46-ounce can unsweetened pineapple juice
  2 bottles (750ml each) dry champagne or sparkling wine

- To prepare ice block, fill mold with water and fresh fruit such as strawberries, cherries or other colorful fruit. Freeze overnight.

- At serving time, mix white wine, lemonade concentrate and pineapple juice in large punch bowl. Unmold ice block into bowl and pour in champagne. Ladle into champagne glasses or punch cups.

Salmon-Caviar Cheesecake

Serve in thin slices accompanied by pumpernickel, rye rounds or bagel chips.

- **Serves 10 to 12 as appetizer**
  20 to 24 as hors d'oeuvre
  1 medium onion, peeled and minced
  2 tablespoons (1 ounce) unsalted butter
  1 teaspoon fresh dill, chopped
  4 8-ounce packages cream cheese, softened
  5 eggs, beaten until frothy
  2 tablespoons red wine vinegar
  2 tablespoons whiskey
  5 ounces lox or smoked Nova Scotia salmon, chopped
  2 3-ounce jars of red caviar
  Sour cream (garnish)
  4 ounces fresh salmon caviar (garnish)

- Preheat oven to 325 degrees.

- In frying pan, sauté onion in butter. Add dill and set aside.

- In food processor, beat cream cheese. Add eggs, red wine vinegar, whiskey and onion-dill mixture and blend thoroughly.

- Remove from processor to mixing bowl. Carefully fold in lox and caviar.

- Turn into greased 8-inch springform pan. Bake 2 to 2½ hours until set. Cool and refrigerate.

- To serve, remove from pan and set on large platter. Decorate top with dollops of sour cream and fresh salmon caviar.

Fabulous French Toasted Croissants

- **Serves 6**
  5 eggs
  ⅔ cup heavy cream
  ⅓ cup orange-flavored liqueur
  2 tablespoons granulated sugar
  Finely grated zest of 1 orange
  2 teaspoons ground cinnamon
  6 stale, plain croissants, cut lengthwise in half
  6 tablespoons (3 ounces) unsalted butter
  Confectioners sugar
  Fresh berries for garnish (optional)

- In a small bowl, beat eggs and cream together.

- Add orange-flavored liqueur, sugar, orange zest and cinnamon and whisk until well blended. Pour into shallow bowl.

- Dip each croissant half into the egg mixture until well coated.

- In a large frying pan, melt 2 tablespoons of butter over medium heat. Add croissants to fit and fry until golden on both sides.

- Repeat with remaining croissants, adding butter to the frying pan as needed.

- Sift confectioners sugar over the croissants and serve with berries.

  Variation: Eliminate orange-flavored liqueur and serve with maple syrup.

Sugar and Spice Muffins

- **Makes 10 to 12**
  1 large egg, beaten lightly
  ½ cup milk
  ⅓ cup (3 ounces) unsalted butter, melted
  1½ cups plus 2 tablespoons all-purpose flour
  ¾ cup granulated sugar
  2 teaspoons baking powder
  ¼ teaspoon salt
  ¼ teaspoon freshly grated nutmeg

  Topping
  ⅓ cup (3 ounces) unsalted butter, melted
  1 teaspoon ground cinnamon
  ½ cup granulated sugar

- Preheat oven to 400 degrees.

- Beat egg, add milk and butter.

- Combine flour, sugar, baking powder, salt and nutmeg. Blend with egg mixture.

- Fill 12 greased muffin tins evenly and bake for 15 to 18 minutes. While baking, mix sugar and cinnamon together in a small bowl.

- Remove muffins from pan and dip tops first in melted butter and then in cinnamon-sugar mixture. Serve warm.

Glazed Blueberry Muffins

A glazed topping over berry-rich muffins

- **Makes 16**
  ½ **cup (4 ounces) unsalted butter**
  1 **cup granulated sugar**
  2 **eggs**
  2 **cups all-purpose flour**
  ½ **teaspoon salt**
  2 **teaspoons baking powder**
  ½ **cup milk**
  2¼ **cups fresh blueberries, washed and drained**
  1 **teaspoon vanilla extract**
  2 **teaspoons granulated sugar for topping**

- Preheat oven to 375 degrees. Grease muffin tins and top surface of pans as well.

- Cream butter and sugar, add eggs 1 at a time and mix until blended.

- Sift dry ingredients and add alternately to butter mixture with the milk.

- Mash ½ cup of berries with a fork and stir into batter. Add rest of whole berries and fold into batter. Add vanilla extract.

- Pile batter high into muffin tins. Sprinkle with sugar. Bake for 30 minutes.

Cranberry Apricot Sauce

The perfect sweet-tart touch for ham or poultry

- **Makes 1 quart**
  1 **pound fresh cranberries**
  2 **cups granulated sugar**
  2 **cups water**
  ¾ **cup apricot preserves**
  ¼ **cup brandy**

- Cook cranberries with sugar and water until they all pop (about 15 minutes).

- Remove from heat. Add apricot preserves and brandy. Refrigerate until ready to serve.

$\int$pring Luncheon for Twelve

- **Asparagus Tea Sandwiches**
- **Shrimp Mousse accompanied by Crispy Crackers**
  Muscadet
- **Annual Meeting Chicken Salad**
- **Confetti Rice Salad in Boston Lettuce Cups**
  Warm Cloverleaf Rolls
  Beaujolais
- **Fresh Strawberry Pie**
- **Kiwi Sorbet**
  Iced Tea

Designed by John LaFarge (American, 1835–1910), assembled by Thomas Wright (American, born England, 1855–1910), and painted by Juliette Hanson (American, active 1882–1902); *Spring*; 1901–2; opalescent glass, painted glass, and lead; approx. 100 x 69 1/2". Gift of Charles S. Payson

LaFarge, a premier nineteenth-century interior designer and mural painter, is credited with reviving the art of stained glass in the United States. His experiments with opalescent glass allowed for infinite modulations of color, which produced an overall harmony as well as the sense of depth needed to depict rounded forms. In *Spring* a winged female figure floats before a naturalistic backdrop of apple blossoms and peonies.

Asparagus Tea Sandwiches

Fresh-as-springtime roll-up canapés

- Makes 24
  1 pound large asparagus spears (12 stalks)
  1 loaf unsliced white sandwich bread
  1 pint Homemade Food-Processor Mayonnaise
  Paprika
  Watercress (garnish)

- Scrape asparagus spears and plunge into a pot of boiling water. Bring back to boil and cook for 5 minutes or until al dente. Immediately plunge into cold water. Drain. Cool. Cut in half horizontally, reserving tips.

- Trim crust off bread. Slice into 24 slices and spread each slice with mayonnaise.

- Roll bread around each half spear as neatly as possible. Trim ends evenly.

- Place on a platter, seam-side down, and sprinkle with paprika. Cover loosely with plastic wrap and a damp towel. Refrigerate overnight.

- To serve, arrange on platter. Decorate with watercress and asparagus tips.

Variations:

- Use a curry or dill-flavored mayonnaise for extra punch.

- Substitute fresh goat cheese for mayonnaise for an interesting contrast of flavors and textures.

Shrimp Mousse

Serve as a flavorful spread, or slice thinly and serve on greens for a first course.

- Serves 8
  ¾ cup Homemade Food-Processor Mayonnaise
  3 ounces cream cheese, softened
  5 ounces canned tomato soup, undiluted
  1 envelope unflavored gelatin
  ½ teaspoon salt (optional)
  1 pound cooked shrimp, chopped
  ½ cup celery, finely chopped
  ¼ cup onion, finely chopped
  Thinly sliced pumpernickel and rye breads
  8 whole shrimp, cooked, shelled and chilled

- Beat mayonnaise with cream cheese.

- Heat soup and add gelatin. Stir until dissolved. Cool.

- Add soup mixture to mayonnaise mixture and fold in chopped shrimp, celery, and onion. Mix thoroughly.

- Pour into oiled 2-cup mold and refrigerate overnight.

- To serve, unmold and decorate with whole shrimp. Serve with pumpernickel and rye breads.

Annual Meeting Chicken Salad

The vinaigrette dressing is a welcome change from the traditional mayonnaise.

- Serves 24
  1½ heads shredded lettuce
  12 green onions, thinly sliced
  9 celery stalks, thinly sliced
  9 large whole chicken breasts, poached
  3 3-ounce cans of chow mein noodles
  6 tablespoons of toasted sesame seeds

  Dressing
  1½ cups olive oil
  ¼ cup red wine vinegar
  3 crushed cloves of garlic
  3 teaspoons salt
  1½ teaspoons pepper

- Cut poached chicken into strips and toss with lettuce, onions, and celery.

- Combine and whisk dressing ingredients.

- Just before serving, toss salad with dressing. Add chow mein noodles and sprinkle with sesame seeds.

Confetti Rice Salad

The tangy dressing enhances the contrasting flavors and textures in this favorite.

- Serves 12
  1 cup cooked rice
  5 tablespoons olive oil
  1 tablespoon wine vinegar
  1 teaspoon salt
  2 tablespoons fresh lemon juice
  ½ tablespoon dry mustard
  1 cup cooked peas (may use frozen peas)
  1 cup cooked diced carrots
  1 cup diced celery
  1 cup diced cucumber
  ¼ cup sliced scallions

- Add the oil, vinegar, lemon juice, salt and mustard to the hot rice.

- Stir in the vegetables and season to taste.

- To serve as a mold, pack into a lightly oiled 2-quart ring mold. Unmold and serve at room temperature.

Variation: The mixture can also be stuffed into hollowed-out tomatoes.

Strawberry Pie

A luscious layer of cream cheese comes between the crust and the berries.

• **Serves 6 to 8**

Crust
1 cup all-purpose flour
½ teaspoon salt
6 tablespoons vegetable shortening
4 tablespoons ice water

• Preheat oven to 425 degrees.

• Mix ingredients for crust until crumbly. Form in a ball, wrap in plastic wrap and refrigerate until ready to roll out.

• Roll out and line a 9-inch pie or tart tin with pastry. Using a fork, prick holes over crust. Bake for 20 minutes or until golden brown. Cool.

Filling
1 quart strawberries
1 cup granulated sugar
3 tablespoons flour
3 ounces cream cheese
½ pint heavy cream

• Sort and hull berries. Save 6 to 8 of the prettiest berries for later. Mash remainder in saucepan. Add sugar and flour. Blend thoroughly. Stirring constantly, cook slowly until juices thicken. Cool.

• Mix cream cheese with a little cream until consistency of whipped cream. Spread in baked and cooled pie shell.

• Cut some of the whole berries in half and place closely together on cream base. Pour cooled strawberry mixture over berries. Chill until serving time.

• To serve, whip remainder of cream until stiff and swirl over pie. Decorate with remaining whole berries.

Variation: Line baked pie shell with 3 ounces melted bittersweet chocolate.

Kiwi Sorbet

Garnish this pale green sorbet with strawberries for a brilliant summer-time dessert.

• **Serves 6 to 8**
1½ cups freshly squeezed orange juice
3 ripe kiwis, room temperature, peeled and chopped
1 banana, peeled and chopped
8 ripe whole strawberries with hulls (garnish)

• Mix orange juice, kiwis and bananas in processor, about 45 to 60 seconds. Do not over-process or kiwi seeds will become bitter.

• Transfer to ice cream maker and freeze according to instructions. For best texture, do not freeze for more than 2 hours before serving or it will become too hard to scoop.

• Serve in stemmed glasses and garnish each with a strawberry.

Variation: Substitute 2 ripe mangoes, peeled and chopped, for the kiwis. Proceed as above and garnish with berries or slivers of candied orange peel.

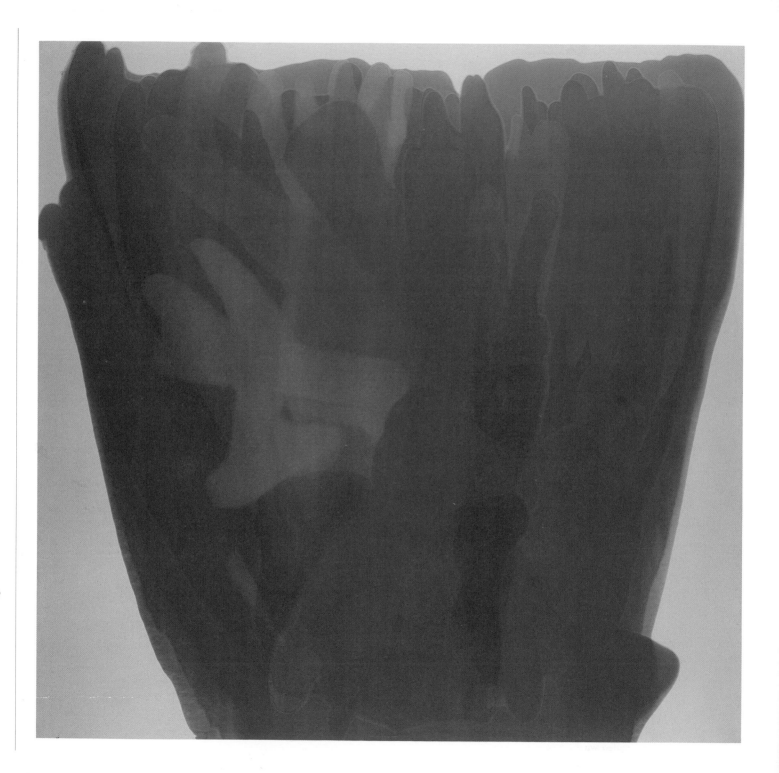

*M*idsummer's Eve Dinner for Eight

- **Buddha's Eye**
  Assorted Nuts
- **Frosted Beet Soup**
- **Deviled Salmon Steaks**
  Pinot Grigio
- **Farmer's Market Sauté**
  Parslied New Potatoes
- **Patrician Peach Pie**
  Hungarian Tokay
  Iced Coffee or Iced Tea

Morris Louis (American, 1912–1962), *Beth*, 1960, acrylic resin paint on canvas, 105 x 106 1/4". Purchased: Adele Haas Turner and Beatrice Pastorius Turner Memorial Fund

The art of Morris Louis is essentially about color, and during the last eight years of his life he explored the technique of staining canvas with thinned acrylic pigments to achieve a figuration at once both emotive and abstract. *Beth* (a transliteration of the second letter of the Hebrew alphabet) belongs to a series of paintings called "Florals" in which hovering masses of intense and discrete hues are chromatically interfused and then unified by a veiled wash of color.

Buddha's Eye

A cool cocktail at the end of a sweltering day

- Serves 4 to 6

  5 parts gin

  5 parts Rose's Lime Juice

  2 parts green crème de menthe

  Ice

  Fresh mint leaves

  Fresh lime slices

- Combine gin, lime juice and crème de menthe and blend well.

- At serving time, pour into an ice-filled pitcher, stir well, and serve in small, long-stemmed glasses. Garnish with a sprig of mint and/or a slice of lime.

Frosted Beet Soup

Its delicate pink color is refreshing.

- Serves 6 to 8

  2 cups beef broth

  1 medium cucumber, peeled, seeded and chopped

  1 large onion, sliced

  ½ bay leaf

  ¼ teaspoon dried basil

  1 16-ounce can sliced beets

1 tablespoon fresh lemon juice

½ teaspoon granulated sugar

½ cup yogurt

Garlic powder to taste

Sliced scallion tops or chopped chives (garnish)

- In 3-quart saucepan, put beef broth, cucumber, onion, bay leaf and basil. Bring to boil, lower heat and cook for 10 minutes until vegetables are tender.

- Remove bay leaf, add beets and beet liquid, lemon juice and garlic powder. Purée in small batches in blender.

- Before serving, stir in ½ cup yogurt and garnish with scallions or chives. Serve in mugs for an interesting appetizer.

Deviled Salmon Steaks

A lively fish dish — try it on the grill for an out-door treat.

- Serves 4

  4 fresh salmon steaks, 1-inch thick

  6 ounces Dijon-style mustard

  6 tablespoons (3 ounces) unsalted butter

  Juice of 1 lemon

- One-half hour before serving, pat salmon steaks dry. Coat each side generously with mustard and place on wire rack to set mustard and dry.

- To cook, melt 4 tablespoons butter in frying pan over medium-high heat. Stir in lemon juice. Add salmon steaks and cook 6 minutes on each side.

- To serve, place each steak on a plate. Melt remaining butter in pan and pour over salmon. Wedges of lemon are a colorful garnish. Serve with steamed buttered peas and parsley-sprinkled boiled new potatoes for this up-to-date version of a New England classic dinner.

Farmer's Market Sauté

A bounty of summer's fresh vegetables

- **Serves 4**
  1 small red bell pepper
  1 small eggplant
  1 small zucchini
  3½ tablespoons olive oil
  2 tablespoons chopped fresh basil
  2 tablespoons chopped fresh parsley
  1 tablespoon unsalted butter
  Salt and pepper to taste

- Cut vegetables into 2½ to 3½ -inch strips.

- Heat 1½ tablespoons oil in a large sauté pan or wok until oil is hot, but not smoking. Sauté eggplant until lightly browned and soft (about 3 minutes). Remove and set aside.

- In same pan, heat 1 tablespoon oil and sauté peppers about 1 minute. Add remaining oil and zucchini and sauté 1 minute.

- Add basil and parsley, salt and pepper. Stir quickly. Add butter and mix lightly until butter melts. Serve at once.

Variation: Yellow peppers can be used; yellow squash can be included. Be certain to cook peppers together and cook squash with the zucchini.

Patrician Peach Pie

Special with a hint of almond — unusual because of the light custard texture

- **Serves 6 to 8**
  5 large, very ripe peaches
  1 9-inch unbaked pie shell
  2 large eggs
  1 cup granulated sugar
  2 tablespoons all-purpose flour
  ½ to 1 teaspoon almond extract (according to taste)

- Preheat oven to 325 degrees.

- Peel peaches by plunging into boiling water for approximately 10 seconds. Slice into pie shell.

- Beat eggs, sugar and flour together until smooth. Add almond extract. Pour over peaches. Bake 1 hour. Serve at room temperature with a scoop of vanilla ice cream and garnish with a few raspberries.

Variation: Ripe nectarines can be substituted for peaches and the pie will be as splendid.

Summer Picnic for Sixteen

- Cold Spicy Carrot Soup   • Cold Cucumber Soup
  Plain and Sesame Breadsticks
- Tangy Baked Chicken for a Crowd
- Caesar Potato Salad
- Summer Seafood Salad in Scooped-out Baguettes
- Crunchy Pea Salad
  California Chardonnay
- Old-Fashioned Ginger Cookies
- Butter Pecan Cookies
- Fudgy Brownies
  Watermelon Wedges
  Lemonade   Iced Tea

Marsden Hartley (American, 1877–1943), *Painting No. 4 (A Black Horse)*, 1915, oil on canvas, 39 1/4 x 31 5/8". The Alfred Stieglitz Collection

Hartley's ability to deal with patterns decoratively was probably aided by his close study of the arts of the American Indian. In this tapestry-like composition, the figurations do not function solely as designs but retain their identity as recognizable objects such as the totem pole, tepee, and reclining horse.

Spicy Carrot Soup

Curry and chili add zest to this smooth, colorful soup.

- **Serves 8 to 10**
- **6 cups chicken stock**
- **1 large clove of garlic, halved**
- **1 medium large onion, quartered**
- **1½ pounds carrots, peeled and sliced**
- **2 medium potatoes, washed and quartered**
- **2 celery stalks, quartered**
- **⅛ teaspoon oregano**
- **1 teaspoon chili powder**
- **1 teaspoon curry powder**
- **Peel of 1 orange, grated**
- **1 cup light cream**
- **Chopped dill or mint (garnish)**
- **Commercial sour cream or yogurt (garnish)**

- Simmer stock, garlic, onion, carrots, potatoes and celery until carrots are tender (20 to 30 minutes).

- Cool and then purée in batches in blender.

- Stir in oregano, chili, curry and orange peel. Add cream to desired consistency.

- Serve hot or cold with chopped dill or mint and a dollop of sour cream or yogurt.

Cold Cucumber Soup

By using yogurt, this soup can be low calorie.

- **Serves 6**
- **2 tablespoons (1 ounce) unsalted butter**
- **½ onion, finely chopped**
- **1 clove of garlic, finely chopped**
- **3 large cucumbers, peeled, seeded and chopped**
- **3 tablespoons all-purpose flour**
- **2 cups chicken broth**
- **1 teaspoon salt**
- **¾ cup commercial sour cream or yogurt**
- **1 tablespoon fresh dill**
- **1 teaspoon grated lemon rind**
- **⅛ teaspoon mace**

- In a heavy frying pan, heat butter and sauté onion, garlic and cucumbers until tender (about 10 minutes).

- Sprinkle with flour, stirring constantly. Gradually stir in the broth. Add salt, if desired, and bring to a boil. Reduce heat and simmer until cucumber is tender.

- Cool and purée in batches in blender.

- Stir in sour cream or yogurt, dill, lemon and mace. Chill for several hours before serving.

Tangy Baked Chicken for a Crowd

The oriental flavor appeals to everyone — can be prepared in advance.

- **Serves 16**

  4 chickens (about 3 pounds each), quartered

  1½ cups soy sauce

  3 tablespoons grated fresh ginger

  3 tablespoons minced garlic

  Salt to taste

  1 bunch scallions, chopped (reserve green tops for garnish)

- Preheat oven to 350 degrees.

- Trim off any excess fat from the chickens. Rinse and pat dry. With a small knife, pierce the pieces of chicken in 2 or 3 of the thickest spots.

- In a large bowl, mix together the soy sauce, ginger, garlic, salt and chopped scallions. Add chicken and toss to coat with the marinade. Let stand at room temperature for 1 hour, turning occasionally, or cover and refrigerate for up to 24 hours.

- Pour off marinade and set aside. Bake chicken, covered, for 30 minutes. Uncover, baste with marinade and continue baking for 30 minutes. May be prepared to this point 24 hours in advance. Either serve at room temperature or reheat. Place on decorative heated serving tray and sprinkle with thinly sliced green scallion rings.

Variation: Marinade is also excellent with duck or pork.

Caesar Potato Salad

An unexpected combination — delicious and simple!

- **Serves 6 to 8**

  8 to 10 medium red potatoes

  5 tablespoons lemon juice

  12 tablespoons olive oil

  3 to 4 large garlic cloves

  1 tablespoon dry mustard

  1 2-ounce can anchovies, undrained

  1 raw egg

  ½ teaspoon Worcestershire sauce

- Boil potatoes until tender, approximately 20 minutes, and then cool.

- Combine all remaining ingredients in the blender.

- Slice the potatoes and mix in the dressing. Top with chopped parsley, chopped chives and freshly ground pepper.

Summer Seafood Salad

Tuna-flavored mayonnaise sets a Mediterranean mood for this mixed seafood salad.

- **Serves 12**
  1½ pounds whole sea scallops, sliced
  ¼ pound bay scallops, whole
  1½ pounds large, unpeeled shrimp
  2 medium carrots, peeled
  2 stalks celery, peeled
  1 medium zucchini, halved and seeded
  1 medium summer squash, halved and seeded
  4 scallions, thinly sliced
  ¼ cup minced parsley
  3 egg yolks, room temperature
  3 ounces fresh lemon juice
  ¾ cup virgin olive oil
  1 7½ -ounce can of oil-packed tuna, undrained
  5 tablespoons heavy cream
  4 anchovies, rinsed and dried
  3 tablespoons capers, rinsed and drained
  12 lemon wedges (garnish)
  Parsley sprigs (garnish)

Court bouillon
  4 cups water
  1 cup dry white wine
  1 carrot, cut into 1-inch pieces
  ½ onion, sliced into rings
  3 sprigs parsley
  1 bay leaf
  1 teaspoon salt
  ½ teaspoon whole peppercorns

- In a large saucepan, bring ingredients for court bouillon to a boil. Reduce heat and simmer for 20 minutes. Strain into another large saucepan. Bring to a boil and add scallops. Cook until scallops turn opaque (2 minutes). Remove scallops with a spoon.

- Return bouillon to a boil and add shrimp. Cook for 3 minutes. Drain and cool. Peel and devein shrimp.

- Cut carrots, celery, zucchini and squash into small cubes.

- To serve, combine diced vegetables with seafood and fold in the mayonnaise. Mix in scallops and mound on a bed of lettuce. Season with salt and pepper to taste and garnish with lemon wedges and parsley.

Mayonnaise
- Mix 3 egg yolks and lemon juice in food processor. With machine running, gradually pour in oil. Add tuna, cream and anchovies. Blend until smooth. Transfer to a bowl and stir in the capers.

Crunchy Pea Salad

A distinctive salad or a delightful vegetable side dish

- **Serves 8 to 10**
  1 package frozen petite peas, defrosted and drained
  ½ cup chopped celery
  ½ cup chopped green onions
  ½ teaspoon salt
  2 tablespoons commercial sour cream
  ¼ cup garden dressing (recipe below)

Additional commercial sour cream

1 cup cashews, coarsely chopped

¼ cup crisp bacon bits

Red leaf lettuce leaves, washed, dried and chilled

- Place peas in a bowl and gently mix in celery, onions, salt, sour cream and dressing. Cover and refrigerate for up to 3 days.

- Remove from refrigerator 30 minutes before serving. Add additional sour cream, if needed, stir in nuts and bacon bits, and turn out on lettuce-lined platter or individual salad plates.

- Garnish with additional nuts, if desired.

Garden Dressing

¾ teaspoon fresh lemon juice

1 cup red wine vinegar

1½ teaspoons salt

1 teaspoon freshly ground pepper

1 teaspoon Worcestershire sauce

1 teaspoon Dijon-style mustard

1 clove of garlic, mashed

1 teaspoon granulated sugar

3 cups corn oil

- In blender, mix juice, vinegar, salt and pepper, Worcestershire sauce, mustard, garlic and sugar. Slowly pour in oil in a steady stream. May be kept for several weeks in refrigerator.

Note: In addition to using on pea salad, this dressing sparks salads of mixed greens, chilled asparagus or blanched and chilled green beans.

Old-Fashioned Ginger Cookies

Perfect for cutting into fanciful shapes and decorating for special occasions

- **About 6 dozen**

⅔ cup vegetable shortening

1 cup granulated sugar

1 egg, lightly beaten

¼ cup light molasses

2 cups sifted all-purpose flour

1 teaspoon salt

1 teaspoon baking soda

1 teaspoon ground cinnamon

½ teaspoon ground ginger

- Preheat oven to 350 degrees.

- In a large bowl, thoroughly cream shortening and sugar. Add egg and molasses and mix well. Add flour, salt, baking soda, cinnamon and ginger. Dough will be soft and sticky. Refrigerate for 1 hour before rolling out.

- On a lightly floured surface, roll dough ⅛-inch thick, dusting rolling pin with flour, if necessary. Cut with floured cutter; arrange on lightly greased cookie sheet. Bake 10 minutes or until brown. Cool on rack. Store in air-tight container or freeze.

Butter Pecan Cookies

Perfect crunchies for ice cream

- **Makes 4 to 5 dozen**
  1 cup (8 ounces) unsalted butter, softened
  ¾ cup light brown sugar, firmly packed
  ¾ cup granulated sugar
  2 eggs
  1 teaspoon vanilla extract
  2¼ cups all-purpose flour
  1 teaspoon baking soda
  ½ teaspoon salt
  1 cup pecans, chopped

- Preheat oven to 375 degrees.

- In a large bowl, cream butter and sugars. Beat in eggs and vanilla.

- Combine flour, baking soda and salt in a separate bowl. Gradually mix into butter mixture until well blended. Fold in pecans.

- Drop from a teaspoon onto ungreased cookie sheet and bake about 10 minutes or until lightly browned.

Fudgy Brownies

Rich, gooey double-chocolate treats

- **About 54 squares**
  1 pound unsalted butter
  8 ounces unsweetened chocolate
  8 eggs, lightly beaten
  4 cups granulated sugar
  2½ cups all-purpose flour
  12 ounces chocolate chips

- Preheat oven to 350 degrees.

- Melt butter and unsweetened chocolate over low heat.

- Mix eggs, sugar and flour. Combine with butter mixture and fold in chips.

- Spread in lightly greased and floured 15-inch x 9-inch x 3-inch pan. Bake 55 minutes. Note: Center will be "soft" when brownies come from oven but will firm up when cool. Cut into squares or bars. Excellent with scoops of vanilla ice cream.

42

Fireworks for Ten

- **Marinated Mushrooms and Artichoke Hearts**
- **Dilled Beans**

  Grilled Spareribs with • **Spicy Bar-B-Q Sauce**

  Grilled Steaks with • **Mustard Sauce**

  Bordeaux   Imported and Domestic Beers

  Grilled Corn-On-The-Cob • **Tangy Horseradish Mold**
- **Tabouli Salad on Romaine Leaves**
- **Rum Macaroon Ice Cream Cake**

  Slices of Summer Melons
- **Macadamia White Chocolate Cookies**

  Iced Coffee

Joseph Mallord William Turner (English, 1775–1851), *The Burning of the Houses of Parliament*, 1834–35, oil on canvas, 36 1/4 x 48 1/2". John H. McFadden Collection

Turner, a witness to the great fire that destroyed the Houses of Parliament in London in 1834, painted the event with a combination of remembered fact and expressive invention. The sky is a furnace, and the towers of Westminster Abbey glow in the background. Boats filled with spectators appear as shadows on the Thames, which is spanned by a stone bridge that fades into the distance.

Marinated Mushrooms and Artichoke Hearts

These will remind you of antipasta in Italy.

• Serves 16 to 20

2 10-ounce packages frozen artichoke hearts, defrosted

2 pounds small mushrooms, cleaned and trimmed

1½ cups water

1 cup cider vinegar

½ cup vegetable oil

1 garlic clove, halved

1½ tablespoons salt

½ teaspoon black peppercorns

½ teaspoon dried thyme

½ teaspoon dried oregano

• Cook artichoke hearts until tender and drain.

• Slice mushrooms in half, if large, and combine with artichoke hearts.

• Combine water with vinegar, oil, garlic and seasonings. Add vegetables and toss lightly.

• Refrigerate, covered, overnight or longer. Bring to room temperature and drain before serving.

Dilled Beans

Crispy as a vegetable or an hors d'oeuvre

• Serves 8

2 pounds fresh whole green beans, blanched

1 cup water

¾ cup white vinegar

½ cup granulated sugar

2 garlic cloves, sliced

1 teaspoon dried tarragon or 2 teaspoons fresh tarragon, finely chopped

1 bay leaf

1 teaspoon salt

1 tablespoon mustard seed

2 tablespoons fresh dill, finely chopped

• In large saucepan, combine water, vinegar and sugar. Add garlic, tarragon, bay leaf, salt and mustard seed. Bring to a boil, stirring constantly. Remove from heat and add dill.

• Pour mixture into a 9 x 13-inch rectangular baking dish. Add cooked beans and coat with liquid mixture.

• Cover dish with wax paper and then with aluminum foil.

• Refrigerate at least 24 hours. Serve chilled or at room temperature.

Spicy Bar-B-Q Sauce

A wonderful all-purpose sauce

- Makes 2 cups

  ¾ cup catsup

  ½ cup olive oil

  ½ cup red wine vinegar

  2 tablespoons garlic vinegar

  1 tablespoon tarragon vinegar

  1 tablespoon Worcestershire sauce

  1 small onion, minced

  2 teaspoons brown sugar

  ¼ teaspoon celery salt

  ¼ teaspoon garlic salt

  ½ teaspoon salt

  ½ teaspoon mustard seed

  ¼ teaspoon celery seed

  ¼ teaspoon ground cloves

  1 teaspoon chili powder

  1 teaspoon oregano

  1 bay leaf

- Place all ingredients in large saucepan and bring to a boil. Reduce heat and simmer sauce for 3 minutes. Store in covered jar. Keeps indefinitely in refrigerator.

Mustard Sauce for Grilled Meat

A splendid accompaniment to grilled filet of beef or broiled sirloin steaks

- Makes 2½ cups

  1 cup heavy cream

  1 cup Dijon-style mustard

  1 cup sherry

  4 egg yolks

  Freshly grated pepper

- In a large heavy saucepan, heat half of the cream to the boiling point, stirring constantly. Reduce heat to low and reduce cream slightly. Remove from heat.

- In a separate bowl, beat the rest of the cream, mustard, sherry, egg yolks and 3 or 4 grinds of pepper.

- Whisk egg yolk mixture into saucepan with heated cream. Return to medium heat stirring constantly. Cook sauce until it starts to simmer and thicken.

- Remove from heat at once or eggs will scramble.

- Sauce can be reheated before serving but do not boil.

Tangy Horseradish Mold

Excellent with beef or grilled meats

• **Serves 8**

1 cup boiling water

1 small package lemon gelatin

4 ounces freshly grated or freshly purchased prepared horseradish

½ cup commercial sour cream

Juice of 1 lemon

2 teaspoons minced fresh onion

1 teaspoon grated lemon rind

Few grinds of freshly ground white pepper

Lettuce leaves, washed, dried and chilled

2 scallions (garnish)

• Dissolve lemon gelatin in boiling water and cool to room temperature.

• Mix horseradish, sour cream, lemon juice, onion, lemon rind and pepper. Stir into gelatin mixture until completely blended. Pour into 2-cup mold and chill about 8 hours or overnight.

• At serving time, line a serving platter with lettuce and turn out mold on the greens. Garnish with shreds of the green tops of scallions.

Tabouli Salad

Bulgur wheat is available at most Middle Eastern grocery stores or in the rice section of supermarkets.

• **Serves 12 to 14**

1½ cups bulgur wheat

1½ cups chopped parsley

1 cup canned chick peas, drained and rinsed

3 tomatoes, peeled, seeded and finely chopped

½ cup scallions, finely chopped

1 cup carrots, cut into 2-inch strips

½ cup fresh mint leaves, finely chopped

½ cup lemon juice

⅔ cup olive oil

1 teaspoon salt

¼ teaspoon freshly ground pepper

Toasted pita bread, cut into quarters

• Soak bulgur in 3 cups boiling water for 1 hour. Drain well and squeeze out excess water.

• Mix bulgur with all other ingredients. Cover and refrigerate overnight.

• Serve on a bed of lettuce with wedges of toasted pita bread.

Rum Macaroon Ice Cream Cake

An outrageous dessert but easy to prepare and needs one or two days to "mellow"

- **Serves 12**
  12 large soft macaroons, 2½ to 3-inches in diameter
  ⅓ cup dark rum
  1 quart coffee, chocolate or mocha ice cream, softened
  1 pint heavy cream, whipped
  1 cup thinly sliced, blanched almonds, lightly toasted

- Split macaroons and brush liberally with rum. Line bottom and side of lightly oiled 9-inch springform pan with the cakes.

- In a large bowl, mix ice cream lightly, then fold in whipped cream. Pack into pan. Pave top with almonds. Cover with plastic wrap and freeze overnight.

- To serve, remove from freezer and unmold. Keep frozen until about 30 minutes prior to presentation. Slice in wedges.

Macadamia White Chocolate Cookies

Grown-up chocolate chip cookies, splendid when served with after-dinner coffee

- **3 to 4 dozen**
  12 tablespoons (6 ounces) unsalted butter, room temperature
  ½ cup light brown sugar, packed
  ½ cup granulated sugar
  1 egg
  1 teaspoon vanilla extract
  1½ cups all-purpose flour
  ½ teaspoon baking powder
  ½ teaspoon salt
  2 tablespoons light corn syrup
  1 cup macadamia nuts, halved
  12 ounces white chocolate, cut in quarter-size chunks

- Preheat oven to 375 degrees.

- In a large bowl, cream butter and both sugars. Add egg and vanilla and mix thoroughly.

- Gradually add flour, baking powder and salt and mix well. Add corn syrup, then nuts and chocolate.

- Drop by the tablespoonful onto ungreased cookie sheets, about 4-inches apart. Bake for 9 to 12 minutes or until golden brown. Cool on rack and store in air-tight container.

48

Celebration Dinner for Eight

- Escargots with Champagne and Hazelnuts
  Côtes de Rhone
- Boneless Leg of Lamb with Artichoke Stuffing
  French Burgundy
- Zucchini-Tomato Fans
- Potatoes Vesuvio
  Mixed Green Salad with · Vinaigrette Dijonnaise
- Grand Philippine Flan
  Sweet Vouvray
  Coffee

Wassily Kandinsky (Russian, active Germany, 1866–1944), *Improvisation No. 29 (The Swan)*, 1912, oil on canvas, 41 3/4 x 38 3/16". The Louise and Walter Arensberg Collection

In his series of paintings entitled "Improvisations," the pioneering abstract artist Kandinsky eliminates recognizable objects and expresses a belief in the ability of color to evoke the basic rhythms of the universe. In *The Swan* vestiges of natural forms, such as the long curved neck of the bird, linger in the swirling shapes. Every area of this canvas comes alive with the saturated color that describes a joyous spiritual state.

Escargots with Champagne and Hazelnuts

Definitely worth the trouble!

- Serves 8

  2 cups (16 ounces) unsalted butter

  4 tablespoons garlic, finely chopped

  2 shallots, finely chopped

  2 teaspoons parsley, chopped

  1 teaspoon dried tarragon

  ⅛ teaspoon dried thyme

  1 bay leaf

  2 tablespoons hazelnuts, chopped

  ½ teaspoon salt

  Freshly ground pepper

  ⅛ teaspoon freshly grated nutmeg

  1 cup premium canned beef consommé

  1 tablespoon unflavored gelatin

  ¾ cup dry white wine

  1 tablespoon demi-glace (optional)

  48 snails, cleaned

  ½ bottle Champagne

- In a heavy 3-quart saucepan, mix together all ingredients up to and including the gelatin. Bring to a boil, add wine and demi-glace. Remove from heat.

- Wash snails and put them into liquid. Cook slowly, uncovered, until reduced by half.

- Add Champagne and reduce by half (about ¾ hour). Remove from heat, cool and refrigerate.

- When ready to serve, remove from refrigerator and lift snails out of jellied butter and put 6 into each ramekin or heat-proof dish. Add 2 tablespoons of jellied butter to each dish. Heat until just boiling.

- Serve with warm crusty French bread to absorb the sauce.

Note: Demi-glace, a reduction of meat juices, is available in many food specialty shops.

Variation: Cut the snails into large pieces and serve with sauce over angel hair pasta for a first course.

Boneless Leg of Lamb with Artichoke Stuffing

Roast lamb with savory stuffing — a decided Italian accent

- Serves 8

  5 pound leg of lamb, boned and flattened

  1 large clove of garlic, finely chopped

  Salt to taste

  Freshly ground pepper

  4 tablespoons olive oil

  1 10-ounce package frozen artichoke hearts, defrosted and chopped

  1 medium onion, finely chopped

  ¼ cup finely chopped parsley

  ½ teaspoon dried oregano

  ½ teaspoon dried thyme

  ½ teaspoon dried rosemary

  ⅓ cup freshly grated Parmesan cheese

  ½ cup fresh bread crumbs

  1 egg, lightly beaten

  1 cup olive oil

  Sprigs of fresh herbs

- Preheat oven to 375 degrees.

- Bring lamb to room temperature. Sprinkle with garlic, salt, pepper and 2 tablespoons olive oil. Set aside.

- Heat remaining 2 tablespoons of oil in frying pan and add artichokes, onion, parsley, oregano, thyme and rosemary. Stir occasionally until onions are soft but not brown, about 3 to 4 minutes. Remove from heat. Add cheese, crumbs and lightly beaten egg. Season with additional salt and pepper.

- Spread artichoke mixture over lamb. Roll meat carefully, keeping mixture well inside the edges. Tie securely several inches apart. Place in shallow roasting pan seam-side down. Rub lamb with a little additional olive oil. Roast in oven for approximately 90 minutes or until meat thermometer registers 140 degrees.

- Let stand 10 minutes before slicing into ¾ to 1-inch slices. Strain and degrease pan juices and spoon over meat. Garnish with herb sprigs. Accompany with steamed green beans and Baked Tomatoes Provençal.

Variation: The filling is a splendid change in roast chicken.

Zucchini-Tomato Fans

Try these fans as either a garnish for an entrée or as a vegetable accompaniment.

- **Serves 10 to 12**

  4 fresh plum tomatoes or 12 cherry tomatoes

  2 teaspoons dried basil, crumbled

  ¾ teaspoon salt, or to taste

¼ teaspoon black pepper

2 large cloves garlic, finely minced

8 zucchini, about 8 inches long

2 tablespoons plus 1 teaspoon extra virgin olive oil

¼ cup grated Parmesan cheese

- Preheat oven to 400 degrees.

- Cut each tomato crosswise into ⅛-inch thick slices. If you are using plum tomatoes, cut each slice in half. Lay the slices on a large plate and sprinkle with basil, salt, pepper and garlic. Set aside.

- Cut off and discard the ends of the zucchini. Slice each zucchini crosswise into 2-inch lengths. Blanch for 2 minutes in boiling water; then immediately plunge into cold water. Drain.

- Stand each zucchini section on a cut end and make 3 evenly spaced 1½-inch deep cuts downward being careful not to cut all the way through.

- Insert ½ round of plum tomato, skin side up or 2 cherry tomato slices into each cut. (The tops of the tomatoes should be almost flush with the tops of the zucchini.)

- Using 1 teaspoon of the oil, lightly coat a shallow casserole just large enough to hold the zucchini. Place the fans upright making certain that they touch each other. Drizzle with the remaining oil. Cover tightly with foil. May be prepared to this point 24 hours in advance. Cover and refrigerate. Bring to room temperature before continuing. Place in upper third of the oven. Bake 25 minutes.

- Remove from oven, remove foil, baste with oil and sprinkle with the Parmesan. Place under broiler and broil for 3 to 5 minutes or until cheese is lightly browned. Remove and serve hot or warm.

Potatoes Vesuvio

The filling is a delightful surprise!

- Serves 8

4 pounds Idaho potatoes

6 tablespoons (3 ounces) unsalted butter or margarine,
   softened

3 teaspoons salt or to taste

2 eggs, beaten

Approximately ¼ cup hot milk

Filling

1 cup coarsely shredded American cheese

3 egg yolks, slightly beaten

4 tablespoons (2 ounces) unsalted butter, melted

1 tablespoon light cream

¼ teaspoon dry mustard

¼ teaspoon salt or to taste

⅛ teaspoon cayenne pepper

¼ cup chopped parsley (garnish)

- Preheat oven to 400 degrees.

- Peel potatoes and cut into quarters. Cook in boiling
salted water until tender. Drain and mash slightly
with electric mixer.

- Add butter, salt and eggs. Add ¼ cup of hot milk.
Beat until smooth.

- Reserving 2 cups of potatoes for border, pour
potatoes into a 10-inch oval casserole. Form a 2-
inch depression in the center of the potatoes for the
filling.

- Combine filling ingredients, beating until well
blended. Pour filling into depression. Sprinkle
paprika over filling. Use reserved potatoes to make
an attractive border around the potatoes. (A large

star-tip pastry tube is helpful but if not available, a
tablespoon can be used.) May be prepared to this
point 24 hours in advance. Cover and refrigerate.
Bring to room temperature before continuing.

- Bake 30 minutes or until delicately browned.
Garnish with chopped parsley and serve.

Vinaigrette Dijonnaise

*Great on strong-flavored greens or
marinated vegetables*

- Makes about ½ cup

2 tablespoons white wine vinegar (or more, to taste)

¼ cup vegetable oil

¼ cup extra virgin olive oil

1 teaspoon salt

½ teaspoon freshly ground pepper

1 tablespoon Dijon-style mustard

1 quart greens, washed and chilled (such as chicory,
   endive, watercress, romaine)

- Using a blender, a large jar or a bowl, combine all
ingredients except greens. Cover and refrigerate for
up to 1 week. Bring to room temperature before
serving.

- To serve, pour dressing over greens and toss gently.
Serve on chilled salad plates.

Variations: Omit mustard and add 1 tablespoon or
more of chopped fresh chives, parsley or capers and
blend well.

Grand Philippine Flan

The Canonigo Order of Philippine monks enjoy this extraordinary treat on feast days.

• Serves 8

Flan

½ cup granulated sugar

½ teaspoon water

8 egg whites

¾ cup granulated sugar

1 teaspoon cream of tartar (optional)

Sauce

12-ounce can evaporated milk

8 egg yolks

¾ cup granulated sugar

½ cup (4 ounces) unsalted butter

2 teaspoons vanilla or lemon extract

Flan

• Preheat oven to 325 degrees.

• In a small heavy saucepan, melt ½ cup sugar with ½ teaspoon water. Pour into 4-cup ring mold and rotate to coat bottom and sides with caramel. Set aside to cool.

• In a large bowl, whip egg whites and gradually add ¾ cup sugar. Beat until stiff peaks form. (Cream of tartar may be added to aid in beating whites.)

• With a rubber spatula, spread egg white mixture in ring mold over the caramel. Bang mold on counter several times to eliminate air pockets. Place mold in larger pan filled with hot water reaching halfway up mold and bake for ½ hour.

• Remove mold from oven and cool. Invert onto large serving platter lightly sprinkled with granulated sugar.

Sauce

• Mix 8 yolks together with ¾ cup granulated sugar and evaporated milk. Strain into top of double boiler.

• Add butter and vanilla or lemon extract and stir constantly over boiling water until mixture thickens slightly. Mixture should coat spoon and not be too thick. Strain into bowl and set aside.

• At serving time, pour custard sauce over the mold or fill center, spooning any extra sauce attractively over the ring. Serve at once.

54

ireside Dinner for Six

- **Consommé Bellevue**

  Marsala

- **Orange, Onion and Avocado Salad**

- **Pork Braised with Bourbon**

  California Cabernet

- **Purée d'Hiver**

  French Beans sprinkled with Toasted Cashew Nuts

- **Candy Trimmed Lemon Crunch Cake**

  Port   Coffee

Simon Jacobsz. de Vlieger (Dutch, c. 1600–1653), *Marine*, oil on panel, 23 5/8 x 32 11/16". John G. Johnson Collection at the Philadelphia Museum of Art

Seascapes such as this reflect the marine interest of seventeenth-century Holland, whose economic stability was inextricably linked to the sea. This painting of calm seas, a vast, gentle sky, and a distant horizon is an excellent example of the tonal style of De Vlieger. By creating a balanced design and exploiting the delicate gradations of color, the artist imparts a sense of quiet composure to the scene.

Consommé Bellevue

• **Serves 6**

3 13¾-ounce cans chicken broth

2 8-ounce bottles clam juice

1 teaspoon sliced garlic

⅛ teaspoon cayenne pepper

3 tablespoons sherry

Grated rind of 1 lemon

Parsley (garnish)

• Combine broth, clam juice, garlic and cayenne. Simmer for 10 minutes.

• Strain and discard garlic. Add sherry.

• Serve in cups with grated lemon rind and chopped parsley.

Orange, Onion and Avocado Salad

A contrast of textures, flavors and colors

• **Serves 6**

Salad

2 heads of Boston lettuce, washed, dried and chilled in damp towels

1 small red onion, thinly sliced

4 navel oranges, peeled and thinly sliced

1 avocado, thinly sliced

12 Nicoise-style olives, pitted and halved

½ cup coarsely chopped walnuts, sautéed in 1 to 2 tablespoons vegetable oil (optional)

Dressing

2 tablespoons cilantro leaves

4 teaspoons red wine vinegar

¾ teaspoon granulated sugar

½ teaspoon Dijon-style mustard

¼ teaspoon salt

Freshly ground pepper

Grated peel from 1 orange

5 tablespoons vegetable or virgin olive oil (or a blend of each)

• Make dressing. Put all ingredients, except oil, in blender and mix well. With blender running, add oil in a slow stream until incorporated.

• Arrange salad. Place lettuce leaves on individual salad plates and top with alternate slices of onion, oranges and avocado. Sprinkle with olives and walnuts. Spoon dressing over salads and serve at once.

Pork Braised with Bourbon

- **Serves 6**

  3 pound pork loin in one piece, boned and tied

  24 pitted prunes

  1½ to 2 cups good quality beef bouillon

  ¼ pound prosciutto, cut in ¼-inch thick slices

  ½ cup Dijon-style mustard

  ⅔ cup dark brown sugar

  2 tablespoons vegetable oil

  ⅔ cup bourbon or sour mash whiskey

  Bouquet garni of thyme, sage and parsley tied in a
    cheesecloth bag or tea strainer

  2 bunches watercress

  6 pitted prunes plumped in warm water

- Preheat oven to 375 degrees.

- Steep 24 prunes in 1 cup tepid bouillon for 30 minutes. Cut prosciutto into strips.

- Dry roast. With tip of small sharp knife, make slits along length of roast and poke prosciutto into incisions. Paint roast with mustard. Roll in brown sugar.

- Heat oil in heavy, ovenproof casserole and brown meat, turning when one side is brown. Sugar will caramelize. Watch that it doesn't burn.

- Pour half of whiskey over meat and ignite. When flames subside, pour on ½ cup of remaining bouillon. Cover pot. May be prepared to this point and refrigerated up to 6 hours prior to roasting. (Remove from refrigerator 1 hour before roasting.)

- Place covered pot in oven and roast for 1¾ hours. Halfway through cooking turn meat, season with salt and pepper, add bouquet garni and lower heat to 350 degrees. About 10 minutes before end of cooking time, add prunes and their liquid.

- Remove meat to warm platter and tent loosely with foil. Strain cooking liquid and remove as much fat as possible. Return liquid to pot and bring sauce to a boil. Add remaining whiskey, stirring briskly.

- To serve, carve roast in thin slices and arrange on platter decorated with bouquets of watercress and plumped prunes.

Purée D'Hiver

Winter vegetables can be boring — but not if you serve this colorful dish that glamorizes the lowly squash.

- Serves 6

1½ cups acorn squash, peeled, seeded and cut into 1½-inch cubes

1½ cups yellow squash, peeled, seeded and cut into 1½-inch cubes

1½ cups butternut squash, peeled, seeded and cut into 1½-inch cubes

3 cups boiling water

½ teaspoon salt

2 tablespoons (1 ounce) unsalted butter

4 tablespoons apple butter

Salt and pepper to taste

Nutmeg (optional)

3 large navel oranges, halved, with insides scooped out

- Cook vegetables together in large saucepan in boiling salted water until barely fork-tender (about 12 minutes).

- Drain thoroughly. Place in a blender or food processor; add butter and apple butter and blend to a smooth consistency. Season with salt and pepper to taste. May be prepared to this point 4 hours in advance. Cover and refrigerate. Bring to room temperature before continuing.

- Heat and serve in orange cups. Sprinkle with nutmeg.

Note: Orange cups will not slide if you cut the bottoms to make them flat.

Variation: Substitute 1½ cups pears, peeled, cored and cut into 1½-inch cubes for 1 of the squash varieties. If using pears, eliminate apple butter and add ¼ cup sugar or to taste.

Candy-Trimmed Lemon Crunch Cake

A gorgeous cake worthy of your best dinner party

- **Serves 14 to 16**
  1 10-inch angel food or sponge cake (purchased or home-made)
  2 cups heavy cream
  ¼ cup confectioners sugar

Lemon Candy Crunch
1½ cups granulated sugar
⅓ cup water
¼ cup light corn syrup
1 tablespoon baking soda
¼ teaspoon lemon extract or oil of lemon

Lemon Candy Crunch
- In a heavy 1-quart saucepan, combine sugar, water and corn syrup. Cook over moderate heat, stirring occasionally, until syrup reaches the hard crack stage (300 degrees on candy thermometer). May take 40 to 45 minutes.

- Line a shallow baking pan or cookie sheet with foil. Butter foil well.

- Remove sugar mixture from heat at once and quickly stir in baking soda and lemon extract (mixture will foam). Stir vigorously until well blended. Pour mixture into pan and let cool.

- Turn out of pan and remove foil. Place in a heavy plastic freezer bag and hit with a mallet to make coarse crumbs.

To assemble
- Split cake into 4 layers.

- Whip cream until stiff, flavor with confectioners sugar.

- Spread ½ of the cream between the layers and the remainder on top and sides of the cake.

- Generously sprinkle crushed candy over top and sides, gently pressing where necessary. Refrigerate until serving time.

Variation: Instead of lemon extract, add 3 teaspoons instant coffee granules to the syrup mixture before cooking and 1 teaspoon instant coffee granules to the whipped cream.

*S*ouper Sunday for Twenty

Baskets of Soft Pretzels with Mustard

• Mushroom and Liver Paté with Crispy Rye Crackers

• Pepperoni and Cheese Tartlets

• Winter Vegetable Soup

• Crab Chowder with Oyster Crackers

• Thousand Bean Soup

White Rhone

Assorted Warm Crusty Breads

Wedges of Cheddar and Imported Swiss Cheeses

Barolo

Basket of Stayman, Winesap and Delicious Apples

Domestic and Imported Beers

• Frozen Chocolate Mousse

• Almond Macaroons

Pablo Picasso (Spanish, 1881–1973), *Three Musicians*, 1921, oil on canvas, 80 1/2 x 74 1/8". A. E. Gallatin Collection

Picasso's *Three Musicians*, monumental in its size and conception, is the culminating statement of Cubism with its intricately balanced composition and brilliant interplay of color. The three traditional figures of the comedy stage — Harlequin, holding a violin and bow, Pierrot, playing a recorder, and a monk, holding an accordion — stare out from the shallow picture space with disquieting smiles.

Mushroom and Liver Paté

The mushrooms add a commendable flavor to this cocktail spread.

- **Serves 12**
  1 tablespoon unflavored gelatin

  ¼ pound chicken livers

  Cognac

  3 slices uncooked bacon, chopped

  3 tablespoons (1½ ounces) unsalted butter

  ½ pound mushrooms, coarsely chopped

  ⅓ cup onion, coarsely chopped

  ¼ pound cream cheese, softened

- Cover chicken livers in Cognac and soak for ½ hour.

- Meanwhile, dissolve gelatin in 2 tablespoons Cognac.

- Sauté bacon until crisp, remove bacon, drain and discard fat.

- Add butter to pan and sauté drained chicken livers, mushrooms and onion until livers are no longer pink.

- Blend liver mixture in food processor, add bacon pieces. Cream the cheese and gelatin and blend until smooth.

- Pour in mold and refrigerate overnight.

- To serve, bring to room temperature and invert on a platter. Serve with crackers or bread rounds.

Pepperoni and Cheese Tartlets

- **Makes 48**
  1 cup (8 ounces) unsalted butter, melted

  2 cups all-purpose flour

  6 ounces cream cheese, softened

  3 eggs

  1 cup light cream

  ½ teaspoon salt

  4 ounces Swiss cheese, shredded

  ¼ pound pepperoni, finely chopped

- Preheat oven to 350 degrees.

- To make the crust, blend butter, flour and cream cheese and form into 48 balls.

- Grease mini-muffin pans with non-stick spray and push each ball into a muffin shell and mold to form a crust.

- Beat eggs. Add cream and salt. Mix in cheese and pepperoni until well blended.

- Pour mixture into uncooked shells. Bake for 25 to 30 minutes. Serve warm.

Winter Vegetable Soup

Ground beef makes this a hearty weekend soup for the family.

- **Serves 6**
  3 onions, coarsely chopped

  2 tablespoons (1 ounce) unsalted butter

  1 pound lean ground beef

1 clove of garlic, minced

3 cups beef stock

2 35-ounce cans tomatoes

1 cup potatoes, diced

1 cup celery, diced

1 cup carrots, diced

1 cup dry red wine

2 tablespoons parsley, chopped

½ teaspoon basil

¼ teaspoon thyme

Salt to taste

Freshly ground pepper to taste

- In a large saucepan, cook onions in butter until translucent.

- Stir in garlic and ground beef and cook until beef is brown.

- Add stock, all vegetables, wine and seasonings.

- Bring to a boil then reduce heat and simmer for 1 hour.

Crab Chowder

Creamy, delicious and welcome on a cold night

- **Serves 8 to 10**

8 cups bottled clam juice

1 cup dry sherry

½ cup brandy

¼ cup minced shallots

1 tablespoon minced garlic

8 fresh parsley stems

4 bay leaves

4 medium potatoes, peeled and cut into ½-inch cubes

2 ounces bacon or salt pork, cut into ⅛-inch cubes

2 cups onion, finely chopped

1½ cups celery, finely chopped

1 tablespoon dried thyme

½ cup all-purpose flour

3 cups heavy cream

¾ pound fresh or frozen crabmeat

Fresh parsley, chopped

Salt to taste

Freshly ground pepper to taste

- In a large pot, heat clam juice, sherry, brandy, shallots, garlic, parsley stems and bay leaves. Bring to a boil and cook for 15 minutes, skimming surface and stirring occasionally. Strain through a fine strainer, reserving liquid.

- In separate saucepan, boil cubed potatoes for 5 minutes and drain.

- In large soup pot, cook bacon or salt pork until crisp. Add onions and celery and sauté in bacon fat for 6 minutes. Add thyme and sauté for an additional minute.

- Make a roux by stirring in flour and cook, stirring constantly over a low heat for 5 minutes. Do not brown the flour.

- Stir clam broth gradually into roux over low heat. When all the broth is added, heat to boiling and then reduce heat and simmer for 20 minutes.

- Stir in cream, potatoes and crab and heat until hot. Garnish with parsley and serve in deep bowls.

Thousand Bean Soup

• **Serves 8**

¼ cup each of any of the following to total 2 cups:

lentils	**navy beans**	**red beans**
black beans	**garbanzos**	**lima beans**
split peas	**red lentils**	**pinto beans**

2 quarts water mixed with 2 tablespoons salt

2 ham hocks

1 large onion, chopped

1 teaspoon chili powder

1 28-ounce can tomatoes

2 tablespoons lemon juice

2 tablespoons herbs (bay leaf, basil, thyme) to taste

2 boneless chicken breasts, raw and diced

1 pound smoked sausage, skinned and sliced

• Wash beans, put them in a large pot, add salt and 2 quarts water and soak overnight.

• Drain, add 2 quarts of water, ham, onion, chili powder, tomatoes, lemon juice and herbs. Simmer for 4 hours.

• Remove ham hocks, leave remaining pieces of meat in the soup.

• Add boneless chicken breasts and sausage. Simmer for 40 minutes. Serve in deep bowls.

Frozen Chocolate Mousse

A fabulous dessert for a crowd

• **Serves 20**

5 ounces unsweetened chocolate

3 ounces dark sweet chocolate

8 eggs, separated

1⅓ cups granulated sugar

4 cups heavy cream

Orange liqueur

• In a double boiler, melt chocolates.

• Beat egg yolks with sugar until thick and light. Blend in chocolate mixture and set aside to cool.

• Whip cream until firm. Fold chocolate mixture into whipped cream. Beat egg whites until stiff and glossy and fold into mixture. Pour in large bowl or individual serving dishes and chill. Freeze at least 3 hours or overnight.

• To serve, drizzle with orange liqueur.

Almond Macaroons

*Good use of extra egg whites — make
sure you bake them on a dry day.*

- **Makes about 2 dozen**
  1¾ cups confectioners sugar

  2 tablespoons granulated sugar

  1½ cups canned almond paste

  2 egg whites from large eggs

- Preheat oven to 350 degrees.

- In a food processor, mix sugars and almond paste.
  Continue to process while adding egg whites, one at
  a time.

- Cover cookie sheets with baking parchment or
  brown paper. Drop walnut-size balls onto paper
  1-inch apart. Partially flatten tops with damp paper
  towel placed over bottom of drinking glass. Bake 12
  to 15 minutes until light brown on top but soft
  inside. Watch carefully.

- Remove from oven and cool completely. Carefully
  remove cookies by dampening back of brown paper,
  waiting for a few minutes, and sliding them off with
  a flat knife or spatula. Store in air-tight container
  or freeze.

Supper After the Concert for Twelve

- **Caviar Dip in Pumpernickel Shell surrounded by Cucumber Circles and Fingers of Black Bread**
  Champagne   Iced Vodka
- **Shrimp and Lobster with Wild Rice**
  Chablis
- **Watercress and Pear Salad**
  Toasted Discs of French Bread
- **Normandy Apple Tart**

Vittorio Crivelli (Italian, Venice, active c. 1481–c. 1502), *Enthroned Virgin and Child with Angels*, 1489, tempera on panel, 55 3/4 x 30". Purchased for the W. P. Wilstach Collection

Venetian painters typically gave their polyptychs the exceptional decorative richness seen in this central panel from Crivelli's altarpiece. The Virgin is enthroned as the Queen of Heaven, dressed in sumptuous garments of gold and brocade patterned with pomegranates. Her crown and the jewels that edge her robe are rendered in relief, thus giving a three-dimensionality to the linear forms. The surrounding fruits, flowers, and bird are symbolic attributes of the Madonna.

Caviar Dip

Consider serving a scoop on bite-size pancakes or thick slices of cucumber.

• Serves 8

1 cup Homemade Food-Processor Mayonnaise

1 cup commercial sour cream

1 jar (3½ ounces) red lumpfish caviar or salmon roe caviar

6 large scallion bulbs, chopped

1 jar (3 ounces) pimiento-stuffed olives, sliced

• Combine all ingredients and chill.

• Serve in a hollowed-out patty-pan squash with an array of raw vegetables and fingers of black bread.

Note: Be sure to use red caviar, black will turn the mixture an unappetizing grey. This is best when made a day ahead.

Shrimp and Lobster with Wild Rice

An exquisite entrée for a glorious party

• Serves 12

1 cup wild rice

3 cups water

1 teaspoon salt

2 tablespoons (1 ounce) unsalted butter

Additional ⅔ cup (6 ounces) unsalted butter

2 pounds fresh white mushrooms, sliced

2 cups celery, finely chopped

2 medium green peppers, chopped

2 medium onions, finely chopped

⅔ cup all-purpose flour

2 cups milk

½ teaspoon salt, or to taste

¼ teaspoon freshly ground pepper

2 teaspoons fresh lemon juice

2 teaspoons Worcestershire sauce

1 tablespoon sherry (optional)

Hot pepper sauce (optional)

4 lobster tails (about 5 ounces each), cooked, cleaned and each cut into 6 pieces

3 pounds medium shrimp, cooked and cleaned

4 ounces pimiento pieces

1 cup slivered almonds, lightly toasted

Sprigs of fresh dill or parsley (garnish)

• Bring water to boil. Add wild rice and salt. Reduce heat to a simmer. Cover and cook over low heat until water is absorbed. Remove from heat. Add 2 tablespoons of butter. Mix well and set aside.

• In a large frying pan, melt the additional ⅔ cup butter. Sauté mushrooms, celery, green pepper and onion until soft and most of liquid has evaporated. Sprinkle flour over vegetables and stir gently. Cook over low heat, stirring for approximately 1 minute.

• Slowly add milk, a little at a time, stirring until all the milk is completely incorporated. Continue cooking for an additional 5 minutes, stirring often. Cook just to boiling. (Be careful that it does not overflow.) Remove from heat. Add salt, pepper, lemon juice, Worcestershire sauce, sherry and hot pepper sauce. Gently fold in lobster, shrimp and rice.

- Lightly butter casserole. Fill with rice and seafood mixture. May be prepared up to 1 day in advance to this point. Cover and refrigerate. Bring to room temperature before continuing. Sprinkle top with toasted almonds. Decorate with pimiento.

- Preheat oven to 350 degrees. Bake for 30 to 40 minutes. Serve at once garnished with sprigs of dill or parsley.

Watercress and Pear Salad

A stylish salad perfect for serving "European style" after the entrée

- **Serves 6**
  2 tablespoons white wine vinegar
  Juice of ½ lemon
  ¼ cup olive oil
  ¼ cup vegetable oil
  2 tablespoons heavy cream
  Salt and freshly ground pepper
  2 bunches watercress, washed, stems removed
  ½ cup Saga Blue cheese, crumbled
  2 Bosc pears, peeled and cubed

- In a small bowl, combine vinegar, lemon juice, olive oil, vegetable oil and heavy cream. Season to taste with salt and pepper and blend thoroughly, either in a jar or using a wire whisk.

- Place watercress, cheese and pears in a salad bowl. Pour on dressing and toss. Serve immediately.

Normandy Apple Tart

This rich, fragrant apple tart is basted with Calvados for a touch of Normandy cuisine.

- **Serves 6 to 8**
  8 Winesap or Granny Smith apples, peeled, cored and sliced
  1 9-inch pie shell, unbaked
  1 12-ounce jar apricot preserves
  2 tablespoons (1 ounce) unsalted butter
  ¼ cup Calvados or applejack
  ¼ cup slivered almonds

- Preheat oven to 425 degrees.

- Line pie shell with apples, arranged carefully. Pack plenty of apples in the shell to compensate for shrinkage.

- In a saucepan, heat preserves, butter and Calvados, mixing well. Pour over apples. Bake 30 minutes. Sprinkle almonds on top and bake an additional 10 to 15 minutes until brown. Serve warm or cool with whipped cream.

$\mathscr{R}$omantic Mediterranean Dinner for Two

- **Fettucine con Quatri Fromaggi**
  Soave
- **Crevettes L'Antiboise over Arborio Rice**
  Frascati
  Warm, Crusty Italian Rolls
  Salad of Radicchio and Romaine with • Parmesan
  Vinaigrette
- **Heart-Shaped Raspberry Meringue Nest**
  Asti Spumanti
  Espresso

Tapestry: *Courtly Life*, French, 1490, wool and silk, 98 1/4 x 62 3/4". Purchased: Museum and Subscription Funds

Fifteenth-century tapestries such as this are woven narratives that offer manifold opportunities for the enjoyment of their poetic themes, rich patterns, and sumptuous color. *Courtly Life* depicts an elegant lord and lady against a background strewn with flowering plants. The bird, perhaps a falcon, perched on the lady's left hand turns inquiringly to the lord, who lightly touches his harp as another bird flutters overhead.

Fettucine con Quatri Fromaggi

Toasted walnuts add crunch to the rich sauce composed of four Italian cheeses – a gorgeous first course!

- **Serves 4 to 6**
½ cup coarsely chopped walnuts
8 ounces egg fettucine (fresh, if possible)
2 cups heavy cream, room temperature
8 ounces whole-milk Mozzarella, shredded
2 ounces sweet or young Gorgonzola cheese, crumbled
3 tablespoons freshly grated Parmesan cheese
2 tablespoons freshly grated Romano cheese
3 tablespoons chopped parsley, preferrably Italian flat-leaf
2 tablespoons finely chopped fresh basil (or ½ teaspoon dried)
½ teaspoon dried oregano
1 tablespoon finely chopped fresh chives
Additional grated Parmesan cheese

- Preheat oven to 300 degrees.

- Toast walnuts in oven until just fragrant (about 5 minutes). Set aside.

- Cook fettucine until al dente and drain retaining some moisture.

- Pour cream into pot in which pasta was cooked. Bring to boil over high heat. Boil 2 minutes, then add all the cheeses and herbs. Lower heat and stir until well blended (about 2 minutes).

- Add fettucine and mix well. Pour onto warmed serving platter and sprinkle with walnuts. Serve at once offering extra grated cheese.

72

Crevettes L'Antiboise

There's a hearty Mediterranean flavor in this shrimp and herb dish.

- **Serves 4**
5 tablespoons olive oil
1 medium zucchini, cut into ½ -inch cubes
Salt to taste
Freshly ground pepper
1 red pepper, roasted, peeled, cored and finely sliced
1 small dried hot chili pepper
1 pound large uncooked shrimp, peeled, deveined and marinated in Madeira for 1 hour
3 large garlic cloves, finely minced
1 large sprig fresh thyme plus 2 tablespoons finely minced thyme
8 to 10 canned Italian plum tomatoes, drained and quartered
3 tablespoons minced parsley
Lemon wedges (garnish)
2 cups cooked rice

- Heat 2 tablespoons of the oil in a medium frying pan.

- Add zucchini and sauté with salt and pepper until nicely browned. Add red pepper and continue cooking for 1 minute. Remove from heat and set aside.

- Heat remaining oil with the chili pepper in a large frying pan over high heat. When pepper has darkened, remove and discard.

- Add shrimp, garlic and thyme sprig. Sauté, shaking pan constantly until shrimp turns bright pink. Season with salt and pepper.

- Add tomatoes and cook until excess liquid has evaporated. This should take 2 to 3 minutes. Add zucchini mixture and parsley.

- Remove from heat, serve over rice or pasta and garnish with lemon wedges.

Parmesan Vinaigrette

- **Makes 2 cups**
  ¼ **cup water**
  2 **teaspoons aromatic bitters**
  1½ **teaspoons garlic salt**
  1½ **teaspoons granulated sugar**
  ½ **teaspoon powdered cumin**
  1 **teaspoon Worcestershire sauce**
  ½ **teaspoon oregano**
  ½ **teaspoon garlic powder**
  ¼ **teaspoon freshly ground pepper**
  6 **tablespoons extra virgin olive oil**
  3 **tablespoons red or white wine vinegar**
  4 **quarts washed and chilled salad greens (such as iceberg lettuce, chicory, romaine, endive)**
  ⅔ **cup freshly grated imported Parmesan cheese**
  1 **or 2 ripe avocados, peeled and sliced**

- Mix first 9 ingredients well and let stand 15 minutes. Beat in oil and vinegar. Chill, covered, until serving time. May be prepared up to 1 week in advance.

- At serving time, arrange salad greens in large bowl. Sprinkle with Parmesan cheese. Pour on dressing and toss gently. Garnish with avocado slices and serve at once.

Raspberry Meringue Nest

- **Serves 10**

  Meringue
  6 **egg whites, room temperature**
  ¾ **cup granulated sugar**
  1 **cup confectioners sugar**
  ¼ **cup cornstarch**

- Preheat oven to 225 degrees.

- Line a baking sheet with baking parchment or brown paper. Draw a 9-inch circle onto the center of the paper.

- Beat egg whites until they form stiff peaks. Gradually beat in granulated sugar.

- Sift together confectioners sugar and cornstarch. Fold gently but completely into egg white mixture.

- Fill a pastry bag, fitted with a large plain nozzle, with meringue mixture. Pipe in a spiral onto prepared baking sheet to make a 9-inch round base. Form the sides of the nest with an edging of meringue rosettes. Bake in oven 12 hours with oven door slightly open. Remove and cool on a rack. Set on metallic doily (meringue will adhere to paper) on serving platter.

  Filling
  1 **cup heavy cream, chilled**
  1 **tablespoon brandy**
  2½ **cups fresh raspberries**

- Whip cream with brandy until stiff. Fill nest with brandy cream and cover with raspberries.

*L*ate Afternoon Reception for Fourteen

- **Caviar Supreme with Toast Triangles**
  Iced Vodka
- **Assorted Tea Sandwiches**
  Sancerre
- **Glazed Brie with Sesame Crackers**
- **Oatmeal Lace Cookies**
- **Petticoat Tails**
- **Butterscotch Brownies**
- **C³ Brownies**
- **Lemony Yogurt Bread**
- **Glazed Pound Cake**
  Bunches of Red and Green Grapes
  Assorted Teas   Cream Sherry

Pierre-Auguste Renoir (French, 1841-1919), *Les Grands Boulevards*, 1875, oil on canvas, 20 1/2 x 25".
The Henry P. McIlhenny Collection in memory of Frances P. McIlhenny

In the full light of a sunny spring day Renoir has depicted the bourgeois prosperity of the pedestrians on the Grands Boulevards. He has portrayed a specific instant of urban street life in which form seems to have dissolved in light. For Renoir, Paris was a city in blossom, which he has painted with an overall luminescence and uniformity of brushstroke that provide unity and rhythm to the scene.

Caviar Supreme

An unusual version of the popular caviar appetizer adds the richness of avocado.

- Serves 12 to 14

1 package unflavored gelatin

¼ cup cold water

4 eggs, hard cooked and chopped

½ cup Homemade Food-Processor Mayonnaise

¼ cup parsley, minced

1 large green onion, minced

¾ teaspoon salt

Dash hot pepper sauce

Freshly ground white pepper

1 medium avocado, puréed just before adding

1 medium avocado, diced just before adding

1 shallot, minced

2 tablespoons fresh lemon juice

2 tablespoons Homemade Food-Processor Mayonnaise

½ teaspoon salt

Dash of hot pepper sauce

Freshly ground pepper

1 cup commercial sour cream

¼ cup onion, minced

1 3½ -ounce jar black caviar

Fresh lemon juice

Thinly sliced pumpernickel bread

- Line bottom of a 1-quart soufflé dish with foil extending 4-inches beyond rim of dish on 2 sides. Oil lightly.

- Soften gelatin in cold water in measuring cup. Set cup in pan of hot water to liquefy gelatin. This gelatin will be divided among 3 layers.

- For egg layer, combine eggs, mayonnaise, parsley, green onion, salt, pepper sauce and pepper with 1 tablespoon gelatin. Neatly spread egg mixture in soufflé dish.

- For avocado layer, combine puréed and diced avocados, shallot, lemon juice, mayonnaise, salt, pepper sauce and pepper with 1 tablespoon gelatin. Gently spread over egg mixture.

- For sour cream layer, mix sour cream and onion with remaining 2 tablespoons gelatin. Spread carefully over avocado layer. Cover dish tightly with plastic wrap and refrigerate overnight.

- Just before serving, lift mixture out of dish using foil as handles. Top with caviar, sprinkle with lemon juice and serve with pumpernickel bread.

Assorted Tea Sandwiches

- Cucumber with Dill Butter on Rounds of White Bread
- Watercress Roll-ups
- Deviled Egg Salad on Fingers of Rye Bread
- Chèvre and Orange Marmalade on Triangles of Wheat Bread
- Westphalian Ham with Honey Mustard on Black Bread Squares

Glazed Brie

A surprise nutty sugar topping

- **Serves 10**

  1 8-inch wheel of Brie cheese, top rind removed

  1 cup chopped pecans or whole blanched almonds

  1 cup light brown sugar

- Preheat oven to 325 degrees.

- Place Brie in oven-proof quiche or pie plate.

- Press nuts into the top and cover with the brown sugar, pressing gently into the Brie.

- Bake for 10 minutes. Then broil until the brown sugar caramelizes (about 3 minutes). Do not burn. Serve warm with hard crackers.

Oatmeal Lace Cookies

This easy variation of a Florentine can be served plain or fancy.

- **Makes 48 cookies**

  ½ cup (4 ounces) unsalted butter or margarine, melted

  1 cup sugar

  1 cup rolled oats

  4 tablespoons all-purpose flour

  ½ teaspoon salt

  1 egg, lightly beaten

  1½ teaspoons baking powder

  ½ teaspoon vanilla extract

- Preheat oven to 350 degrees.

- In a large bowl, mix butter, sugar, oats, flour, salt, egg, baking powder and vanilla extract until thoroughly blended.

- Line cookie sheets with aluminum foil or baking parchment lightly coated with non-stick cooking spray. Drop cookie mixture by ⅓ teaspoons on sheets 2 to 3 inches apart. Be sure cookies are not too close together. Bake 6 to 10 minutes or until golden in color. Remove from oven and cool on foil or paper for 15 minutes (otherwise cookies will stick or break apart).

Variation: Glaze cookies with chocolate

5 tablespoons (2½ ounces) unsalted butter

4 tablespoons light corn syrup

5 ounces bittersweet chocolate bits

1 tablespoon rum, orange liqueur or raspberry liqueur

- Combine butter and corn syrup in a saucepan. Bring to a simmer over low heat stirring constantly, then continue stirring and simmering for 1 minute. Remove from heat and whisk in chocolate and liqueur until chocolate has melted and glaze is smooth.

- Let cool for 8 minutes, then pour and spread glaze over cookies and let dry; or spread glaze over bottom of one cookie, sandwich with a second cookie and let dry.

Petticoat Tails

A classic shortbread, named for the shape of ladies' petticoats in the 18th century

- **Makes 32 pieces**
  1 cup (8 ounces) unsalted butter, softened
  ½ cup granulated sugar
  3 cups all-purpose flour, sifted
  ½ teaspoon baking powder
  1 teaspoon vanilla or almond extract

- Preheat oven to 350 degrees.

- In the bowl of an electric mixer, cream butter and sugar. Resift flour with baking powder and add to mixture gradually. Add vanilla or almond extract. Dough will be crumbly.

- Press dough into 4 7-inch round pans and prick all over with a fork. Bake for 20 minutes or until golden. Cool in pans.

- With a table knife, gently mark off 8 wedges and carefully lift out of pan. Store in air-tight container.

Butterscotch Brownies

Chewy, crunchy brownies to try with chocolate sauce.

- **16 to 20 squares**
  4 tablespoons (2 ounces) unsalted butter
  1 cup brown sugar
  1 egg, lightly beaten
  1 teaspoon vanilla
  ½ cup all-purpose flour
  1 teaspoon baking powder
  ¼ teaspoon salt
  ½ to 1 cup finely chopped pecans or walnuts

- Preheat oven to 350 degrees.

- In a saucepan, melt butter and stir in sugar until dissolved. Cool slightly and beat in egg and vanilla.

- Sift flour, baking powder and salt together and blend into butter mixture. Mix well. Fold in nuts.

- Spread batter into a lightly greased and floured 8-inch x 8-inch pan and bake 30 minutes. Cool and cut into squares.

C³ Brownies

Chocolate brownies with chocolate chips and chocolate frosting – scrumptious!

- 24 to 32 squares

  12 tablespoons (6 ounces) unsalted butter, softened

  1 cup granulated sugar

  ½ cup firmly packed brown sugar

  ⅔ cup light corn syrup

  1 teaspoon vanilla extract

  3 large eggs

  4 ounces unsweetened chocolate, melted

  1 cup all-purpose flour

  ⅛ teaspoon salt

  8 ounces pecans or walnuts (whole or chopped)

  4 ounces chocolate chips

- Preheat oven to 350 degrees.

- Cream together butter and sugars until well-blended. Add corn syrup, eggs and vanilla. Add melted chocolate.

- Sift flour and salt together and add to batter, gradually. Fold in nuts and chocolate chips.

- Pour into greased and floured 13-inch x 9-inch pan and bake 25 to 35 minutes. Do not overbake. These are very "fudgy". Cool.

Frosting
½ cup heavy cream
4 ounces semi-sweet chocolate

- Melt chocolate and cream in a double boiler, whisking constantly until thick and smooth. Spread on brownies and cut in bars or squares.

Lemony Yogurt Bread

Makes a nice gift!

- Makes 2 loaves

  1 cup vegetable shortening

  2 cups granulated sugar

  4 eggs, well-beaten

  3 cups all-purpose flour

  ½ teaspoon salt

  2 teaspoons baking powder

  1 8-ounce container lemon yogurt

  1 lemon, juice and rind

Topping
Lemon juice
⅓ cup granulated sugar

- Preheat oven to 350 degrees. Grease two 8-inch loaf pans.

- Cream shortening and sugar and add 4 beaten eggs and mix well.

- Sift flour, salt and baking powder and add to egg mixture alternating with yogurt.

- Grate rind of lemon and add to mixture with ½ the juice from the lemon.

- Pour mixture into greased loaf pans and bake for 45 minutes.

- As soon as loaves are baked, drizzle top with lemon-sugar mixture. Cool in pan.

Glazed Pound Cake

- **Serves 16 to 20**

Cake

3 cups granulated sugar

1½ cups (12 ounces) unsalted butter, softened

6 eggs, at room temperature

8 ounces cream cheese, at room temperature, in 8 pieces

3 cups all-purpose flour

1 teaspoon vanilla extract

3 tablespoons orange liqueur

- Preheat oven to 325 degrees.

- In a large mixing bowl, cream sugar and butter until fluffy. Add eggs, one at a time, until fully incorporated. Add cream cheese, piece by piece, until mixture is smooth. Slowly fold in flour and mix well. Add vanilla and liqueur.

- Grease 10-inch tube or 12-cup fluted tube pan. Pour in batter. Bake 1½ hours, checking for doneness after 1¼ hours. (Cake tester should come out clean. Do not over-bake.)

- Cool cake in pan. Invert on serving plate. Serve garnished with fruit and whipped cream, or glaze.

Glaze

½ cup (4 ounces) unsalted butter

¼ cup water

1 cup granulated sugar

½ cup orange liqueur

½ pint heavy cream, whipped

- Melt butter in saucepan. Stir in water and sugar. Boil 5 minutes, stirring constantly. Remove from heat. Stir in liqueur.

- Prick top of cake with skewer. Spoon and brush glaze evenly over top and sides. Repeat until glaze is used up. Decorate with border of whipped cream.

Variation: Other flavors may be substituted such as raspberry liqueur or dark rum.

$\mathcal{A}$PPETIZERS AND HORS D'OEUVRES

Henri de Toulouse-Lautrec (French, 1864-1901), *At the Moulin Rouge: The Dance*, 1890, oil on canvas, 45 1/2 x 59". The Henry P. McIlhenny Collection in memory of Frances P. McIlhenny

The Parisian dance hall and cabaret called the Moulin Rouge was Lautrec's greatest single source of material, although he rarely gave clues to its exact appearance. It was rather the people of the café who held his interest: the female dancer, her partner in the top hat, and the woman in the foreground. Here the spectators are unmoved and only half-interested in the dance as they remain isolated by their own expressions.

Ceviche

The scallops "cook" in the lime juice for this version of the Latin American appetizer.

- **Serves 8**
  2 pounds bay scallops
  1 cup fresh lime juice (8 to 10 limes)
  ¼ cup parsley, chopped
  ½ cup scallions, chopped
  ½ cup green pepper, chopped
  ½ cup red pepper, chopped
  1 to 2 jalapeño peppers, seeded and diced (optional)
  ¼ cup celery, chopped
  ½ cup olive oil
  Salt and pepper to taste

- Marinate scallops in lime juice in the refrigerator for at least 3 hours, stirring occasionally.

- Drain. Add remaining ingredients and mix thoroughly.

- Serve with crackers and a spoon to put the ceviche on the cracker or serve on a lettuce leaf as a first course.

Crab and Caviar Spread

Perfect for a last minute party as many of the ingredients can be kept in the pantry

- **Serves 10 to 12**
  1 6-ounce can jumbo lump crabmeat
  ½ cup mayonnaise
  ¼ cup catsup
  2 tablespoons chives, chopped
  1 tablespoon parsley, chopped
  2 hard boiled eggs, chopped
  1 medium onion, finely chopped
  1 tablespoon fresh lemon juice
  Pinch of dried dill weed
  3½-ounce jar red caviar
  Unsalted Melba rounds

- In a large bowl, mix together all ingredients except the caviar and toasts.

- Gently fold in caviar and refrigerate to chill.

- Garnish with parsley and serve with unsalted Melba rounds.

Note: Do not prepare more than 2 hours before serving as mixture gets runny if it stands too long.

Dilled Shrimp with Savory Sauce

More exciting than plain boiled shrimp

- **Serves 6**
  1½ pounds large shrimp, cooked, cleaned with tails left
      on
  ½ cup tarragon vinegar
  8 peppercorns, bruised
  1 whole bay leaf
  4 whole sprigs of fresh dill
  ⅛ teaspoon dried thyme
  Lettuce leaves (Boston, Bibb, red leaf)
  Fresh dill (garnish)

- Put shrimp in large, non-metallic bowl. Add vinegar, peppercorns, bay leaf, dill and thyme. Mix well; cover and refrigerate at least 2 hours but preferably overnight. Turn shrimp several times while marinating.

- At serving time, drain shrimp and arrange on bed of various lettuces. Accompany with Lamaze Sauce for dipping.

Shrimp Seurat

So simple, but results are simply sensational

- **Serves 8 to 10**
  3 pounds medium shrimp, cooked and cleaned
  1 large Bermuda onion, sliced thinly
  Juice of one lemon
  1 pint prepared mayonnaise-type salad dressing

- In a large bowl, place shrimp, sliced onion, lemon juice and salad dressing. Mix well.

- Store in covered container and refrigerate for 24 to 48 hours. Present in a large glass bowl with wooden skewers.

Salmon-Walnut Paté

A colorful canapé

- **Serves 10**
  8 ounces cream cheese, softened
  2 tablespoons onion, finely chopped
  1 tablespoon fresh lemon juice
  1 tablespoon prepared horseradish
  ¼ teaspoon liquid smoke
  1 12-ounce can red salmon, drained
  1 cup chopped walnuts
  1 bunch parsley (garnish)

- Beat softened cream cheese with onion, lemon, horseradish and liquid smoke. Fold in salmon.

- Form mixture into a ball and roll in chopped walnuts.

- Present on a bed of parsley and serve with black bread squares.

Note: Liquid smoke is available in the spice section of the market.

Variation: Use chopped pecans instead of walnuts.

Tricolor Seafood Mousse

A very showy appetizer or first course for a special dinner party

- **Serves 20 to 24**
  2 pounds fillet of sole, puréed and chilled

  2½ cups heavy cream

  2 egg whites

  1½ teaspoons salt

  ½ teaspoon white pepper, freshly ground

  ½ teaspoon grated nutmeg

  2 pounds fillet of salmon, puréed and chilled (reserve 4 slices)

  1¾ cups heavy cream

  2 egg whites

  1 teaspoon salt

  ¾ teaspoon cayenne pepper

  ¾ teaspoon grated nutmeg

  1½ pounds scallops, puréed and chilled (reserve 16)

  2¼ cups heavy cream

  1½ teaspoons salt

  ½ teaspoon white pepper, freshly ground

  ½ teaspoon grated nutmeg, freshly ground

  2 bunches spinach, washed, stemmed and blanched

- Preheat oven to 300 degrees.

- Transfer chilled sole to stainless steel bowl and set in larger bowl filled with ice.

- Whisking constantly, gradually add cream in a slow steady stream until well blended.

- Beat egg whites in medium bowl until frothy and fold into fish mixture.

- Season with salt, pepper and nutmeg.

- Repeat procedure in separate bowls with salmon and scallop mixtures. Refrigerate all 3 bowls.

- Line two 9 x 5-inch loaf pans with oiled parchment paper. Divide sole mousse evenly between prepared pans, smoothing carefully.

- Arrange 1 slice salmon over top of sole mousse and cover with 3 to 4 spinach leaves.

- Spread ¼ of salmon mousse evenly over spinach leaves in each pan.

- Spread out 6 to 8 spinach leaves overlapping on work surface. Arrange 8 of the reserved scallops down center of leaves and roll up leaves around scallops in a cylinder. Transfer to center of loaf pan and repeat for second loaf pan.

- Cover cylinders with remaining ¼ of salmon mousse, then a single layer of spinach leaves, then another salmon slice. Fill each pan with ½ of the scallop mousse mixture.

- Cover pans with oiled parchment paper and set pans in large shallow pan. Add boiling water up to 2-inches on sides of loaf pans. Bake 1 to 1¼ hours until mousse is set. Cool.

- To serve, run sharp knife around edges of molds. Dip briefly into hot water and then invert on platter. Remove parchment paper and discard. Slice mousse using a damp sharp knife. Serve with Sauce Verte.

Sauce Verte

1 cup Homemade Food-Processor Mayonnaise

½ cup parsley, finely chopped

½ cup watercress, finely chopped

1 tablespoon fresh lemon juice

1½ teaspoons fresh tarragon

¾ teaspoon Worcestershire sauce

¼ teaspoon minced garlic

• Blend all ingredients and chill.

Caponata

This luscious Italian bread spread is a favorite canapé.

• Serves 12 to 16

½ cup olive oil

2 cups celery, chopped

1 medium-sized eggplant, unpeeled, diced

2 cups white onion, chopped

2 cups peeled canned tomatoes, chopped, with juice

⅓ cup vinegar

½ cup green olives, chopped

½ cup black olives, chopped

1 whole sweet pimiento, chopped

1 tablespoon capers, chopped

Handful of parsley, chopped

Salt and pepper

• Sauté celery in olive oil until soft.

• Add eggplant and cook until soft.

• Add onion and cook until translucent.

• Add chopped tomatoes, juice and vinegar and simmer for 5 minutes. Add olives, pimiento, capers and parsley and simmer for ½ hour.

• Cool. Season with salt and pepper to taste. Serve at room temperature with crackers or thin rounds of Italian bread.

Vegetable Cheese Wheel

Vegetable bits sparkle like confetti

• Serves 16 to 20

4 ounces cheese-flavored crackers

½ cup stuffed green olives, chopped

½ cup celery, chopped

1 small green pepper, finely chopped

1 small sweet red pepper, finely chopped

1 small onion, finely chopped

2 tablespoons fresh lemon juice

1 teaspoon salt

Dash of paprika

Dash of hot pepper sauce

2 cups commercial sour cream

4 ounces cream cheese

¼ teaspoon dry mustard

Parsley sprigs (garnish)

• Crush cheese crackers and place ½ of the crumbs on buttered bottom and sides of a 10-inch springform pan.

• Blend all other ingredients in food processor and spread over crumbs.

• Cover with remaining crumbs. Cover and chill overnight.

• To serve, remove sides of pan, garnish with parsley and serve with crackers.

Marinated Roasted Red Bell Peppers

For an unusual presentation, serve with Saga Blue Cheese and wheat crackers.

- Serves 6 to 8
  4 large red bell peppers
  Virgin olive oil
  1 teaspoon white vinegar
  2 garlic cloves, sliced
  Salt and freshly ground black pepper
  ½ cup chopped parsley

- Preheat oven to 400 degrees.

- Place whole peppers on foil-lined cookie sheet and roast for 40 minutes, turning once after 20 minutes.

- Remove from oven and cool in paper bag. Peel off skin, remove seeds and stem. Slice into ¼-inch strips.

- Place into a bowl and add olive oil to cover. Add vinegar, garlic slices, salt and pepper to taste. Cover with plastic wrap and refrigerate at least 2 hours. Serve at room temperature sprinkled with parsley.

Variation: Arrange with fillets of anchovies and oil-cured olives for an Italian-style appetizer.

Marinated Carrots

Favorites with the calorie-counting crowd

- Serves 6
  6 to 8 carrots, quartered and sliced into 3-inch lengths
  ½ cup virgin olive oil
  ¼ cup white wine vinegar
  ½ red onion, thinly sliced
  2 garlic cloves, minced
  1 teaspoon fresh basil, chopped
  1 teaspoon salt
  ½ teaspoon freshly ground pepper
  Juice of one lemon

- Parboil sliced carrots for 3 minutes. Drain.

- Mix remaining ingredients, pour over carrots and refrigerate overnight.

- Drain thoroughly before serving as finger food.

Layered Crêpes

A wonderful way to use left-over crêpes

- 8 to 10 slices
  3 to 4 crêpes, 7-inches in diameter
  ½ cup Homemade Food-Processor Mayonnaise
  8 ounces cream cheese, softened
  2 tablespoons milk
  1 tablespoon minced onion

1 tablespoon minced green pepper

2 ounces dried beef, minced

Sautéed almonds (garnish)

- Mix together all ingredients except the crêpes.
- Layer mixture between crêpes. Cover top and sides.
- Garnish with almonds and chill.
- To serve, slice in tiny pie-shaped wedges.

Variation: Mound mixture into center of a platter, garnish with parsley and surround with crackers for an appealing cocktail spread.

Clam Pie

Also good when baked in individual ramekins and served as a first course

- Serves 6

2 10-ounce cans minced clams with juice

1 teaspoon fresh lemon juice

1 medium onion, coarsely chopped

1 small green pepper, coarsely chopped

¼ teaspoon parsley flakes

3 to 4 garlic cloves

1 teaspoon dried oregano

4 tablespoons (2 ounces) unsalted butter, melted

¾ cup plain bread crumbs

Parmesan cheese

- Preheat oven to 350 degrees.
- Simmer clams and juice with lemon juice for 10 minutes.

- In blender, chop onion, pepper, parsley, garlic and oregano.
- Put vegetable mixture in a frying pan with melted butter and sauté briefly.
- Add clams and lemon juice to bread crumbs and transfer to the frying pan with the vegetable mixture. Pour into 1-quart casserole. May be prepared ahead to this point and frozen. Bring to room temperature before baking.
- Bake for 15 minutes. Serve with crackers.

Hot Shrimp Dip

Gentlemen love it

- Serves 8

6 ounces cream cheese, softened

Splash of milk (¼ cup at most)

½ teaspoon minced garlic

1 4½-ounce can of tiny shrimp, drained

Paprika

Toast points

- Preheat oven to 350 degrees.
- Blend cream cheese and milk until smooth, then add garlic and shrimp.
- Bake in a small greased casserole dish for 20 minutes. Set in center of round basket and surround with toast points.

Variation: For individual canapés, spread uncooked dip on toast points and bake at 350 degrees for 8 to 10 minutes.

89

Herbed Scallops

Elegant served warm or chilled

• **Serves 10**

1 pound bay scallops

1 cup Homemade Food-Processor Mayonnaise

1 teaspoon capers, washed in cold water, drained and minced

1 tablespoon dried dill

1 teaspoon dried tarragon

1½ tablespoons fresh parsley, minced

2 large garlic cloves, finely minced

1 hard boiled egg, chopped

½ teaspoon salt

Freshly ground pepper to taste

2 tablespoons chives, minced

• Boil scallops for 2 minutes (do not over-cook). Remove from heat, drain and cool.

• Mix mayonnaise in a bowl with capers, herbs, parsley, garlic, egg, salt and pepper.

• Add scallops and combine thoroughly.

• To serve, place scallops on a flat platter and sprinkle with chives. Serve with crackers or tooth-picks for spearing.

Hot Crabmeat Appetizer

Elegant beginning for a meal

• **Serves 8 to 10**

2 8-ounce packages cream cheese, softened

Juice of one lemon

1 large garlic clove, minced

1½ teaspoons Worcestershire sauce

Salt and pepper to taste

Hot pepper sauce, to taste

12 ounces lump crabmeat

• Preheat oven to 350 degrees.

• Beat all ingredients together except crabmeat.

• Gently fold in crabmeat.

• Pour into 6-cup casserole. May be prepared ahead to this point and frozen. Defrost before baking. Bake for 20 to 30 minutes or until hot and bubbly. Serve with French bread rounds.

Variation: Bake in individual ramekins and present as a first course.

Pork Pasties

Packets of phyllo stuffed with a savory pork filling are splendid hot hors d'oeuvres.

- **Makes 24 pieces**
  ½ **pound ground pork**
  ¼ **cup onion, finely chopped**
  1½ **cups cabbage, finely shredded**
  2 **medium apples, finely chopped**
  3 **tablespoons cold water**
  1 **tablespoon Dijon-style mustard**
  2 **teaspoons all-purpose flour**
  ½ **teaspoon salt**
  ½ **teaspoon ground cinnamon**
  3 **tablespoons fine bread crumbs**
  1 **package frozen phyllo dough, defrosted overnight in refrigerator**
  ½ **cup (4 ounces) unsalted butter, melted**

- Preheat oven to 400 degrees.

- In a large frying pan, cook pork and onion until browned. Drain.

- Place cabbage and apple over the meat mixture, cover and cook over low heat for 10 minutes.

- Combine cold water, mustard, flour, salt and cinnamon. Add to meat mixture, stirring. Stir in bread crumbs and cool.

- Unfold phyllo dough. Spread 1 sheet flat and brush with melted butter. Top with a second sheet and brush with butter. Cut into strips measuring 2-inches wide.

- Spoon 2 teaspoons of filling near one end of a strip of phyllo dough. Fold end over the filling at a 45-degree angle and continue folding to form triangles (like folding an American flag). Brush top with butter.

- Repeat process until all filling is used. May be frozen at this point. Can go directly from freezer to oven. Bake for 25 minutes. Serve at once.

Note: When working with phyllo dough, it is important to work quickly as it dries out very fast. While working with the sheets of dough, keep unused sheets moist by placing a damp dish towel over them.

Cheese Onion Pennies

Heavenly!

- **Serves 4 to 6**
  1 **cup mayonnaise**
  6 **tablespoons Parmesan cheese, freshly grated**
  2 **tablespoons finely chopped onion**
  24 **to 30 rounds of white bread (cut out with a 1¾-inch canapé cutter or small glass)**

- Blend mayonnaise, cheese and onion in food processor until smooth.

- Spread about 2 teaspoons on each round, and place on cookie sheet. May be prepared ahead to this point and frozen. Defrost before broiling.

- Broil about 6 inches from heat for 2 to 3 minutes or until top is browned and bubbly.

Variation: Double recipe and put in small soufflé dish or quiche dish. Heat until bubbly and serve, surrounded by melba rounds.

Mushrooms Stuffed with Clams and Walnuts

Arrange these on a bed of sprouts to keep them from slipping around when passed.

- Serves 10
  1 pound large mushrooms
  ½ cup (4 ounces) unsalted butter, melted
  1 garlic clove, minced
  1 can minced clams, drained
  3 slices bread, crusts removed and chopped into bread crumbs
  ½ cup walnuts, chopped
  ¼ cup parsley, chopped
  ¼ teaspoon salt
  ¼ teaspoon pepper
  Parmesan cheese, grated

- Preheat oven to 350 degrees.

- Clean mushrooms and remove stems. Brush caps with butter. Chop stems finely.

- Cook garlic and mushroom stems in butter for 2 minutes. Add clams, crumbs, parsley, seasonings and walnuts.

- Stuff the mushroom caps and top with Parmesan cheese. Bake for 15 minutes.

Cheese Bacon Squares

Zesty pick-ups

- Makes 12 squares
  1 8-ounce can refrigerated dinner roll dough
  ¾ cup shredded Swiss cheese
  ¾ cup shredded Mozzarella or Monterey Jack cheese
  1 egg, beaten
  ¼ cup onion, finely chopped
  ¾ cup milk
  ½ cup or 4-ounce can of mushroom stems and pieces, drained
  6 slices of bacon, fried, drained and crumbled
  1 tablespoon minced parsley

- Preheat oven to 375 degrees.

- Separate dough into 2 rectangles and place in an ungreased 9 x 13-inch pan. Make a crust by pressing dough over the bottom and ½-inch up the sides of the pan. Be sure to seal perforations.

- Sprinkle cheeses over the dough. Combine egg, onion, milk and mushrooms and pour over cheeses.

- Sprinkle with bacon and parsley.

- Bake for 22 to 28 minutes or until crust is golden brown. Cool for 5 minutes and cut into squares. Serve warm or at room temperature.

Gougère

A cheese-flavored cream puff pastry — serve as an hors d'oeuvre or as an accompaniment to soups or salads.

- **Serves 10 to 12**
  ⅔ **cup chicken stock**
  4 tablespoons (2 ounces) unsalted butter
  ¼ teaspoon grated nutmeg
  ½ teaspoon salt
  Freshly ground pepper
  1 cup sifted all-purpose flour
  4 eggs
  ⅔ **to 1 cup grated Gruyère cheese**
  1 egg yolk mixed with 3 tablespoons milk
  ½ to 1 cup diced Gruyère cheese

- In a saucepan, bring stock, butter and seasonings to boil.

- Remove from flame and add flour all at once. Mix with wooden spoon until a ball is formed.

- Return to flame and cook for several minutes to remove raw flour taste.

- Remove from heat and place in food processor. Using metal blade, mix well and add eggs one at a time through the feed tube.

- Add grated cheese and mix just a few seconds.

  The Gougère can be presented in two ways:

- Preheat oven to 400 degrees.

- Grease and flour a cookie sheet. Using a 9-inch cake pan, draw a circle on the floured surface.

- Place batter is a pastry bag with a large round tip (#7 or #9). Squeeze batter in a large ring following circle.

- Brush the top of the batter with the egg and milk mixture and sprinkle with diced Gruyère.

- Bake for 30 to 35 minutes. Cut into wedges. Serve immediately. Gougère will rise dramatically and then deflate as it cools.

OR

- Preheat oven to 400 degrees.

- Grease and flour large cookie sheet.

- Spoon batter in small dollops onto cookie sheet.

- Brush tops with egg and milk mixture.

- Sprinkle with diced Gruyère.

- Bake 20 to 25 minutes until puffed and golden. Serve immediately.

Cheese Puffs

French toast tidbits for the cocktail hour

- Serves 12 to 14
  1 day-old baguette French bread, crusts removed, cut into ½-inch cubes
  1 cup (8 ounces) unsalted butter, softened
  ½ pound cream cheese, softened
  ½ pound sharp Cheddar cheese, softened
  1 egg, lightly beaten

- Preheat oven to 350 degrees.

- Melt butter, cream cheese and Cheddar in a double boiler. Remove from heat and cool. Mix egg into the mixture.

- Dip bread cubes into the cheese mixture and place on cookie sheet lined with waxed paper. Refrigerate for 4 hours. May be prepared to this point and frozen. Defrost before proceeding.

- Transfer to a lightly greased cookie sheet and bake for 12 to 15 minutes until brown and melted. Serve at once with toothpicks.

Spanikopita

This Greek classic brings kudos from your guests.

- Makes 18 to 24 pieces
  1 package frozen phyllo dough, defrosted overnight in refrigerator
  2 tablespoons (1 ounce) unsalted butter
  1 large onion, chopped
  2 cloves garlic, chopped
  3 10-ounce packages frozen chopped spinach, cooked and drained
  8 eggs
  2 8-ounce packages cream cheese
  24 ounces cottage cheese
  1 pound feta cheese
  Freshly ground pepper to taste
  1 cup (8 ounces) unsalted butter
  Juice of 1 lemon

- Preheat oven to 325 degrees.

- In a small frying pan, sauté onion and garlic in 2 tablespoons melted butter.

- Combine spinach with eggs and cheeses. Add garlic and onion.

- In small saucepan melt 1 cup butter. Add lemon juice. Set aside.

- Remove phyllo from refrigerator and unfold so that it lies at full length. In a greased 11 x 14-inch baking dish layer 6 sheets of phyllo alternately with melted lemon butter. (Use a pastry brush). Spoon a layer of spinach mixture over phyllo. Continue layering phyllo and lemon butter until phyllo is used up. Brush top with lemon butter.

- Bake, uncovered 45 to 60 minutes. Cool 10 minutes before cutting into squares. May be prepared 8 hours in advance or frozen and reheated prior to serving.

Zucchini Squares

Serve with cocktails or a luncheon salad.

- **Serves 8 to 10**
  - **4 small zucchini**
  - **1 cup prepared biscuit mix**
  - **½ cup onion, finely chopped**
  - **½ cup Parmesan cheese, grated**
  - **2 tablespoons parsley, chopped**
  - **½ teaspoon salt**
  - **½ teaspoon dried oregano**
  - **1 garlic clove, minced (optional)**
  - **Dash of pepper**
  - **½ cup vegetable oil**
  - **4 eggs, slightly beaten**

- Preheat oven to 350 degrees.

- Split zucchini lengthwise and slice thinly (3 to 4 cups).

- In a large bowl, combine biscuit mix, onion, cheese, parsley, salt, oregano, garlic, pepper, oil and eggs thoroughly. Fold in zucchini.

- Spread in greased 13 x 9 x 2-inch pan. Bake 40 minutes until golden. Cut into squares and serve warm.

Water Chestnuts Wrapped in Bacon

A new twist on an old favorite

- **Serves 6**
  - **12 slices bacon**
  - **¼ cup dry sherry**
  - **2 tablespoons soy sauce**
  - **2 tablespoons water**
  - **1 teaspoon sugar**
  - **⅛ teaspoon ground ginger**
  - **1 8-ounce can whole water chestnuts, drained**
  - **24 toothpicks**

- Cut bacon in half and fry until brown but not stiff. Blot and cool.

- Combine sherry, soy sauce, water, sugar and ginger in a bowl. Add water chestnuts and marinate for at least 1 hour.

- Wrap 1 slice of bacon around each water chestnut and secure with a toothpick. (Larger water chestnuts may be cut in half.) Place on a cookie sheet.

- Broil 5 to 7 minutes or until bacon is crisp.

$\mathcal{S}$OUPS

97

Suzuki Harunobu (Japanese, 1725?-1770), *The Three Sake Tasters*, 1765, color woodblock print, *chūban* (approx. 10 x 7"). Gift of Mrs. John D. Rockefeller

Harunobu played a pivotal role in the history of Japanese printmaking by introducing the full polychrome woodblock print. In *The Three Sake Tasters*, the women standing around a huge jar of sake are enacting a traditionally male subject representing Shaka (Buddha), Kōshi (Confucius), and Rōshi (Lao Tsze). The moral of the tale is that all religions have a common source, with their differences lying only in interpretation.

Chilled Strawberry and Wine Soup

Excellent as a dessert for brunch

• Serves 6

2 cups strawberries

½ cup granulated sugar

1 cup water

1 cup white wine

1½ tablespoons fresh lemon juice

1 teaspoon grated lemon peel

½ pint heavy cream, whipped

• Place strawberries, sugar and water in the blender. Cover and purée.

• Add white wine, lemon juice and lemon peel. Fold in whipped cream. Chill and serve in glass bowls or stemmed goblets.

Cold Zucchini Soup

• Serves 6

½ cup (4 ounces) unsalted butter

1½ pounds unpeeled zucchini, grated

¾ cup celery, chopped

½ cup onion, finely chopped

3 cups chicken stock

½ cup all-purpose flour

3 cups heavy cream

¼ cup flaked lump crabmeat

Bouquet garni (1 bay leaf, 5 fresh basil leaves, thyme and peppercorns tied in cheesecloth)

• Melt 3 tablespoons butter in a large saucepan. Add zucchini, celery and onion and cook until tender (about 15 minutes).

• Add stock and bouquet garni. Bring to a boil. Reduce heat and simmer for 3 minutes.

• Meanwhile, in a large saucepan, melt 5 tablespoons butter. Whisk in flour and cook, stirring, for 3 minutes.

• Gradually whisk soup into butter and flour mixture. Simmer 5 minutes and remove the bouquet garni.

• When cool, purée soup in blender and add 2 cups cream.

• Strain mixture into a bowl. Season with salt and pepper and refrigerate 2 hours.

• Just before serving, whip the remaining cup of cream to stiff peaks. Ladle soup into bowls and garnish each with whipped cream and 2 teaspoons flaked crabmeat.

Memphis Melon Soup

*An attractive dish for summertime —
be sure the melons are ripe!*

- **Serves 8**
  1 ripe cantaloupe
  1 ripe honeydew melon
  2 tablespoons fresh lemon juice
  2 tablespoons fresh lime juice
  Fresh mint leaves

- Purée cantaloupe, add lemon juice. Set aside.

- Purée honeydew, add lime juice.

- Line up serving bowls. Pour simultaneously into each bowl so that the cantaloupe and honeydew stay separated. Garnish with mint leaves.

Senegalese Soup

Rich, creamy and subtly spiced with curry, apples and wine

- **Serves 6 to 8**
  3 tablespoons (1½ ounces) unsalted butter
  2 tart apples, peeled, cored and chopped
  1 medium onion, finely chopped
  1 tablespoon curry
  2½ tablespoons all-purpose flour
  ½ teaspoon salt
  3 cups chicken stock
  ¾ cup dry white wine
  ¾ cup light cream
  2 egg yolks
  1 cup cooked chicken, diced (optional)
  Salt to taste
  Freshly ground pepper to taste

- In large saucepan, melt butter and cook apples and onion until onion is translucent. Add curry, flour and salt and cook for 2 minutes, stirring constantly. Slowly add stock and wine, stirring constantly. Bring to a boil, reduce heat and simmer 10 minutes.

- Cool and purée in blender, 2 cups at a time.

- Beat egg yolks, add to cream and slowly add to puréed mixture. Stir to blend.

- Add chicken, if desired, and correct seasoning with salt and pepper. Serve in shallow soup dish with a sliver of unpeeled apple as garnish. Serve hot or cold.

99

Zucchini Gazpacho

A splendid variation of a summertime staple

- Serves 6

2 medium zucchini, peeled, seeded and chopped

2 scallions, finely chopped

1 garlic clove, crushed

1 tablespoon fresh dill, chopped

1 teaspoon honey

4 cups tomato juice

1 red pepper, seeded and chopped

1 cup plain yogurt

1 tablespoon Worcestershire sauce

Extra zucchini slices for garnish

- Mix all ingredients in a large bowl and then process in batches in a blender.

- Serve chilled in shallow bowls with slices of zucchini for garnish.

Spiced Tomato and Tarragon Soup

A favorite from the Lake District in England

- Serves 6

4 cups onion, finely chopped

½ cup (4 ounces) unsalted butter

2 35-ounce cans Italian plum tomatoes, with juice

1½ cups white wine

2 tablespoons granulated sugar

2 tablespoons fresh tarragon, chopped or 1 tablespoon dried tarragon

- In large frying pan, sauté onions in butter until golden (approximately 30 minutes).

- Add tomatoes, wine, sugar and tarragon. Cover with buttered round of waxed paper. Place frying pan lid over paper-covered mixture. Simmer 45 minutes. Let cool for 10 minutes.

- In a blender, purée the mixture in small batches.

- May be served chilled or warm with garnish of sour cream and chopped chives.

Variation: May be prepared with 3 pounds of fresh tomatoes.

Belgian Winter Soup

Perfect for the day after Thanksgiving

- Serves 4

1½ cups chicken stock

½ pound fresh Brussels sprouts, chopped

1 sweet red pepper, chopped

1 fresh tomato, chopped

½ pound cooked turkey, cubed

½ teaspoon freshly ground black pepper

¼ teaspoon fresh basil

- Bring chicken stock to a low boil and add chopped Brussels sprouts, red pepper and tomato. Cook for 5 to 7 minutes.

- Add cubed turkey and seasonings. Simmer for 10 minutes before serving in deep bowls accompanied by corn muffins.

Bombay Chicken Soup

Garnishes make this soup unique.

- **Serves 4 to 6**
  1 small onion, finely chopped
  1 celery stalk, finely chopped
  2 tablespoons unsalted butter
  4 cups chicken broth
  ⅓ cup long grain rice, uncooked
  1 cup milk
  1 cup light cream
  1½ cups cooked chicken, diced
  ½ cup raisins
  2 tablespoons curry powder
  1 hard boiled egg, chopped
  ½ cup peanuts, chopped

- In a 3-quart saucepan, sauté onion and celery in 2 tablespoons butter.

- Add chicken broth and rice. Lower heat to simmer, cover and cook 20 minutes until rice is done.

- Stir in milk, cream, chicken, raisins and curry. Simmer for 20 minutes.

- When ready to serve, garnish with chopped egg and peanuts.

Corn Chowder

Robust and really good!

- **Serves 6 to 8**
  3 tablespoons (1½ ounces) unsalted butter
  3 onions, sliced
  6 stalks celery, leaves removed, finely chopped
  4 10-ounce packages frozen shoe peg corn
  1 quart chicken stock
  2 pints light cream (or more to taste)
  2 tablespoons (1 ounce) additional unsalted butter
  Paprika (garnish)

- Sauté onions in butter and add chopped celery. Cook until lightly browned.

- Boil corn in chicken stock until soft. Drain stock into onion-celery mixture.

- Force corn through food mill, if desired, and add to pot along with cream and butter.

- Heat until very hot. Do not boil. Serve in deep bowls garnished with a dash of paprika.

101

California Fish and Vegetable Soup

A lovely soup for an entrée, served with salad and French bread

- Serves 6

  8 ounces clam juice

  3 cups chicken stock

  ¾ cup water

  1 medium onion, finely chopped

  Grated peel and juice from ½ fresh lemon

  3 sprigs fresh tarragon or 1 teaspoon dried

  2 sprigs fresh dill or ½ teaspoon dried

  4 tablespoons chopped fresh basil or 1¼ tablespoons dried

  1 bay leaf

  1 pound cod or haddock fillets

  1 35-ounce can tomatoes, undrained

  1 8-ounce can tomato sauce

  1½ tablespoons salt, or to taste

  ½ teaspoon red pepper flakes

  1 tablespoon sugar, or to taste

  1½ cups curly or spiral macaroni

  2 medium zucchini, unpeeled, sliced into ⅛-inch rounds

  ½ pound mushrooms, sliced

  Freshly ground pepper

  ½ lemon, thinly sliced (garnish)

- In large soup kettle, combine clam juice, chicken stock, water, onion, lemon peel, lemon juice, tarragon, dill, basil and bay leaf. Bring to boil.

- Add fish fillets and simmer for 15 minutes. Remove fish and set aside. Add tomatoes and tomato sauce to stock. Return to boil, lower heat and simmer for 2 minutes. Add macaroni and boil for an additional 7 minutes. Add salt, red pepper flakes and sugar, to taste.

- Reduce heat. Add zucchini and mushrooms. Simmer for 4 minutes.

- Flake fish. Return to soup mixture and heat thoroughly. Serve in shallow bowls sprinkled with freshly ground pepper and garnish with lemon slices.

Cream of Leek Soup with Stilton

The crumbled Stilton garnish adds zest to this classic French soup.

- Serves 4

  1 tablespoon unsalted butter

  1 tablespoon finely chopped shallots

  2 cups coarsely chopped leeks

  ½ cup peeled and diced potato

  2 cups vegetable or chicken stock, heated

  1½ cups light cream

  Salt, freshly ground pepper, nutmeg to taste

  Lemon juice to taste

  2 ounces Stilton cheese, crumbled

- Melt butter in a 2-quart saucepan. Add shallots and leeks, cover and cook over medium heat until translucent.

- Add potato and hot stock. Cover and cook until potato is tender (about 20 minutes).

- Place in a blender or food processor and purée.

- In a 1-quart saucepan, bring cream to a gentle boil. Reduce heat to very low and cook, stirring frequently, until reduced and slightly thickened (about 45 minutes).

- Add to leek and potato mixture and bring to a boil. Add salt, pepper, nutmeg and lemon juice to taste. May be prepared 24 hours in advance. Reheat at serving time.

- Pour into individual bowls and top with crumbled Stilton cheese.

Curried Crab Soup

A truly splendid soup, suitable for the most elegant dinner party

- **Serves 6 to 8**
  ½ cup (4 ounces) unsalted butter
  1 cup onion, finely chopped
  2 cloves of garlic, minced
  1 cup apple, peeled and chopped
  1 tablespoon curry powder
  6 tablespoons all-purpose flour
  1 cup ripe tomatoes, peeled, seeded and chopped
  6 cups chicken broth
  Salt to taste
  Freshly ground pepper to taste
  1 pound crabmeat, shells removed
  2 cups heavy cream

- In a heavy saucepan, melt butter, add the onion and cook until soft and wilted. Add the garlic and apple. Cook, stirring, until soft and sprinkle with curry powder and flour. Cook, stirring, for 3 minutes.

- Add the chopped tomato. Add chicken broth, a small amount at a time, until well incorporated.

Whisk the soup until smooth and thickened. Add salt and pepper to taste. Simmer 15 minutes.

- Remove from heat and cool. Purée in small batches in blender or processor until smooth. May be prepared in advance to this point and refrigerated or frozen.

- To serve, bring to room temperature, add crabmeat and stir lightly. Simmer for 10 minutes, then add heavy cream. Heat, but do not boil. Serve in small bowls.

Cold Peach Soup

A refreshing summer soup

- **Serves 4**
  4 ripe peaches
  2 cups dry white wine
  1 cup water
  3 tablespoons sugar
  ¼ teaspoon cinnamon
  ¼ teaspoon curry
  3 whole cloves
  1 navel orange, peeled and sliced

- Plunge peaches in boiling water for 1 minute. Remove skins and pits.

- Purée in a blender or food processor and transfer purée to an enameled saucepan. Add wine, water, sugar, cinnamon, curry and cloves. Bring to a boil and simmer, stirring, for 10 minutes.

- Remove cloves. Cool soup. Chill for at least 4 hours.

- Serve in chilled bowls, garnished with thin slices of orange.

Far East Pea Soup

Another vegetable may be substituted for the peas. Spinach, broccoli, carrots or cauliflower are all good suggestions.

- Serves 4 to 6
  1 cup fresh or frozen peas
  1 small onion, diced
  1 small carrot, sliced
  1 stalk celery, diced
  1 potato, peeled and diced
  1 teaspoon curry powder
  3 cups chicken broth
  1 cup light cream
  Salt to taste
  Freshly ground pepper to taste
  2 tablespoons thinly sliced scallions (garnish)

- Simmer vegetables, curry powder and chicken broth for 15 minutes, or until vegetables are tender. Cool.

- When cooled, purée in batches in blender.

- Return to saucepan and add cream and seasonings.

- Heat and serve. Sprinkle with scallions.

Old-Fashioned Cabbage Soup

Here's a hearty soup that's at its best when made a day or two in advance.

- Serves 6
  4 quarts water
  2 pounds short ribs of beef
  1 large cabbage
  1 large onion, chopped
  1 whole carrot, sliced
  4 to 5 sprigs of parsley
  1 35-ounce can crushed tomatoes
  1 12-ounce can peeled, whole tomatoes
  ¾ cup sugar
  3 teaspoons salt
  1 teaspoon pepper
  2 teaspoons sour salt
  6 small potatoes, peeled and boiled

- Cut cabbage in quarters. Core and slice.

- In a large soup pot, put cabbage, onion, carrot, parsley, crushed tomatoes, whole tomatoes, sugar, salt, pepper and sour salt. Bring to a boil, then reduce and simmer for 3 hours.

- Cool soup. Skim fat from the top and remove meat from short ribs. Keep the meat but discard the bones. Return meat to soup.

- When ready to serve, heat and pour over sliced, boiled potatoes in individual shallow bowls.

Onion Soup Gratinée

Thick and flavorful and makes a novel presentation when served in baked squash "bowls".

- **Serves 8 to 10**
  10 cups water
  8 beef bouillon cubes
  Rib roast bone, or 2 pounds soup bones
  ½ cup (4 ounces) unsalted butter
  4 large Spanish onions, sliced
  2 medium carrots, sliced
  2 celery stalks, sliced
  1 bay leaf
  2 teaspoons fresh thyme
  ¼ cup sherry
  4 ounces Gruyère cheese, grated

- Simmer rib roast bone in 10 cups water with bouillon cubes for 2 hours. If using soup bones, cook an additional 2 hours. Add carrots, celery, thyme, bay leaf and simmer for an additional ½ hour.

- In large frying pan, sauté onion slices in the butter.

- Remove bones from stock and add sautéed onions. Simmer for 15 minutes. Add sherry.

- Ladle soup into bowls and top with grated Gruyère (which will melt).

  Variation: For an elegant dinner, instead of soup bowls, present the soup in acorn squash. Allow one squash per person.

- Cut top off squash and save.

- Cut small piece off bottom so squash will stand up and scoop out pulp and seeds.

- Cook squash for 20 minutes at 400 degrees, then fill with onion soup and top with cheese.

Russian Sweet and Sour Cabbage Soup

This Russian peasant soup is tasty and unusual with the addition of raisins and apples.

- **Serves 6 to 8**
  ¾ pound beef chunks
  1½ quarts beef stock
  1 medium red cabbage, coarsely chopped
  3 carrots, sliced into rounds
  2 medium onions, sliced
  1 35-ounce can peeled, whole tomatoes
  2 to 3 hard, crisp apples, peeled, cored and sliced (keep in cold water)
  ½ cup raisins
  ¼ cup brown sugar
  2 tablespoons fresh lemon juice

- In 6-quart soup pot, simmer beef cubes in beef stock for 45 minutes. Add chopped cabbage, onions, carrots and tomatoes and cook for 30 minutes.

- Add apples and raisins, simmer 10 minutes.

- Add brown sugar and lemon juice to taste. Serve with black bread, butter, fruit and cheese.

105

Sweet Red Pepper Soup

A wonderful way to use all those extra summertime peppers

- Serves 6

2 tablespoons (1 ounce) unsalted butter

2 large onions, chopped

2 medium carrots, peeled and sliced

6 cups chicken stock

2½ pounds sweet red peppers, chopped

1 cup skim milk

Salt

Freshly ground pepper

⅛ teaspoon dried thyme

Commercial sour cream or yogurt (garnish)

- Melt butter and sauté onions over low heat until translucent.

- Add carrots and chicken stock and bring to a boil. Reduce heat and simmer for 20 minutes.

- Add chopped red peppers and cook for 20 minutes until peppers are soft.

- Remove from heat and add milk, salt, pepper and thyme.

- When soup is cool, purée in batches in blender.

- To serve, reheat but do not boil. Add dollop of sour cream or yogurt.

106

Tuscan Minestrone

At the table, a Florentine would stir in a little extra olive oil.

- Serves 12

1½ quarts chicken broth

5 cloves garlic, peeled

1 large white onion, chopped

2 12-ounce cans Italian white cannellini beans

1 28-ounce can Italian peeled tomatoes, chopped, with juice

3 carrots, sliced

1 medium cauliflower, coarsely chopped

4 celery stalks, thinly sliced

1 pound green beans, ends trimmed and halved

1 bay leaf

2 tablespoons extra virgin olive oil

Salt to taste

Freshly ground pepper to taste

1 cup tubetti pasta or any small tubular pasta

½ cup parsley, chopped

1 cup Parmesan cheese, freshly grated

- In a large pot, combine broth, garlic, onion, beans, tomatoes, carrots, cauliflower, celery, string beans, bay leaf and olive oil. Bring to boil, reduce heat and simmer 1½ hours.

- When ready to serve, cook pasta separately and put into serving bowls. Pour minestrone over pasta, sprinkle with parsley and cheese.

Potage St. Germain

*Makes a lovely luncheon main course
served with fruit, bread and cheese.*

- **Serves 4 to 6**
  4 tablespoons (2 ounces) unsalted butter

  2 ounces salad oil

  1 bunch scallions, chopped

  1 clove garlic, minced

  1 teaspoon curry (or to taste)

  1 teaspoon tumeric (or to taste)

  2 tablespoons flour

  1 head lettuce, shredded

  1 lemon, juice and zest

  1⅔ pounds peas (may be frozen)

  1 teaspoon sugar

  4 cups chicken stock

  1 cup light cream

- In large pot, heat butter and oil. Add scallions and garlic. Stir and cook on low heat until soft. Add curry, tumeric and flour. Stir.

- Add shredded lettuce, lemon (juice and zest), peas and sugar, stirring constantly. Add stock slowly and stir. Bring to a boil, reduce heat to low and simmer 15 minutes, covered.

- Let mixture cool slightly.

- Place in bowl of food processor and with motor running add light cream in thin stream until incorporated.

- Soup can be served hot or well chilled.

107

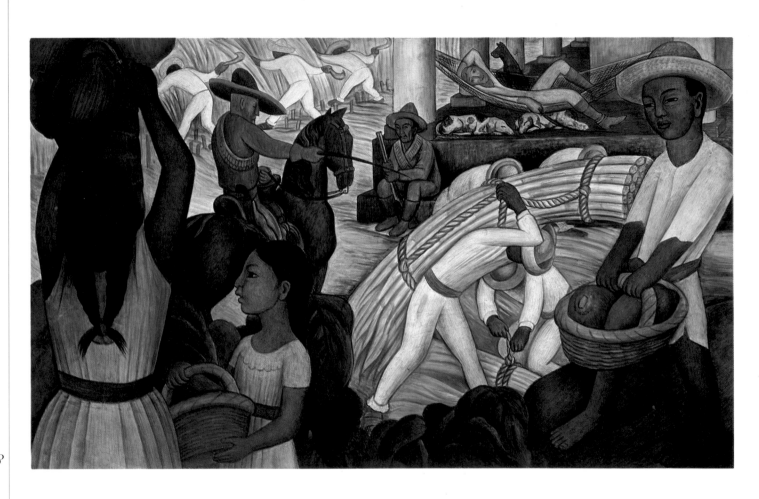

BREAKFAST AND BRUNCH

Diego Rivera (Mexican, 1886–1957), *Sugar Cane*, 1931, fresco, 57 1/8 x 94 1/8". Gift of Mr. and Mrs. Herbert Cameron Morris

Rivera communicated his deep affection and concern for his fellow Mexicans with the dazzling force and beauty of his brilliantly personal use of images, color, and masterful composition. *Sugar Cane*, one of a series of eight "movable frescoes," depicts oppressed workers on a sugar plantation during the Mexican colonial period. Here a mounted foreman directs the heavily laden workers as the cruel-faced owner reclines on a hammock in the background.

Cheddar Cheese Muffins

The combination of cheese, cornmeal and red pepper make these a tasty addition to grilled or baked ham.

- Serves 10
  4 ounces Cheddar cheese, grated
  1 large green onion, including top, minced
  1 cup all-purpose flour
  ⅓ cup yellow cornmeal
  2 teaspoons baking powder
  ½ teaspoon red pepper flakes
  ½ teaspoon salt
  1 tablespoon granulated sugar
  ¾ cup commercial sour cream
  ⅓ cup vegetable oil
  2 large eggs

- Preheat oven to 375 degrees.

- In a large bowl, combine cheese and green onion.

- In a separate bowl, combine flour, cornmeal, baking powder, red pepper flakes, salt and sugar. Add cheese and onion mixture, blending thoroughly.

- In a separate bowl, mix sour cream, oil and eggs thoroughly. Add to dry ingredients. Mix only until dry ingredients are moistened.

- Pour batter into greased muffin tins and fill ⅔ full. Bake 18 minutes. Serve warm. (Can be frozen and reheated.)

Sour Cream Apple Coffee Cake

Certainly worth getting up for!

- Serves 10 to 12
  8 tablespoons (4 ounces) unsalted butter
  1 cup granulated sugar
  2 eggs, beaten lightly
  1 cup commercial sour cream mixed with 1 teaspoon baking soda
  1½ cups all-purpose flour
  1½ teaspoons baking powder
  1 tablespoon vanilla extract
  5 cooking apples, cored, pared and sliced in thin wedges
  ½ cup pecans, chopped
  ¼ cup walnuts, chopped
  ¼ cup granulated sugar
  2 teaspoons ground cinnamon

- Preheat oven to 350 degrees. Grease and flour a 9 x 13-inch shallow baking pan.

- Cream butter and sugar. Add eggs one at a time.

- Add sour cream with soda, vanilla extract and dry ingredients and mix well.

- Pour ½ of batter into the pan. Place half the apple slices on top of the batter. Combine sugar and cinnamon and sprinkle half of mixture over apples.

- Pour remaining batter over apple slices and spread evenly with rubber spatula.

- Cover with remaining apple slices and sprinkle with topping of pecans, walnuts, and remaining sugar and cinnamon mixture. Dot generously with extra butter and bake 45 minutes or until cake tester comes out clean. Open oven door and allow cake to cool in oven. To serve, cut in squares.

Cinnamon Walnut Coffee Cake

This freezes very well.

• **Serves 10**

Cake

½ **cup (4 ounces) unsalted butter, room temperature**

1 **cup granulated sugar**

2 **large eggs**

1 **teaspoon vanilla extract**

½ **pint commercial sour cream mixed with ½ teaspoon**
  vanilla extract

2 **cups all-purpose flour**

½ **teaspoon baking powder**

½ **teaspoon salt**

1 **teaspoon baking soda**

• Preheat oven to 350 degrees. Grease and flour a 10-inch tube pan.

• Cream butter and sugar until smooth. Beat in eggs one at a time. Add vanilla extract.

• In a separate bowl, combine flour, baking powder, salt and baking soda. Combine sour cream mixture with butter mixture and fold in flour mixture until well blended.

Topping

½ **cup granulated sugar**

1 **teaspoon ground cinnamon**

½ **cup chopped walnuts**

3 **tablespoons unsalted butter, melted**

• Combine sugar, cinnamon, walnuts and butter.

• Pour half the batter into a greased and floured 10-inch tube pan. Sprinkle ½ the topping plus ⅓ the melted butter on top of batter.

• Layer rest of batter on top and cover with remainder of topping and butter. Bake 55 minutes. Serve warm.

Cinnamon Toast Fingers

Wonderful breakfast treat and just as good when included on a tea tray

• **Serves 12**

⅔ **cup granulated sugar**

4 **teaspoons ground cinnamon**

6 ½**-inch thick slices of day old homemade white bread,**
  crusts removed and each slice cut into four strips

10 **tablespoons (5 ounces) unsalted butter, melted**

• Preheat oven to 375 degrees. Grease cookie sheet.

• In a shallow wide bowl, combine sugar and cinnamon.

• Dip each bread strip first into the melted butter, coating well, and then into sugar mixture. Place on greased cookie sheet.

• Bake 10 minutes until crisp. Transfer to a rack and let cool for 2 minutes. Serve at once.

Creamy Mushrooms

Elegance from the microwave!

• Serves 8

2 pounds mushrooms, trimmed and quartered

6 tablespoons (3 ounces) unsalted butter or margarine, softened

3 tablespoons all-purpose flour

¼ cup chopped onion

½ cup chopped celery

½ cup chopped green pepper

1 pint commercial sour cream

2 teaspoons prepared mustard

¼ teaspoon freshly grated nutmeg

2 teaspoons salt, or to taste

¼ teaspoon freshly ground pepper

8 slices homemade-style bread, toasted

• Gently combine all ingredients except toast. Place in a 3-quart microwave-safe casserole. May be prepared 4 to 6 hours in advance. Cover and refrigerate. Bring to room temperature before continuing.

• Bake, uncovered, at MEDIUM power for 15 minutes or until cooked through, stirring every 5 minutes. In conventional oven, bake at 350 degrees for 45 minutes.

• Serve at once over wedges of toast.

Variation: For a lower calorie, lower cholesterol combination, omit the sour cream and substitute 1 pint cottage cheese blended with 4 tablespoons milk and 2 tablespoons lemon juice.

Custardy French Toast

A treat for brunch — also a wonderful dessert for bread pudding lovers

• Serves 6

2 large eggs

1 tablespoon confectioners sugar

2 cups light cream

Pinch of salt

½ teaspoon vanilla extract

½ cup rum

3 tablespoons (1½ ounces) unsalted butter

12 slices day-old French bread

Custard Sauce

1 egg, beaten

1 tablespoon granulated sugar

½ teaspoon vanilla extract

¼ cup applesauce

½ cup milk

• In a blender mix eggs, sugar, light cream, salt, vanilla extract and rum. Submerge the French bread in mixture. Meanwhile, in a large, heavy frying pan, melt butter. Sauté slices on each side until golden.

• In a shallow baking casserole, place sautéed bread in one layer.

• In a separate bowl, combine 1 beaten egg, sugar and vanilla extract. Add ½ cup milk which has been heated to the boiling point. Stir in applesauce.

• Pour custard sauce over French bread and bake at 400 degrees for 15 minutes. Serve with syrup.

Do-Ahead Cheese Soufflé

It's foolproof!

- Serves 6

  6 tablespoons (3 ounces) unsalted butter

  6 tablespoons all-purpose flour

  1 teaspoon salt

  Freshly ground pepper

  ½ teaspoon paprika

  Dash of cayenne

  6 ounces sharp Cheddar cheese, diced

  1½ cups milk

  6 eggs, room temperature, separated

- In a large saucepan, melt butter over low heat. Stir in flour and seasonings, then add milk all at once. Cook, stirring constantly, until mixture is smooth and thick, about 3 to 4 minutes. Add cheese and stir until melted. Remove from heat.

- Beat egg yolks to ribbon stage and gradually add to cheese mixture. Beat egg whites until soft peaks are formed. Stir ⅓ of egg whites into cheese mixture to lighten; then gently fold in remaining whites.

- Grease 2-quart soufflé dish. Carefully spoon in cheese mixture. Recipe may be prepared to this point up to 18 hours in advance. Store in refrigerator. Recipe may be frozen.

- Bake in a 350 degree oven for 45 minutes or until tester comes out clean.

- If made in advance, place soufflé in cold oven, set at 350 degrees and bake about 50 minutes or until tester comes out clean. If frozen, place in cold oven, set at 350 degrees and bake about 1 hour or until tester comes out clean. Accompany with grilled ham slices or bacon.

Kedgeree

This is a variation of a British classic that's smashing for a brunch buffet.

- Serves 3 to 4

  1 pound salmon, haddock, cod or halibut, cooked and flaked

  3 hard-cooked eggs, finely chopped

  ¾ cup cooked white rice, cooled

  4 ounces half-and-half

  ½ teaspoon salt

  Freshly ground black pepper

  ½ teaspoon paprika

  6 to 8 slices bacon, crisply fried

- Preheat oven to 350 degrees.

- Lightly butter 1-quart baking dish. Spread fish on bottom. Top with layer of hard-cooked eggs, then rice.

- Mix half-and-half with salt, pepper and paprika and pour over casserole contents. (If mixture looks too dry, add a little more half-and-half.) Bake for 20 minutes or until bubbly. Serve at once garnished with bacon.

Variation: Mix all ingredients lightly and heat in chafing dish. Serve with bacon.

Miniature Cheese and Herb Soufflés

A very special first course guaranteed to impress

- **Serves 8**

  ½ **pound thinly sliced bacon, cut into ½-inch cubes**

  1 **cup heavy cream**

  1 **cup milk**

  5 **eggs**

  1 **teaspoon salt**

  Dash of hot pepper sauce

  ½ **teaspoon freshly ground pepper**

  1 **tablespoon unsalted butter**

  8 **slices white bread, crusts removed, cut in half lengthwise**

  1 **pound Camembert cheese, rind removed, coarsely shredded**

  ¼ **cup fresh rosemary leaves, finely chopped, or 1 tablespoon dried (crumbled)**

- Preheat oven to 350 degrees.

- Sauté bacon in a heavy frying pan over medium heat until crisp. Drain on paper towels.

- To make custard: in a medium bowl, whisk together cream, milk, eggs, salt, hot pepper sauce and pepper.

- Butter 8 6-ounce soufflé dishes.

- Lay ½ slice of bread onto the bottom of each dish. Sprinkle evenly with half of the cheese, bacon, and rosemary. Add another ½ slice of bread and repeat a full second layer.

- Carefully spoon the custard mixture over the bread and cheese mixture to approximately ½ inch from the top of each soufflé dish. Press gently with the back of a spoon, then set aside, covered, for 30 minutes.

- Line an 11 x 17-inch jelly roll pan with aluminum foil. Place soufflé dishes, uncovered, on lined pan. Bake for 30 minutes, until bubbling and golden on top. Serve immediately.

Leek and Onion Pie

Try this for brunch, a light lunch or a first course.

- **Serves 6 to 8**

  1 **unbaked 9-inch pastry shell**

  1 **cup onions, thinly sliced**

  2 **cups leeks, cleaned and thinly sliced (white parts only)**

  2 **tablespoons (1 ounce) unsalted butter**

  3 **eggs**

  ½ **cup milk**

  ½ **cup heavy cream**

  ½ **teaspoon salt, or to taste**

  ¼ **teaspoon white pepper**

- Preheat oven to 400 degrees. Line a 9-inch pie plate with pastry. Crimp the edges.

- In a large heavy frying pan, melt butter and sauté the onions and leeks until translucent.

- In a small bowl, beat the eggs. Add the milk, cream, salt and pepper. Blend well.

- Combine egg mixture with onions and leeks.

- Pour into pie shell and bake 30 minutes. Place under broiler to brown top slightly before serving.

Sausage, Apple and Bean Casserole

This is a "man pleaser".

- Serves 4

1½ pounds mild bulk sausage

2 to 3 apples

1 20¾-ounce can pork and beans

½ cup maple syrup

½ cup brown sugar

¼ cup prepared mustard

½ cup catsup

½ cup grated Cheddar cheese

- Preheat oven to 350 degrees.

- Fry sausage, drain and crumble.

- Pare and slice apples.

- Drain beans and add any or all of the following: maple syrup, brown sugar, mustard or catsup.

- In a 1-quart casserole dish, layer beans, apples and sausage twice. Top with grated Cheddar cheese and bake 25 minutes.

Spinach-Tomato Bake

Try for brunch topped with poached eggs.

- Serves 4

2 large tomatoes

1 slice bread, toasted dry and crumbled coarsely

1 10-ounce package frozen, chopped spinach, cooked and drained

4 tablespoons (2 ounces) unsalted butter, melted

¼ teaspoon salt, or to taste

⅓ cup grated Parmesan cheese

1 clove garlic, crushed

½ teaspoon dried thyme

2 eggs, beaten lightly

- Preheat oven to 350 degrees.

- Thickly slice tomatoes and place in a shallow, greased 1-quart baking dish.

- Combine toast crumbs with spinach and remaining ingredients. Spoon mixture on top of tomato slices. May be prepared 6 to 8 hours in advance. Cover and refrigerate. Bring to room temperature before continuing. Bake for 15 to 20 minutes. Serve piping hot.

Tahoe Brunch

A variation of an Italian "strata"

- **Serves 8 to 10**

  12 slices white bread, crusts removed

  3 tablespoons (1½ ounces) unsalted butter, softened

  1½ pounds mild Italian bulk sausage

  8 tablespoons (4 ounces) unsalted butter

  ½ pound sliced mushrooms

  2 cups thinly sliced onions

  ¾ pound sharp Cheddar cheese, grated

  5 eggs

  3 teaspoons Dijon-style mustard

  1 teaspoon dry mustard

  1 teaspoon ground nutmeg

  1 teaspoon salt

  ⅛ teaspoon freshly ground pepper

  2½ cups milk

  2 tablespoons parsley, chopped

Note: Must be prepared 24 hours in advance.

- Butter bread with softened butter.

- In frying pan, cook sausage breaking it into bite-sized pieces. Set aside.

- In frying pan, melt butter. Add onions and cook until translucent and add mushrooms and cook several minutes until brown.

- Grease a 9 x 13-inch shallow casserole. Layer one half of bread, mushroom mixture, sausage and cheese in that order. Repeat second layer of same ingredients.

- Beat eggs. Add both mustards, nutmeg, salt and pepper. Add milk.

- Pour mixture over sausage and cheese casserole and cover and refrigerate 24 hours.

- To serve, bring to room temperature and bake at 350 degrees for one hour. Present with a garnish of chopped parsley.

Tomato-Cheese Tart

Reminiscent of a deep-dish pizza, but more elegant

- **Serves 6 to 8**

  1 frozen or refrigerated 9-inch pie crust

  ⅓ cup Dijon-style mustard

  1 pound Mozzarella cheese, thinly sliced

  8 ripe tomatoes, thinly sliced, seeds removed

  1 tablespoon finely chopped garlic

  1 teaspoon dried oregano

  1 tablespoon fresh basil, chopped or 1 teaspoon dried

  Salt and pepper, to taste

  2 tablespoons olive oil

- Preheat oven to 400 degrees.

- Place pie crust into 9-inch pie plate. Brush mustard onto bottom and halfway up sides of crust.

- Cover bottom with Mozzarella, then starting at the center, place tomatoes in concentric circles. Sprinkle with garlic, salt, pepper, oregano and fresh basil. Drizzle with olive oil. May be prepared to this point 3 to 4 hours in advance. Cover and refrigerate. Bring to room temperature before continuing.

- Bake 40 minutes, and serve hot or slightly warm.

- Fresh Italian-style plum tomatoes are best for this recipe.

Variation: Layer thin slices of ham between the cheese and tomatoes for a savory accent.

Baked Grits with Cheese

Interest in Americana cooking has made this a new hit in "fancy" restaurants!

- **Serves 6 to 8**
  5 cups water
  1 cup coarse grits
  2 tablespoons (4 ounces) unsalted butter
  ¾ pound sharp Cheddar cheese, grated
  2 eggs, well beaten
  ¼ cup milk
  Salt and pepper

- Preheat oven to 425 degrees.

- Bring water to rapid boil and stir in grits. Stir for about 2 minutes. Reduce heat and cook at slow boil for 20 minutes, stirring frequently.

- Remove from heat and stir in butter. Add cheese and stir until melted in. Set aside and cool for 5 minutes.

- Add eggs, milk, salt and pepper and mix completely. Pour into greased 2-quart casserole. May be prepared to this point 24 hours in advance. Refrigerate covered but bring to room temperature before baking.

- Bake for 45 minutes until thick and brown.

Variation: Add ½ cup chopped green onions and 3 seeded and diced fresh or canned jalapeño peppers.

Southern Spoon Bread

Even Yankees like this!

- **Serves 4 to 6**
  2 cups milk
  ½ teaspoon salt
  ¾ cup ground cornmeal (white or yellow)
  4 tablespoons (2 ounces) unsalted butter
  4 eggs, separated

- Preheat oven to 350 degrees.

- Heat milk in saucepan and slowly add cornmeal and salt with wire whisk.

- Bring to a boil, stirring constantly. The batter will lump easily.

- Stir until thick and add butter, blending it in as it melts.

- Remove from heat, cool a bit and add egg yolks, one at a time. Cool. May be prepared to this point 1 day in advance. Cover and refrigerate. Bring to room temperature before continuing.

- Beat egg whites until stiff and fold into batter mixture.

- Pour into a well-buttered 1½-quart casserole and bake for 35 to 40 minutes.

- Do not open oven while baking. Serve at once as it is like a soufflé. Best when buttered.

Variation: For additional zip, add ½ cup shredded Cheddar cheese and a pinch of cayenne pepper, while blending in butter.

$\mathcal{S}$ALADS

Vincent van Gogh (Dutch, 1853–1890), *Sunflowers*, 1888–89, oil on canvas, 36 3/8 x 28". The Mr. and Mrs. Carroll S. Tyson, Jr. Collection

Sunflowers, one of Van Gogh's best known works, conveys the warmth of color he found at Arles. One of seven paintings of this subject that the artist made to decorate his rooms, this version shows twelve flowers, all in various stages of bloom. The yellows and ochers are applied with great vigor, and the thickness of the paint makes the petals stand out in relief against the turquoise background.

Salade de Boeuf Vinaigrette

An appealing main-course salad for a sweltering summer evening

• **Serves 6 to 8**

Salad
2½ pounds beef brisket cooked and cut into bite-sized cubes totalling 4 cups
2 ribs celery trimmed into 1-inch lengths and julienned
1 small red onion, peeled and thinly sliced
2 tomatoes, peeled, seeded and cubed
4 to 6 cornichons (imported sour gherkins), trimmed and julienned
1 clove garlic, finely minced
2 tablespoons chopped fresh parsley

Dressing
1½ tablespoons Dijon-style mustard
3 tablespoons red wine vinegar
⅔ cup peanut or corn oil, chilled
Salt
Freshly ground pepper

• Place meat in a 1½-quart bowl. Add celery, onion, tomatoes, cornichons, garlic and parsley. Toss gently.

• In a small bowl, combine mustard and vinegar. Gradually whisk in oil. Add salt and pepper to taste.

• Pour dressing over meat mixture. Toss to blend.

• Serve at room temperature on a bed of lettuce and watercress. Garnish with extra cornichons, radish roses and carrot curls.

Variation: Any cooked beef — even leftovers — is splendid prepared this way.

Apricot Chicken Salad

The subtly sweet-spicy dressing is one of the surprises in this entrée salad.

• **Serves 6 to 8**
3 pounds boneless chicken breasts, cooked
1 cup dried apricots, cut into ¼-inch strips
⅓ cup cream sherry
3 ribs celery, chopped
4 scallions, trimmed and sliced on the diagonal
⅓ cup slivered almonds
1 teaspoon dried rosemary
2 cups Homemade Food-Processor Mayonnaise
2 tablespoons Dijon-style mustard
¼ cup honey mustard

• Cut chicken breasts into strips and put into a mixing bowl.

• Put apricots and sherry into a small saucepan and boil. Reduce heat and simmer for 3 minutes.

• Add apricots and liquid to chicken. Add celery, scallions, almonds and rosemary to salad and toss to combine.

• Mix mayonnaise with the two mustards and add to chicken and fruit.

Chicken Almond Mousse

A molded chicken salad with a wonderful variety of textures and flavors

- Serves 6 to 8
  1 tablespoon plain gelatin

  ¼ cup cold water

  2 egg yolks, slightly beaten

  ½ teaspoon salt

  ¼ teaspoon pepper

  Dash paprika

  ½ teaspoon curry powder (optional)

  1 cup chicken stock

  1 cup cooked chicken, ground

  1 cup almonds, ground

  1 cup heavy cream, whipped

- Soften gelatin in cold water.

- Mix egg yolks, salt, pepper, paprika and curry powder in 3-quart saucepan.

- Add chicken stock and cook over low heat, stirring constantly until mixture coats spoon.

- Add gelatin and stir until dissolved.

- Stir in ground chicken and almonds and chill for ½ hour.

- Fold in whipped cream when gelatin begins to thicken. Turn into 1-quart oiled mold.

- Unmold on a bed of lettuce. Garnish with tomatoes, parsley and watercress.

Lime-Curry Chicken Salad

A refreshing and pretty salad that should be made in advance

- Serves 6 to 8
  1¼ pounds chicken breasts, cooked and cubed

  2 cups cooked rice

  2 green onions, sliced thin

  ¾ cup mayonnaise

  Grated rind and juice of 1 lime

  1½ teaspoons curry powder

  ½ teaspoon salt

  ¼ teaspoon white pepper

  1 cup honeydew melon balls

  1 cup cantaloupe balls

  2 tablespoons toasted sliced almonds

- Mix cooked chicken with rice and onion.

- Mix dressing ingredients and pour over chicken and rice. Refrigerate for at least several hours.

- One hour before serving, remove from refrigerator. Add melon balls and sprinkle with toasted almonds. Serve on a bed of greens.

Duck Salad with Oranges and Onions

A lavish luncheon salad or a special appetizer

- **Serves 6 to 8**
  1 roast duck (see below)
  4 seedless oranges, peeled and thinly sliced
  1 small red onion, peeled and thinly sliced into rings
  1 teaspoon finely minced garlic
  24 imported black olives, drained and pitted
  ½ teaspoon ground cumin (or more, to taste)
  3 tablespoons red wine vinegar
  6 tablespoons pure virgin olive oil
  ½ teaspoon salt (or more to taste)
  Freshly ground pepper to taste
  1 tablespoon finely chopped, fresh coriander (optional)
  Assorted washed and chilled greens (such as watercress, red leaf lettuce, Boston lettuce, radiccio)
  Additional orange slices, olives, onion rings, coriander, and 1 avocado, sliced for garnish

Roast duck
1 fresh duck, about 4½ pounds
Salt
Pepper

- Preheat oven to 450 degrees.

- Have butcher cut duck in quarters. Sprinkle inside and out with salt and pepper. Place skin-side up on a rack in a roasting pan. Put in oven and roast about 1 hour or until juices in thigh run clear.

- Pour off excess fat. Heat broiler. Place pan about 3 to 4 inches from source of heat and broil about 5 minutes until skin is crisp. Remove from oven and allow to cool.

Salad
- Remove all the meat from the duck and discard bones. Cut meat into bite-size chunks (there should be about 2 cups) and place in large mixing bowl.

- Add oranges, onion rings, garlic and olives.

- Make dressing. In a blender or large jar, combine cumin, vinegar, olive oil, salt and pepper.

- Pour dressing over duck mixture, add coriander and mix well. May be prepared to this point up to 8 hours in advance. Cover and refrigerate. Bring to room temperature before continuing.

- Arrange greens on a large platter. Spoon the duck salad on top. Garnish with additional onion rings, orange slices, olives, coriander and avocado wedges.

Note: You may wish to double the recipe for the dressing to serve on the side for those who want additional dressing on greens.

The Queen's Chicken Salad

Elizabeth II dined on this during her 1976 visit — it's a royal recipe!

- **Serves 6**
  2 cups cooked white meat of chicken, cubed

  ¼ cup sliced water chestnuts

  ½ pound seedless grapes, halved

  ½ cup chopped celery

  ½ cup toasted slivered almonds

  1 8-ounce can drained pineapple chunks

Dressing

¾ cup Homemade Food-Processor Mayonnaise

1 teaspoon fresh curry powder

2 teaspoons soy sauce

2 teaspoons fresh lemon juice

- In a large bowl, toss salad ingredients together.

- Mix salad dressing and fold into salad mixture. Chill for several hours.

- Serve on a bed of Bibb or Boston lettuce with triangles of buttered white toast or crusty rolls. Garnish with extra chunks of pineapple and slivers of toasted almonds.

Oriental Turkey Salad

Exotic variation of a luncheon favorite — and a smart idea for leftover turkey

- **Serves 8 to 10**
  6 cups cubed, cooked turkey (breasts preferred)

  2 cups seedless white grapes, halved

  1 8-ounce can water chestnuts, thinly sliced

  1 cup celery, chopped

  ½ cup green onion, chopped

  2 cups Homemade Food-Processor Mayonnaise

  2 tablespoons soy sauce

  2 tablespoons lemon juice

  1 tablespoon curry powder

  1 tablespoon minced mango chutney (optional)

  6 to 8 ounces dry-roasted cashews

  1 pound fresh bean sprouts

  8 to 10 small bunches of white grapes (garnish)

- In a large bowl, gently toss turkey, grapes, water chestnuts, celery and green onions. Set aside if serving within an hour. Otherwise, refrigerate until 1 hour before serving time.

- Mix mayonnaise, soy sauce, lemon juice, curry powder and chutney until well blended. Fold in nuts.

- To serve, mix dressing with turkey mixture. Either arrange sprouts on individual plates or on a serving platter. Mound turkey salad attractively in center. Garnish with sprigs of grapes.

Variation: Cubed cooked chicken can be substituted for turkey.

Hawaiian Lobster Salad

Elegant!

• Serves 6 to 8

1 whole pineapple

2 pounds lobster tails, boiled

2 pounds shrimp, boiled, shelled and cleaned

2 apples

1 tablespoon chopped tarragon

1 tablespoon chopped parsley

3 tablespoons Homemade Food-Processor Mayonnaise

6 tablespoons catsup

¼ ounce orange liqueur

¼ ounce port wine

• Cut pineapple in half. Remove flesh and cut away core, keeping pineapple shell intact. Dice pineapple.

• Dice cooked seafood. Core and dice apples. Add seafood and apples to diced pineapple. Add tarragon and parsley. Chill.

• Mix mayonnaise, catsup, orange liqueur and port wine. Fold into seafood and fruit. (Salad should be prepared no more than 3 to 4 hours prior to serving.)

• Fill pineapple halves with salad. Decorate with fresh flowers.

Japanese Summer Salad

Complex in flavor, but easy to assemble

• Serves 6

1 pound dried linguine, broken in half

1½ pounds medium shrimp, cooked

1 bunch green onions, thinly sliced

¼ cup sesame oil, mixed with ¼ cup peanut oil

½ pound mushrooms, sliced

1 bunch broccoli, trimmed and sliced

⅓ cup soy sauce

¼ cup sake

¼ cup toasted sesame seed

2 tablespoons grated fresh ginger

2 garlic cloves, mashed

• Bring large pot of salted water to a boil. Add noodles and cook until al dente (about 10 minutes). Drain, rinse and pat dry.

• Put noodles into a large bowl and stir in shrimp and onions.

• In a large frying pan, heat 2 tablespoons of oil and sauté mushrooms and broccoli for 5 minutes. Add to shrimp mixture.

• Blend soy sauce, sake, sesame seed, ginger, garlic and remaining oil mixture. Toss with shrimp mixture and refrigerate for up to 2 hours.

• Serve in large bowl and garnish all around with alfalfa sprouts. Serve cold or at room temperature.

Salade Niçoise

A glamorous entrée salad reminiscent of southern France

• **Serves 6**

Vinaigrette
⅔ **cup virgin olive oil**

1 tablespoon fresh lemon juice

2 tablespoons white wine vinegar

2 tablespoons Dijon-style mustard

1 garlic clove, minced

1 tablespoon fresh parsley, chopped

• Whisk oil, lemon juice, vinegar and mustard until well-blended.

• Stir in garlic and herbs. Set aside.

Salad
8 new potatoes, steamed for 15 to 20 minutes, peeled and sliced

1 minced scallion

3 tablespoons dry vermouth

Salt and freshly ground pepper

½ **pound fresh green beans, blanched**

2 heads Bibb or Boston lettuce, washed and chilled

2 7-ounce cans Italian style oil-packed tuna, drained

3 tablespoons capers, drained

½ **cup Niçoise olives, pitted**

1 2-ounce can rolled anchovies, drained

3 hard-cooked eggs cut into wedges

4 summer-ripe tomatoes, cut into wedges

• Toss potatoes, scallion, vermouth, salt and pepper gently in 2 tablespoons of the dressing. Set aside.

Toss beans in 2 tablespoons of the dressing. Set aside.

• Arrange lettuce leaves on 6 plates. Make a dome of tuna in the center of each, then surround with bundles of beans and slices of potatoes. Decorate with anchovies, olives and capers. Garnish with tomatoes and eggs. Spoon on remaining dressing and serve at once.

German Potato Salad

Great for picnics since there is no mayonnaise to spoil

• **Serves 6 to 8**

2 pounds new potatoes, cooked

2 tablespoons white vinegar

4 tablespoons vegetable oil

1 teaspoon salt (or to taste)

½ **teaspoon pepper (or to taste)**

½ **pound sliced bacon, fried crisp and crumbled**

4 tablespoons finely chopped onion

3 tablespoons finely chopped parsley

4 tablespoons finely chopped celery

1 tablespoon finely chopped parsley (garnish)

• While potatoes are warm, cut into ¼-inch slices and put in large mixing bowl.

• Whisk oil, vinegar, salt and pepper together. Pour over potatoes while warm and mix gently.

• Mix onion, parsley and celery together. Fold into potatoes. Add crumbled bacon, reserving 2 tablespoons for garnish. Set salad aside, but do not refrigerate if serving the same day. If salad is to be refrigerated, bring to room temperature and toss gently before serving. Garnish.

125

Shrimp Mousseline

A delicate molded luncheon salad

• Serves 4 to 6

2 4¼-ounce cans medium shrimp, rinsed and drained

1 6½-ounce can minced clams, drained, reserving juice

1 envelope plain gelatin

1 8-ounce package cream cheese, softened

1 cup premium mayonnaise

½ cup minced onion

1 cup celery, finely chopped

1 teaspoon fresh lemon juice

Tabasco to taste

Salt and freshly ground pepper to taste

Boston and Bibb lettuces, washed and chilled

4 to 6 whole shrimp, cooked and cleaned (garnish)

4 to 6 wedges of lemon (garnish)

4 to 6 slices of cucumber (garnish)

• Heat reserved clam juice. Remove from heat and stir in gelatin. Set aside.

• In a food processor, blend cream cheese and mayonnaise. Add shrimp, clams, onion, celery, lemon juice and seasonings. Blend in gelatin mixture.

• Pour into lightly oiled 4-cup mold. Cover and refrigerate until firm (about 6 hours). May be prepared to this point 24 hours in advance.

• At serving time unmold onto a bed of lettuce leaves. Garnish with whole cooked and cleaned shrimp and decorate with wedges of lemon and a ring of cucumber slices.

Variation: Pour into lightly oiled individual molds, chill and unmold onto each serving plate lined with lettuces and garnished as above.

Apple-Peanut Salad with Curry Dressing

Inventive and different

• Serves 4

Salad

1 tart green apple (Granny Smith is perfect), cored and thinly sliced, unpeeled

1 avocado, peeled and thinly sliced

2 teaspoons fresh lemon juice

½ cup dry-roasted peanuts

4 tablespoons chopped green onions

8 ounces fresh spinach leaves, heavy stems and ribs removed, washed, dried and chilled

Dressing

4 tablespoons white wine vinegar

2 teaspoons minced mango chutney

½ teaspoon curry powder

½ teaspoon dry mustard

½ teaspoon salt

5 drops hot pepper sauce

6 tablespoons vegetable oil

• Prepare salad up to 3 hours in advance of serving time by mixing apple and avocado slices with lemon juice and tossing with peanuts, onions and torn spinach. Cover and refrigerate.

• Prepare dressing by combining all ingredients, except oil, in blender. Add oil in a slow, steady stream. Refrigerate up to 3 days. Remove from refrigerator 30 minutes before serving time.

• At serving time, arrange salad in a glass bowl. Pour on dressing, and toss gently.

Greek Romaine Salad

Romaine holds up well on a buffet.

• **Serves 10 to 12**
 ¼ **pound sun-dried tomatoes**
 1 **cup red wine**
 1 **cup extra virgin olive oil**
 2 **heads romaine lettuce**
 10 **to 15 leaves of fresh basil**
 ¼ **to ½ pound Feta cheese**
 ¼ **cup balsamic vinegar**

• Several days in advance, place sun-dried tomatoes in bowl and cover with red wine. Let stand for 20 minutes.

• Drain and place tomatoes in a jar and cover with olive oil. Marinate for several days in the refrigerator.

• Wash and dry romaine and basil leaves and tear into pieces in a salad bowl.

• Crumble Feta cheese on top of lettuce.

• Add drained sun-dried tomatoes, reserving olive oil.

• Make vinaigrette by mixing reserved olive oil with balsamic vinegar. Combine and mix with the salad.

Spinach Salad Piquant

A light yet full-flavored version of one of the most popular contemporary salads

• **Serves 8**
 1¼ **pounds fresh spinach, washed and trimmed**
 4 **ounces bean sprouts**
 1¼ **pounds fresh mushrooms, sliced**
 ¾ **pound bacon, fried crisply and crumbled**

Dressing
 ⅓ **cup catsup**
 ⅓ **cup extra virgin olive oil**
 ⅓ **cup red wine vinegar**
 1 **teaspoon brown sugar**
 ⅛ **teaspoon steak sauce**
 ⅛ **teaspoon onion powder**
 ⅛ **teaspoon garlic powder**
 ⅛ **teaspoon salt**
 ⅛ **teaspoon pepper**

• Toss the spinach, sprouts, mushrooms and bacon in large bowl.

• Combine all dressing ingredients and whisk until blended.

• Pour over salad and toss well.

Summer Basil Salad

Use only the best summer tomatoes.

• Serves 6

Dressing

½ cup fresh basil leaves

½ cup extra virgin olive oil

2 tablespoons red wine vinegar

1 small garlic clove, peeled

½ teaspoon granulated sugar

½ teaspoon salt

Pinch of freshly ground pepper

• Place all ingredients in blender or food processor. Blend or process until smooth. Chill for 30 minutes before serving. Can be made up to 24 hours before serving.

Salad

2 ripe medium tomatoes sliced ¼-inch thick

½ small avocado, peeled and sliced into ¼-inch wedges

8 ounces Mozzarella cheese (preferably fresh) sliced ¼-inch thick

½ small red onion, sliced ¼-inch thick and separated into rings

• Arrange alternate slices of tomato, avocado and cheese on platter. Top with onion rings. Just before serving, drizzle on dressing.

Gazpacho Mold with Avocado Dressing

A new twist on an old favorite

• Serves 8 to 10

Salad Mold

2 envelopes unflavored gelatin

1 18-ounce can tomato juice

⅓ cup red wine vinegar

¾ teaspoon salt

¾ teaspoon hot pepper sauce

1 cup diced, peeled tomato

1 cup diced, peeled cucumber

½ cup diced green pepper

⅓ cup red onion, finely chopped

• In medium saucepan over low heat, dissolve gelatin in ¾ cup tomato juice, stirring constantly.

• Remove from heat. Add rest of tomato juice, vinegar, salt and hot pepper sauce.

• Put pan in bowl of ice water and stir until mixture thickens (about 15 minutes).

• Fold in tomato, cucumber, green pepper and onion.

• Pour into 1½-quart mold which has been oiled. Chill until firm.

Avocado Dressing

1 large ripe avocado

½ cup commercial sour cream

½ cup light cream

1 tablespoon grated onion

¾ teaspoon salt

⅛ teaspoon sugar

1 garlic clove, crushed

1 tablespoon fresh lemon juice

Freshly ground pepper

- Combine all ingredients in a blender until smooth. Cover and chill. Stir before serving.

Green Beans Vinaigrette

An intriguing dressing sparks this perfect picnic salad.

- Serves 6

1 pound fresh green beans, washed, trimmed and halved

3 tablespoons vegetable oil

¾ teaspoon salt

⅛ teaspoon freshly ground pepper

½ teaspoon Dijon-style mustard

1 small fresh tomato, seeded and chopped

1 small onion, minced

2 tablespoons chopped cornichons (imported sour gherkins) or dill pickle

2 teaspoons capers, rinsed and drained

1 hard-cooked egg, cut into 4 wedges

4 cherry tomatoes (garnish)

- Cook beans in boiling water until crisp-tender about 3 to 5 minutes.

- In a 6-ounce jar, combine oil, seasonings, mustard, tomato, onion, pickles and capers. Shake until well-blended. Pour dressing over beans and refrigerate.

- About ½ hour before serving time, remove beans from refrigerator and mix. Mound beans on a platter and surround with wedges of egg. Garnish with cherry tomatoes.

Variations: For a Mediterranean touch add 1 garlic clove, minced, to dressing and garnish with four pitted Niçoise olives and four fillets of anchovy. Can also be served as an appetizer on individual salad plates, lined with lettuce leaves.

Hearts of Palm Salad

Wonderful for a crowd

- Serves 16 to 20

1 head iceberg or romaine lettuce, washed, dried and chilled

2 heads Boston lettuce, washed, dried and chilled

1 pound fresh spinach, washed, trimmed, dried and chilled

2 avocados, peeled and diced

3 14-ounce cans hearts of palm, drained and thinly sliced

¼ cup vinegar

¾ cup vegetable oil

1 teaspoon salt

¼ teaspoon freshly ground pepper

- Toss lettuces, spinach, avocado and hearts of palm in a large bowl, preferably glass.

- Place remaining ingredients in a jar or blender and mix well. At serving time, pour over salad and toss gently.

Variations: Garnishes such as slivers of pimiento, trimmed watercress, chopped chives, minced parsley or cherry tomatoes are decorative and tasty additions.

129

Italian Summer Salad

The smell and flavor of summer, any time of the year!

• Serves 8

Marinade

½ cup olive oil

1 cup red wine vinegar

1 garlic clove, crushed

1½ teaspoons salt

½ teaspoon freshly ground pepper

½ teaspoon dried thyme

½ teaspoon dried oregano

1 tablespoon freshly chopped parsley

1 tablespoon freshly chopped basil

2 tablespoons granulated sugar

Salad Vegetables

1 medium purple onion, sliced into rings

1 pound fresh mushrooms, halved

1 7-ounce can hearts of palm, drained and cut into small pieces

2 7-ounce cans drained artichokes, halved or quartered

1 6-ounce can pitted black olives, drained and halved

1 pint cherry tomatoes, halved

Romaine lettuce

• Make marinade by combining all the ingredients and mixing well.

• Combine all vegetables except romaine in a large bowl and pour marinade over them.

• Cover and chill 24 hours, mixing at least once.

• Before serving, drain and place on an arrangement of romaine lettuce.

Sweet and Sour Broccoli Salad

An oriental touch

• Serves 10 to 12

2 heads raw broccoli, washed and dried

⅔ cup raisins

½ cup finely chopped onion

1 cup Homemade Food-Processor Mayonnaise

¼ cup granulated sugar

2 tablespoons white vinegar

10 slices bacon, crisply fried and crumbled

1 hard-cooked egg, sliced

¼ pound grated Cheddar cheese

• Cut flowers off broccoli head and break into bite-size pieces. Toss with raisins and onion and chill.

• Whisk mayonnaise, sugar and vinegar together until well blended.

• Arrange broccoli mixture in a salad bowl. Just before serving, add bacon bits to dressing and pour over broccoli. Toss well. Garnish with egg slices and shredded Cheddar cheese. Serve at once.

Summer Tomato Soufflé

Best with homegrown, summer tomatoes!

• **Serves 4 to 6**

1 pound ripe tomatoes, peeled and seeded

1 cup Homemade Food-Processor Mayonnaise

¼ cup grated onion

¾ teaspoon salt (optional, to taste)

⅛ teaspoon black pepper

1½ tablespoons unflavored gelatin

¼ cup tomato juice

½ cup heavy cream, whipped

2 tablespoons chopped fresh parsley (garnish)

• Dice ¼ pound of the tomatoes and refrigerate. Purée the remaining ¾ pound through a sieve.

• Combine mayonnaise, onion, salt and pepper in a 1-quart mixing bowl.

• In a small saucepan, combine gelatin and tomato juice. Heat gently to dissolve gelatin, stirring constantly. Add sieved tomatoes.

• Add tomato mixture to mayonnaise mixture. Fold in whipped cream.

• Spoon into a lightly oiled ring mold. Refrigerate 3 hours.

• When ready to serve, unmold and fill center with diced tomatoes, seasoned with salt and pepper. Sprinkle with parsley.

Mixed Greens and Mandarin Orange Salad

A colorful touch to a green salad

• **Serves 6 to 8**

½ head iceberg lettuce, washed and shredded

½ head romaine, washed and torn

½ bag spinach, washed and thick stems removed

1 small head Boston lettuce

2 cups celery, thinly sliced

3 tablespoons minced parsley

6 scallions, washed and chopped

2 cups mandarin oranges, drained

¾ cup toasted almonds, sliced

• Combine lettuces and spinach in a large bowl. Toss with celery, parsley, and scallions. Can be prepared ahead to this point.

• Just before serving, add mandarin oranges and almonds.

Dressing

1½ teaspoons salt

¾ teaspoon hot pepper sauce

¾ cup salad oil

6 tablespoons sugar

6 tablespoons tarragon vinegar

• Combine dressing ingredients and pour over salad. Toss well.

Variation: Substitute grapefruit juice for tarragon vinegar.

FISH AND SEAFOOD

Roy Lichtenstein (American, born 1923), *Still Life with Goldfish Bowl,* 1974, oil and Magna on canvas, 80 x 60". Purchased: Edith H. Bell Fund

Lichtenstein often employed imagery from the history of art in structuring his compositions. In this still life of a fish bowl, he reflects the joyful spirit of the work of Matisse, rendering each object in a flat, schematic fashion to heighten its abstract quality.

Baked Bluefish with Creamy Dill Sauce

Quick and easy when your fisherman brings home a treat

- **Serves 8**
  1 4-pound bluefish, cleaned and split
  4 strips of bacon
  Chopped parsley (garnish)
  Lemon wedges (garnish)

- Preheat oven to 425 degrees.

- Place fish, skin side down on an oiled baking sheet and place the bacon across the fish.

- Bake, uncovered, until the fish flakes easily when tested with a fork (20 to 25 minutes). Sprinkle with parsley and serve with lemon wedges and sour cream dill sauce. Accompany with Corn Pudding and a mixed green salad.

Sour Cream Dill Sauce

- **1 egg**
  1 teaspoon salt
  ⅛ teaspoon pepper
  ⅛ teaspoon sugar
  4 teaspoons fresh lemon juice
  1 teaspoon grated onion
  2 tablespoons dill, finely chopped
  1½ cups commercial sour cream

- Beat egg until fluffy. Add remaining ingredients ending with sour cream. Mix well and chill.

Crusty Broiled Fish Fillets

A simply splendid way to quickly prepare any fish fillets

- **Serves 2**
  2 fresh fish fillets, about ½ pound each
  4 tablespoons (2 ounces) unsalted butter
  ½ cup fresh bread crumbs
  Freshly ground pepper and salt to taste
  ½ teaspoon paprika
  Lemon wedges and parsley sprigs (garnish)

- Preheat broiler to high. Select a baking dish large enough to hold fillets in one layer. Grease bottom of dish with 1 tablespoon butter. Sprinkle with salt and pepper to taste.

- Arrange fillets, skin side down, in the dish and sprinkle with salt and pepper to taste.

- Mix bread crumbs with paprika and sprinkle on fish fillets. Melt remaining butter and sprinkle on crumbs. Broil about 6 inches from heat until golden brown. Bake in 400 degree oven 10 minutes for 1-inch thick fillets; longer for thicker fillets. Serve at once, garnished with lemon wedges and parsley bouquets. A quick sauce of mayonnaise diluted with lemon juice and warmed is a sprightly accent.

Fragrant Fish

An intriguing sauce flavors any firm, fresh white fish fillets

- **Serves 6**
  3 tablespoons (1½ ounces) unsalted butter
  1 onion, chopped

2 ripe tomatoes, peeled, seeded and chopped

Salt and freshly ground pepper

6 tablespoons chopped fresh dill

Flour

¼ cup Pernod

¾ cup water

2 pounds fresh fish fillets such as sea trout, haddock or
    sea bass

- Melt butter in frying pan. When foam subsides, add onion and sauté until translucent. Stir in tomatoes, salt, pepper and dill. Set aside.

- Mix Pernod and water.

- Lightly season fish fillets with salt and pepper and dust with flour. Arrange in one layer in a large baking dish. Arrange tomato and onion mixture around fish and pour Pernod and water over fillets. Bake at 350 degrees for 10 to 15 minutes, until fish flakes. (The sauce will evaporate, so watch carefully and add more Pernod and water if needed.)

- Serve at once accompanied by sautéed potatoes. Garnish with sprigs of fresh dill.

Note: The proportions of Pernod and water are arbitrary. If you do not wish to use Pernod, dry vermouth is a satisfactory substitute.

Fillets en Papillote

Fish and shrimp bathed in a mushroom sauce are baked in envelopes of foil to capture all the flavor.

- **Serves 4**

8 small or 4 large white fish fillets

Aluminum foil

½ pound fresh mushrooms

6 tablespoons (3 ounces) unsalted butter

½ pound small shrimp, cooked in the shell, then cleaned

4 tablespoons all-purpose flour

1 cup milk

1 teaspoon salt

2 tablespoons fresh lime juice

¼ cup chopped parsley

Paprika (garnish)

- Preheat oven to 425 degrees.

- Cut aluminum foil in 4 squares. Dry fish and arrange on foil.

- Chop stems from mushrooms and sauté stems and buttons in 2 tablespoons butter.

- Divide shrimp and mushrooms into 4 equal portions and place on top of fish.

- Melt 4 tablespoons of butter in a saucepan. Blend flour and salt and cook for 1 minute. Gradually pour in milk, stirring constantly, until smooth and thickened. Add lime juice.

- Divide sauce into 4 servings and pour over fish, mushroom and shrimp. Sprinkle with parsley.

- Fold foil together to make a tight seal. Place on flat baking pan. Bake for 40 minutes.

- To serve, place on platter, slit top open like a baked potato and sprinkle with paprika. Accompany with French-fried eggplant strips and wedges of lime.

Flounder Florentine

So easy, yet dressy

- **Serves 6 to 8**

  2 10-ounce boxes of frozen chopped spinach, partially thawed and drained

  2 pounds fresh flounder fillets (or other mild fish)

  ½ cup commercial sour cream

  ⅔ cup mayonnaise

  1 8-ounce can water chestnuts, thinly sliced

  ½ pound sliced mushrooms, sautéed in a little butter for 5 minutes (optional)

  ¼ cup sherry

  Salt and freshly ground pepper to taste

- Preheat oven to 350 degrees.

- Spread partially thawed spinach in a baking dish. Place fillets in a single layer on top and scatter with water chestnuts.

- Mix sour cream, mayonnaise, mushrooms, sherry, salt and pepper. Pour over fish. Bake for 45 minutes. Serve at once.

- May be accompanied by tomatoes stuffed with bread crumbs, parsley and minced garlic which have been baked in the oven for 15 to 20 minutes, along with the fish.

Coulibiac of Salmon with Fresh Asparagus

A most elegant dish worthy of the fanciest dinner parties

- **Serves 8**

  2 6-ounce cans of salmon, drained

  1 cup mayonnaise

  2 tablespoons capers

  2 hard boiled eggs, chopped

  ½ cup wild rice, cooked

  1 bunch fresh dill, chopped

  ⅛ teaspoon salt

  ⅛ teaspoon granulated sugar

  1 9 x 14-inch sheet of puff pastry

  1 raw egg

Salmon

- Drain salmon well. Mix in mayonnaise, capers, rice, dill, eggs, salt and sugar. The result should look like tuna salad.

- Spread the sheet of puff pastry on a floured cutting board and cut into rectangles approximately 3 x 4½-inches.

- Place a large spoonful of salmon mixture in middle of pastry and wrap the pastry completely. Place seam side down on baking sheet that has been covered with waxed paper. Put in refrigerator to stand for at least 6 hours.

- When ready to cook, brush the pastry with an eggwash (equal parts beaten whole egg and cold water). Place in preheated 350 degree oven for 30 minutes until golden.

Garnish

36 fresh asparagus spears

4 tablespoons unsalted butter

- Cut the asparagus on a bias so that it will be placed next to the pastry in the plate in a fleur-de-lis pattern, 2 spears on each side. Immerse in boiling water for 3 to 4 minutes and plunge into cold water. When ready to serve, reheat quickly in sauté pan with butter.

Buerre Blanc

2 shallots

3 tablespoons good quality vinegar

3 tablespoons dry white wine

½ pint heavy cream

¼ pound (4 ounces) whipped butter

- Mince shallots. Place in sauté pan with wine and vinegar and reduce until shallots are just moist.

- Lower heat and add heavy cream. Cook, stirring constantly, until it turns pale yellow.

- Remove from heat and whisk in butter, a little at a time, until it looks like Hollandaise. Strain the sauce through a sieve to separate shallots.

- To serve, pour sauce on plate, place the puff pastry on the sauce and arrange asparagus in a fleur-de-lis on each side of the pastry. Slice thickly and serve with the sauce and additional asparagus.

Stuffed Shad Roe

Doubles nicely for a splendid dinner party

- **Serves 4**

  2 tablespoons (1 ounce) unsalted butter

  2 tablespoons all-purpose flour

  1 cup light cream

  ½ teaspoon salt

  ½ teaspoon pepper

  ⅛ teaspoon mace

  4 large pairs shad roe

  6 tablespoons (3 ounces) unsalted butter

  ½ pound lump crabmeat, picked over

  Lemon wedges

- Preheat oven to 375 degrees.

- Make cream sauce by melting 2 tablespoons butter. Blend in flour and cook, stirring, for 1 minute. Slowly add the cream and cook, constantly stirring, until smooth and thick. Season with salt, pepper and mace.

- In a large heavy frying pan, melt 6 tablespoons butter and sauté the roe over medium heat until brown on both sides. Set aside on warm dish and reserve browned butter.

- Carefully mix crab lumps in just enough cream sauce to bind together. Keep warm in a double boiler.

- Carefully split each half roe and stuff with crab, using toothpicks to hold it together.

- Place on ovenproof serving platter and bake 10 minutes.

- Serve with browned butter and lemon wedges.

137

Baked Stuffed Red Snapper

The almond-studded stuffing adds a
special touch.

- Serves 6

  1 4-pound red snapper, cut for stuffing

  4 tablespoons (2 ounces) unsalted butter

  1 large onion, chopped

  1 clove of garlic, minced

  3 cups dried bread crumbs

  1 cup minced cucumber

  ½ cup toasted almonds, chopped

  1 teaspoon dried thyme

  ⅛ to ¼ cup white wine or sherry

  Salt and pepper to taste

- Preheat oven to 425 degrees.

- Rub inside of fish with salt, pepper and 1 tablespoon butter.

- Melt butter and sauté onion and garlic until soft.
  Add bread crumbs, cucumber and almonds. Season
  with salt, pepper and thyme. Moisten with wine or
  sherry.

- Stuff the fish lightly and sew it up.

- Place fish on well-greased baking pan. Add a little
  wine or sherry to the pan. Bake for 25 to 30 minutes, basting occasionally. Serve with a wreath of
  parsley, wedges of lemon and slices of cucumber.
  Accompany with Baked Lettuce.

Lemon Soy Swordfish

Delicious either broiled or grilled –
fresh tuna is a savory alternative.

- Serves 8

  ⅓ cup soy sauce

  1 teaspoon grated lemon peel

  ¼ cup fresh lemon juice

  1 clove of garlic, crushed

  2 teaspoons Dijon-style mustard

  ½ cup vegetable oil

  8 small swordfish steaks or 4 large ones, halved

- Combine soy sauce, lemon peel, lemon juice, garlic,
  mustard and oil, blending well.

- Place fish in a 9 x 13-inch baking dish. Pour marinade over fish, pricking the steaks with a fork so
  marinade can penetrate. Cover and refrigerate 1 to
  3 hours, turning occasionally.

- Heat broiler and broil fish in marinade 5 to 6
  minutes on each side. (Thick steaks may require
  longer.) If grilling, remove from marinade and cook
  over moderately hot coals, brushing regularly with
  marinade. Serve garnished with lemon wedges and
  parsley. Baked Tomatoes Provençal and steamed
  rice mixed with a teaspoon of grated lemon peel are
  attractive accompaniments.

Crab au Gratin

A classic presentation of crab, lightly flavored with wine and cheese

- Serves 6

  ½ cup (4 ounces) unsalted butter

  ¼ cup all-purpose flour

  1 cup milk

  1 cup light cream

  ½ cup dry white wine

  ½ teaspoon salt

  ¼ teaspoon paprika

  2 tablespoons grated onion

  ¼ pound fresh mushrooms, sliced

  1 cup sharp Cheddar cheese, grated

  1 pound backfin crabmeat, picked over

  ⅓ cup bread crumbs

- Preheat oven to 400 degrees.

- Melt butter in 1½-quart saucepan. Stir in flour and cook 2 minutes.

- Add milk, cream and wine, stirring until thick and smooth. Add salt, paprika, onion, mushrooms and cheese. Stir over low heat until cheese melts.

- Fold in crabmeat. Spoon into 1½ to 2-quart casserole, sprinkle with crumbs and bake for 10 to 12 minutes. Serve at once on toast triangles accompanied by Broiled Deviled Tomatoes and lemon wedges.

Crab in Whiskey Cream Sauce

The spinach and whiskey sauce is a complement to the delicate crab.

- Serves 6

  1 pound lump crabmeat, shells removed

  6 tablespoons (3 ounces) unsalted butter

  Salt and pepper (optional, to taste)

  2 ounces whiskey

  2 ripe tomatoes, peeled, seeded and finely chopped

  1 cup heavy cream

  1 pound spinach, washed with stems removed

- In a large frying pan, sauté crabmeat in 4 tablespoons of the butter until slightly browned – about 8 minutes. Salt and pepper to taste.

- Add whiskey and flambé. Add tomatoes and heavy cream. Continue cooking until liquid is reduced by half.

- Meanwhile, sauté spinach in 2 tablespoons butter in a 10-inch frying pan until just limp. Place spinach on the bottom of a 12-inch gratin dish. Place crabmeat mixture over spinach and place under broiler for a few minutes until top is golden brown.

Crabmeat Imperial

This traditional entrée is also an elegant first course or luncheon dish.

• **Serves 4**

1 small green pepper

½ small jar pimiento, drained

2 green onions

1 pound jumbo lump crabmeat

2 egg yolks

1 scant tablespoon Worcestershire sauce

Dash hot pepper sauce

1 tablespoon Dijon-style mustard

2 tablespoons mayonnaise

4 additional tablespoons mayonnaise

• Preheat oven to 350 degrees.

• Chop green pepper, pimiento and scallions.

• Gently mix vegetables with crabmeat, egg yolks, Worcestershire sauce, pepper sauce and 2 table-spoons mayonnaise.

• Put into 4 individual ramekins and spread 1 table-spoon mayonnaise on each ramekin.

• Bake for 10 to 12 minutes until browned. Serve in the center of a plate surrounded by a tangle of shoestring potatoes and spears of steamed aspara-gus.

Crab Louis

A cold dish perfect for a hot summer evening

• **Serves 4 to 6**

2 pounds lump crabmeat, shells removed

1 cup mayonnaise

⅓ cup plus 1 tablespoon heavy cream

¼ cup chili sauce

4 tablespoons minced scallions

2 tablespoons minced green pepper

1 tablespoon horseradish

1 tablespoon Worcestershire sauce

Salt and pepper to taste

• Mix mayonnaise, cream, chili sauce, scallions, green pepper, horseradish and Worcestershire sauce together. Season to taste with salt and pepper.

• Gently mix just enough sauce with the crabmeat to moisten crabmeat. Reserve the rest of the sauce to pass when served.

• Refrigerate until ready to serve.

Lump Crab Cakes

There are no fillers in these heavenly crab cakes.

- **Makes 6 cakes**
  1 pound lump crabmeat, picked over
  1 large egg
  ¼ cup mayonnaise
  1 teaspoon Worcestershire sauce
  1 teaspoon dry mustard
  ½ teaspoon salt
  ¼ teaspoon pepper
  4 tablespoons (2 ounces) margarine
  ¼ cup oil for frying

- In a small bowl, mix egg, mayonnaise and seasonings.

- Add crabmeat and mix gently but thoroughly. If mixture is too dry, add a little more mayonnaise. Shape into 6 cakes.

- Fry cakes 5 to 6 minutes each side in mixture of margarine and oil. Serve with tartar sauce, lemon wedges and mounds of Parmesan Potato Sticks.

Variation: Mixture can be turned into ramekins and baked at 350 degrees for 20 minutes.

New England Lobster Pudding

A special entrée that can be assembled early and baked just before presenting

- **Serves 6**
  2 tablespoons (1 ounce) unsalted butter
  2 tablespoons all-purpose flour
  ½ teaspoon dry mustard
  Salt to taste
  1 cup light cream
  3 tablespoons white rum or vermouth
  3 chicken lobsters (1 pound each) boiled, meat removed from shells, or 12 ounces lobster meat
  5 slices bread, crusts removed, broken in pieces
  1 cup fresh bread crumbs
  1 additional ounce unsalted butter
  Paprika

- In a large saucepan, melt butter. Add flour, mustard, salt and paprika. Cook for 1 minute until paste is formed.

- Slowly add cream and stir constantly until smooth and thickened. Add rum or vermouth. Add lobster meat and pieces of bread. Mix well and pour into 2-quart casserole. May be prepared to this point up to 6 hours in advance. Refrigerate.

- Top casserole with bread crumbs and dot with butter. Bake in 350 degree oven for 15 minutes. Serve at once.

Coquille St. Jacques

Splendid as an entrée, this classic is also a beautiful first course.

• **Serves 6**
  3 pounds scallops
  ½ cup vermouth
  ½ cup heavy cream
  1½ cups (12 ounces) unsalted butter
  Salt
  Freshly ground white pepper
  ½ carrot, julienned
  ½ turnip, julienned
  ½ leek, julienned
  Green peppercorns
  Chopped fresh parsley (garnish)

• Cut scallops in half if they are large. In a saucepan, bring scallops and vermouth to a boil. Immediately remove scallops and place in a gratin dish or shallow heat-proof casserole. Continue heating vermouth until it starts to caramelize. Whisk in ½ cup heavy cream and reduce until it is thick enough to coat a spoon. Remove from heat.

• Whisk in butter, a little at a time. Season with salt and pepper to taste.

• In boiling water, blanch carrot, turnip and leek for about 1 to 2 minutes. Refresh immediately under cold water and drain. Arrange vegetables on top of scallops. Sprinkle with green peppercorns. Cover with sauce and garnish with parsley. Warm on stove or in a 350 degree oven and serve immediately accompanied by steamed rice and asparagus or tiny green beans.

Variation: To serve as an appetizer, divide mixture among individual shells or gratin dishes and proceed as above. Serves 8 to 10.

Moules à la Provençal

The garlic adds a zest to this Mediterranean favorite.

• **Serves 4 to 6**
  48 extra-large scrubbed, debearded mussels
  12 tablespoons (6 ounces) unsalted butter, softened
  3 tablespoons finely minced shallots or scallions
  1 to 3 cloves of garlic, mashed
  ¼ cup minced parsley
  ½ cup fine white dry bread crumbs
  Salt and pepper to taste
  ½ pound linguine
  Lemon wedges (garnish)

• In a large covered kettle, steam mussels with 2 cups water or wine over high heat tossing frequently just until shells open. Discard half shells.

• Beat butter in mixing bowl until light and fluffy. Beat in rest of ingredients and taste for seasoning.

• Spread a bit of mixture over each mussel. Recipe may be prepared to this point, covered with wax paper and refrigerated until needed.

• Just before serving, broil under very hot broiler until butter bubbles in shells. Serve on a bed of linguine and garnish with wedges of lemon.

Scallops Florentine

A classic seafood dish

- Serves 6
  2 shallots, minced
  1 garlic clove, minced
  8 tablespoons (4 ounces) unsalted butter
  1 cup heavy cream
  1 teaspoon nutmeg
  ½ teaspoon white pepper
  2 10-ounce packages frozen chopped spinach, defrosted and drained
  8 ounces small shell pasta, cooked al dente (8 minutes), drained and mixed with 1 tablespoon vegetable oil
  1¼ pounds bay scallops, rinsed and drained
  3 ounces Parmesan cheese, grated
  Parsley (garnish)

- Preheat oven to 350 degrees.

- In large sauté pan, melt butter. Add minced garlic and onion and cook until translucent. Add cream and reduce by half (about 3 to 5 minutes). Stir in nutmeg and pepper.

- Squeeze excess water from defrosted spinach and add to cream mixture. Gently fold in cooked pasta and scallops.

- Transfer to shallow 4-quart gratin dish and sprinkle with cheese. May be prepared in advance to this point. Bake for 10 to 12 minutes until scallops are opaque. Do not overcook. Serve immediately garnished with bouquets of parsley.

Scallops Marsala

Mushrooms and cream enrich the fragrant sweet wine-based sauce.

- Serves 6
  1½ pounds scallops
  3 tablespoons (1½ ounces) unsalted butter
  2 tablespoons shallots, finely chopped
  ½ pound small mushrooms, sliced
  ¾ cup heavy cream
  3 to 4 tablespoons Marsala wine
  Salt and pepper to taste
  ¼ cup parsley, finely chopped

- Cut large scallops in half.

- In large frying pan, melt 1½ tablespoons butter. Add shallots and mushrooms and sauté for 3 minutes. Spoon into a bowl and set aside.

- Melt remaining 1½ tablespoons butter and add scallops. Sauté 1 to 2 minutes until opaque. Do not overcook. Use slotted spoon to add scallops to mushroom mixture and set aside.

- Add cream and wine to liquid in frying pan. Drain the liquid from the scallop and mushroom mixture and add to frying pan. Cook over medium-high heat until sauce reduces to ¾ cup and thickens to coat a spoon lightly.

- Add mushroom and scallop mixture and heat. Sprinkle with parsley and season to taste. Serve over angel hair pasta and accompany with buttered frenched green beans.

143

Vodka Steamed Scallops

A spirited scallop recipe with an Oriental touch

• Serves 4

1 pound bay scallops

1 tablespoon vodka

½ teaspoon cornstarch

1 tablespoon minced fresh ginger

¼ cup chopped scallions

1 tablespoon chopped fresh cilantro or parsley (optional)

1 tablespoon peanut oil

2 cloves of garlic, peeled and crushed

1 tablespoon soy sauce

2 cups cooked rice, kept warm

• In a large bowl, toss scallops with vodka and cornstarch. Place in steamer and top with ginger, scallions and cilantro (if used). Steam over boiling water for 5 minutes or until scallops are barely firm to the touch.

• While scallops steam, in a small frying pan, heat oil. Add garlic and cook until garlic begins to brown. Remove garlic, add soy sauce and blend.

• To serve, mound ½ cup cooked rice on each plate. Remove scallops with slotted spoon and arrange over rice. Drizzle a little of the garlic-soy oil over scallops and serve at once. Accompany with curly chicory sautéed in olive oil and garlic.

Scallops and Mussels with Saffron Sauce

A cold main course in which the scallops are "cooked" by marinating in lime and orange juice

• Serves 6

1½ pounds bay scallops, rinsed and drained

½ cup fresh orange juice

½ cup fresh lemon juice

½ pound fresh asparagus, trimmed, peeled and cut diagonally into 2-inch pieces

3 medium shallots, minced

½ cup dry white wine

3 pounds mussels, scrubbed and debearded (or 2 packages frozen mussel meat)

½ teaspoon fresh lemon juice

⅛ teaspoon saffron

⅛ teaspoon grated nutmeg

½ pound fresh spinach torn into bite-sized pieces

1 tablespoon olive oil

½ teaspoon freshly ground pepper

½ cup (or more) Fromage Blanc (recipe follows)

• Spread scallops in a single layer in a glass flat-bottomed casserole. Combine orange and lemon juice and pour over scallops. Cover and marinate in the refrigerator for 4 hours. Scallops will become opaque as if cooked.

• Blanch asparagus until crisp tender, about 1 minute. Rinse with cold water and pat dry.

• In a large heavy saucepan, combine shallots and wine. Bring to boil over high heat. Add mussels, cover and cook, shaking gently, until mussels open (5 to 6 minutes).

- Remove pan from heat, discarding any unopened mussels (or use frozen mussels which are already shelled). Strain cooking liquid and reserve.

- Rinse saucepan. Return cooking liquid and reduce to 3 tablespoons.

- Remove mussels from shells and place in a bowl.

- In a small bowl, whisk Fromage Blanc, lemon juice, saffron, nutmeg and 1 tablespoon of reduced cooking liquid until smooth.

- Toss spinach with olive oil, remaining cooking liquid and pepper. Arrange spinach on large serving platter.

- Drain scallops and add to mussels. Toss with saffron sauce.

- Arrange in mound on torn spinach leaves and garnish with asparagus, extra sauce and sprinkle with pepper and a pinch of saffron threads.

Fromage Blanc
1 15-ounce container part-skim ricotta cheese
¼ cup plain yogurt
¼ teaspoon salt

Combine ingredients in blender until smooth. Refrigerate, covered, for 12 hours.

Shrimp Curry

Guests help themselves to classic condiments.

- **Serves 8**
6 tablespoons vegetable oil
2 onions, finely chopped

1 onion, sliced
4 cloves of garlic, chopped
5 to 6 peppers, finely chopped
4 teaspoons ginger, freshly grated
3 teaspoons ground cumin
2 teaspoons ground turmeric
2 teaspoons salt
1 teaspoon ground coriander
1 teaspoon ground cardamom
½ teaspoon ground cloves
Juice of 1 lemon
2 pounds medium shrimp, shelled and deveined
1½ cups chicken broth

Condiments
Shredded coconut
Chutney
Scallions
Peanuts
Raisins

- Combine chopped onion, garlic, peppers, ginger, cumin, turmeric, salt, coriander, cardamom and cloves.

- Heat 6 tablespoons of oil and sauté 1 sliced onion until golden.

- Add previously combined ingredients. Cook slowly and thoroughly stirring often.

- Add shrimp and cook until opaque. Add lemon juice and chicken broth.

- Serve with steamed rice and accompany with condiments served in individual bowls.

145

Baked Shrimp and Artichokes

Perfect for a party – can be assembled ahead.

- **Serves 8**
  2 packages frozen artichokes
  1 medium onion, finely chopped
  3 tablespoons (1½ ounces) unsalted butter
  2 tablespoons all-purpose flour
  1½ cups chicken broth
  1 cup heavy cream
  ⅔ cup white burgundy
  ¼ cup ripe olives, sliced
  1¾ pounds small shrimp, cooked and cleaned
  ½ cup Parmesan cheese, grated

- Cook artichokes according to package instructions, drain and set aside.

- Melt butter over medium-high heat and sauté onion until translucent. Add flour and cook for 2 to 3 minutes. Add chicken broth, cream and wine and cook, stirring constantly, until thickened. Add shrimp and olives to sauce and mix well.

- Arrange artichoke hearts on bottom of a 9x13-inch casserole. Pour shrimp sauce over artichoke hearts. Top with grated Parmesan cheese and bake for ½ hour at 350 degrees. Serve over orzo accompanied by slivers of steamed carrots.

Shrimp Newburg

Classically correct as an entrée or a first course – lobster is a luxurious substitute.

- **Serves 4**
  2 tablespoons (1 ounce) unsalted butter
  2 tablespoons all-purpose flour
  1 cup heavy cream
  3 tablespoons catsup
  ½ tablespoon Worcestershire sauce
  Salt and pepper, to taste
  2 tablespoons sherry
  1 pound shrimp, cooked and cleaned

- Melt butter and stir in flour. Cook for 2 minutes then stir in cup of cream. Stir constantly until sauce thickens.

- When thick, stir in catsup and Worcestershire.

- Combine above with shrimp, salt, pepper and sherry. Serve with wide noodles or over triangles of toast.

Shrimp Orientale

The Chinese touches include water chestnuts and snow peas.

• Serves 10 to 12

4 tablespoons salad oil

4 pounds uncooked shrimp, peeled and deveined

2 scallions, minced

1½ cups sliced water chestnuts

1 pound fresh snow peas

1 cup hot chicken broth

1 teaspoon powdered ginger

2 teaspoons salt

4 tablespoons soy sauce

4 tablespoons sherry

4 tablespoons cornstarch

2 tablespoons water

2 bunches green onions, chopped (garnish)

• Heat salad oil in large frying pan or wok and sauté scallions until translucent and shrimp until pink.

• Make sauce by combining ginger, salt, soy and sherry with cornstarch which has been dissolved in 2 tablespoons water. Whisk mixture into hot chicken broth.

• Add water chestnuts and peas to shrimp and pour sauce over all. Cook 3 minutes until sauce thickens.

• Serve over rice with a garnish of chopped green onions.

Paprika Shrimp

Colorful and easy with a bit of a bite

• Serves 3 to 4

2 tablespoons (1 ounce) unsalted butter

24 medium-size shrimp, peeled and deveined

Salt and freshly ground pepper

¼ teaspoon cayenne pepper (or to taste)

1 teaspoon paprika

3 tablespoons finely chopped shallots or mild onion

⅓ cup heavy cream

2 teaspoons Dijon-style mustard

⅓ cup commercial sour cream

Chopped fresh parsley (garnish)

Strips of pimiento (garnish)

• In a frying pan, heat butter and when hot, add shrimp. Sprinkle with salt and pepper to taste, cayenne pepper and paprika. Stir and cook shrimp until they turn pink, turning each shrimp once. Do not overcook.

• Sprinkle with shallots and add heavy cream. Stir the mustard into sauce and remove pan from heat.

• Stir in sour cream and heat thoroughly without boiling.

• Serve immediately with rice or noodles and garnish with parsley and strips of pimiento. Accompany with shredded romaine dressed in a lemon vinaigrette.

147

Shrimp Sauté Provençal

A perfect last-minute dish

- Serves 4

8 tablespoons olive oil

32 to 36 large uncooked shrimp, peeled and deveined

1 teaspoon chopped garlic

1 cup white wine

8 tablespoons fresh chopped tomatoes

4 tablespoons fresh chopped basil

4 tablespoons (2 ounces) butter, cold

- In a sauté pan, heat olive oil. Add shrimp and sauté 2 minutes on each side. Remove shrimp and add garlic and sauté without burning.

- Deglaze pan with wine and add basil and tomatoes. Reduce by one-third. Add chilled butter and swirl slowly until melted.

- Add salt and pepper to taste and serve in a nest of spaghetti accompanied by Zucchini with Pesto.

Shrimp in Zucchini Boats

A most entrancing luncheon entrée – can be prepared in advance.

- Serves 4

8 small zucchini

4 medium tomatoes, diced

2 tablespoons (1 ounce) unsalted butter

2 shallots, finely chopped

1 teaspoon cayenne pepper

Salt to taste

½ pound uncooked medium shrimp, shelled

1¼ cup Mornay sauce

2 tablespoons Parmesan cheese

- Trim ends of zucchini and boil whole in salted water for 5 minutes. Drain and refresh under cold water.

- When cool, remove a thin slice lengthwise from the side of each zucchini and scoop out flesh with the tip of a teaspoon. Chop the flesh and reserve the zucchini boats.

- Melt butter in saucepan and add shallots. Cook until soft.

- Add zucchini flesh and tomatoes and cook briskly for 2 to 3 minutes.

- Cut each shrimp into 4 to 5 pieces and add to mixture in saucepan.

- Place zucchini boats in a buttered 9x13-inch baking dish. Fill boats with zucchini, tomato and shrimp mixture.

- Top with Mornay sauce, sprinkle with Parmesan and bake 10 to 12 minutes at 425 degrees.

- Serve on a bed of spaghetti tossed with butter and finely diced sweet red pepper.

Mornay Sauce

2 tablespoons (1 ounce) butter

2 tablespoons all-purpose flour

1¼ cups milk, scalded

2 ounces Parmesan cheese, finely grated

- Melt butter and add flour. Cook, stirring, for 2 minutes.

- Add milk and bring to a boil, whisking constantly.

- Add Parmesan and stir until thickened.

Linguine with Shrimp and Anchovy Tomato Sauce

The flavor of anchovies is hardly detectable. The overall taste is surely delectable!

- Serves 6

  5 tablespoons olive oil

  4 tablespoons (2 ounces) unsalted butter

  4 cloves of garlic, minced

  6 anchovies, drained and chopped

  2 tablespoons fresh lemon juice

  ⅔ cup dry white wine

  4 ripe tomatoes, peeled and chopped

  ½ cup chopped basil

  3 to 4 tablespoons heavy cream

  24 large uncooked shrimp, peeled and deveined

  ¾ pound linguine

  Parmesan cheese

- Melt 2 tablespoons oil and 1 ounce butter in frying pan over medium heat. Add 3 minced cloves of garlic and stir for 2 to 3 minutes; do not let burn.

- Add chopped anchovies and stir 1 to 2 minutes. Add lemon juice and white wine and boil for 2 to 3 minutes.

- Add tomatoes and simmer for 5 minutes. Add basil and simmer an additional minute.

- Add 3 to 4 tablespoons heavy cream until incorporated. Add remaining 1 ounce butter, bit by bit, until incorporated.

- In another large frying pan, heat 2 tablespoons oil at medium heat. Add remaining garlic and stir for 1 minute.

- Add raw shrimp and sauté until cooked through and opaque.

- Add cooked shrimp to tomato-anchovy sauce.

- Cook linguine in large pot of boiling salted water. Drain well. Toss with 1 tablespoon of olive oil and 1 tablespoon of Parmesan cheese.

- Place linguine on platter and top with sauce. Pass Parmesan cheese. Accompany with florets of steamed broccoli.

Shrimp and Scallops à la Lyonnaise

Tomatoes, onions and peppers give this dish a French accent.

- **Serves 6**

  ¼ cup virgin olive oil

  4 tablespoons (2 ounces) unsalted butter

  1½ red onions, julienned

  ½ teaspoon marjoram

  ⅛ teaspoon freshly grated nutmeg

  ⅛ teaspoon cayenne

  1½ red peppers, julienned

  1 pound medium shrimp, shelled

  1 pound sea scallops

  2 dozen cherry tomatoes, halved

  ½ cup dry white wine

  Chopped fresh parsley

- In a large frying pan, heat olive oil and butter until hot and foam has subsided. Add onions and sauté until translucent. Stir in marjoram, nutmeg and cayenne.

- Add shrimp and scallops and sauté for a minute or two until shrimp turns pink and scallops whiten. Add peppers, cherry tomatoes and wine and simmer until seafood is cooked through, about 5 minutes. Serve with slices of boiled potato and garnish with parsley.

Neptune's Casserole

A wonderful seafood mélange

- **Serves 8**

  1½ cups cooked rice

  ½ pound raw shrimp, cleaned

  ½ pound sea scallops

  ½ pound crabmeat, shells removed

  ½ cup red or green pepper, chopped

  ½ cup onion, chopped

  1 cup celery, chopped

  1 cup fresh mushrooms, sliced

  1 tablespoon Worcestershire sauce

  Dash white pepper

  ½ teaspoon salt

  1 cup mayonnaise

  1 cup light cream

  1½ cups white Cheddar cheese, grated

  ½ cup dry bread crumbs

  4 tablespoons (2 ounces) unsalted butter, melted

- Preheat oven to 375 degrees.

- Spoon cooked rice into a greased 9 x 13-inch pan.

- Combine next 12 ingredients and pour over the rice. Bake, covered for 30 minutes.

- Remove from oven. Cover with grated cheese and bread crumbs and drizzle with butter. Return to oven and bake, uncovered, for 15 minutes. Serve at once accompanied by a mix of green beans and wax beans.

Paella

Clear directions make this easy to prepare.

- Serves 12

  1 teaspoon oregano

  2 crushed peppercorns

  1 clove garlic, peeled and crushed

  1½ teaspoons salt

  2 tablespoons olive oil

  1 teaspoon vinegar

  1½ pounds chicken drumsticks and thighs, separated

  Additional 4 tablespoons olive oil

  ¼ pound ham, cut into 3-inch julienne strips

  1 hot Italian sausage, sliced

  1 ounce salt pork, chopped

  1 medium onion, peeled and chopped

  1 green pepper, seeded and chopped

  ½ teaspoon ground coriander

  1 teaspoon capers

  3 tablespoons tomato sauce

  2¼ cups rice, washed and drained

  4 cups boiling water or chicken broth

  1 teaspoon saffron

  1 package frozen peas

  1½ pound lobster, cooked with meat removed

  1 pound shrimp, shelled and deveined

  1 dozen small clams

  1 quart mussels, rinsed and cleaned

  1 jar pimientos, cut in ⅛-inch slices

  ¼ cup chopped parsley

- Combine oregano, peppercorns, garlic, salt, olive oil and vinegar. Rub chicken with the mixture.

- Heat remaining 4 tablespoons of oil in heavy, large casserole and brown chicken over moderate heat.

- Add ham, sausage, salt pork, onion, green pepper, coriander and capers. Cook 10 minutes over low heat.

- Add tomato sauce and rice and cook 5 minutes.

- Add boiling water (or broth) and saffron. Mix well and cook, covered, over medium-high heat until the liquid is absorbed, about 20 minutes.

- Turn rice over from top to bottom with a large spoon. Add peas, lobster meat and shrimp. Cook 6 minutes longer.

- Steam the mussels and clams together in a little water until the shells open. Place the mussels, clams and pimiento on top of the mixture.

- Sprinkle with chopped parsley.

MEATS

Eduard Charlemont (Austrian, 1848–1906), *Moorish Chief*, c. 1880, oil on panel, 59 1/8 x 38 1/2". John G. Johnson Collection at the Philadelphia Museum of Art

In this portrait Charlemont has depicted elements of the North African culture that his contemporary Europeans found so exotically fascinating. He used methods that are subtle yet theatrical to represent the strong light falling across the figure in the doorway, the bronze and gold smoldering in the dim background, and the gleam of the drawn sword resting in the hand of the chief.

Carbonnades of Beef à la Flamande

A Belgian classic in a simpler guise – a favorite for winter nights

- Serves 6 to 8

  5 tablespoons (2½ ounces) unsalted butter

  5 tablespoons vegetable shortening

  4 pounds round steak or chuck, cut into 1-inch cubes

  4 to 5 onions, thinly sliced

  ¼ cup all-purpose flour

  1½ cups beer

  1 clove of garlic, finely minced

  1 bay leaf

  3 sprigs parsley

  ½ teaspoon dried thyme

  Salt

  1 teaspoon granulated sugar

  1 tablespoon wine vinegar

  Freshly grated nutmeg

  French bread, sliced

  Dijon-style mustard

- Preheat oven to 325 degrees.

- In a large frying pan, melt butter and shortening over moderate heat. Brown a few cubes of beef at a time and remove with a slotted spoon to a large, heavy casserole with a lid.

- Add onions and sauté until golden. Add flour and cook, stirring, until it starts to brown. Slowly add beer, stirring and scraping until mixture is thickened and smooth. Add garlic, bay leaf, parsley, thyme, salt, sugar, vinegar and a grating of nutmeg. Mix well and pour over meat.

- Cover casserole and bake 2 hours or until meat is fork tender. Fifteen minutes before finishing, spread mustard on bread and place on top of stew to brown. Serve with buttered noodles or steamed potatoes and plenty of cold beer.

Grilled London Broil Moutarde

A brilliant barbecue suggestion

- Serves 8

  4 pound flank steak

  2 cups soy sauce

  1 cup vegetable oil

  2 cloves of garlic, chopped

  ½ cup dry sherry

  3 tablespoons brown sugar

  Salt

  1 teaspoon freshly ground pepper

  1 teaspoon ground ginger

  ¾ cup mayonnaise

  ¾ cup commercial sour cream

  ¼ cup Dijon-style mustard

  2 tablespoons chopped fresh parsley for garnish

- Place flank steak in 9 x 13-inch baking dish. Mix soy sauce, vegetable oil, garlic, sherry, brown sugar, salt, pepper and ginger until thoroughly blended. Pour over steak and marinate 8 hours or overnight.

- Prepare grill as for any meat or heat broiler. Remove steak from marinade and grill or broil 6 or 7 minutes on each side for rare meat.

- Meanwhile, blend mayonnaise, sour cream and

MEATS

mustard, and pour in sauce boat. When steak is done, carve across the grain on the diagonal in thin slices. Garnish with parsley. Serve at once or at room temperature with sauce. Serve with toasted French bread and a salad of thick slices of ripe tomatoes alternated with slices of onion.

Variation: The sauce is also superb on grilled sirloin steak.

Steak Salad

A twist on grilled steak for a buffet or picnic

- **Serves 6 to 8**

Marinade
⅓ cup sesame oil
⅓ cup Hoisin sauce
⅓ cup soy sauce
2 tablespoons finely chopped scallion
2 tablespoons finely grated fresh ginger
2 to 3 black peppercorns, crushed
1 clove garlic, crushed
1 bay leaf, crumbled
1½ to 2 pounds boneless sirloin, flank steak, "London Broil" or filet

- Mix ingredients for marinade in glass baking dish large enough to hold meat. Pour over beef and marinate 6 hours.

- Remove meat, pat dry, and broil or grill until rare to medium rare (135 to 150 degrees). Cool to room temperature and slice thinly.

Creamy Dressing
1 egg
Juice of 1 lemon
1 teaspoon Dijon-style mustard
⅛ teaspoon salt
½ cup olive oil
12 pimiento-stuffed olives, drained
2 teaspoons capers, drained
1 small garlic clove, peeled
White pepper

- Place egg, lemon juice, mustard and salt in food processor and run until blended. With machine still running, slowly add olive oil in drops and then in slow stream. Add remaining ingredients and purée.

Garnishes
½ cup finely chopped celery
½ pound Gruyère cheese, julienned
1 medium red onion, thinly sliced
1 pint cherry tomatoes
3 hard-boiled eggs, quartered
Mixed salad greens

- Mix slices of beef with celery, cheese and red onion. Arrange on a large platter covered with greens. Garnish and chill.

- At serving time, toss salad lightly with some of the dressing and pass the rest in a sauce boat. Accompany with slices of Italian or French bread spread with butter and crushed garlic and toasted until bubbly.

155

Baked Steak Citron

Steak for a crowd with a scrumptious topping

- Serves 8

 1 3-inch sirloin steak

 1 cup bottled chili sauce

 4 tablespoons (2 ounces) unsalted butter

 ½ teaspoon salt

 ⅛ teaspoon paprika

 2 medium onions, thinly sliced

 1 large lemon, thinly sliced and seeded

 2 large summer-ripe tomatoes, thickly sliced

 ½ pound fresh mushrooms, sliced

- Preheat oven to 450 degrees.

- Place steak in a shallow baking dish. Spread with chili sauce and dot with 2 tablespoons butter. Season with salt and paprika.

- Cover steak with alternating overlapping slices of onion, lemon and tomato. Bake 45 to 50 minutes for rare. Let stand for 10 minutes before carving.

- Sauté mushrooms in remaining 2 tablespoons of butter for about 8 to 10 minutes. Top steak with mushrooms. Present steak on a platter and carve into ½-inch slices. Accompany with pan juices. Serve with Italian bread and a mixed green salad.

Hungarian Beef Goulash

Use the best Hungarian paprika you can find to give this favorite a true taste of Budapest.

- Serves 4 to 6

 3 tablespoons (1½ ounces) unsalted butter

 1 pound round steak or chuck, cut into 1-inch cubes

 2 medium onions, diced

 1 clove of garlic, minced

 1 green pepper, diced

 2 teaspoons paprika

 1 8-ounce can tomato sauce

 1 8-ounce can water or beef stock

 1 teaspoon salt

 Freshly ground black pepper

 ½ pound wide egg noodles

 ¼ cup chopped fresh parsley

- Heat butter in large heavy casserole. Brown beef cubes a few at a time. Remove with a slotted spoon and reserve. Add onions and garlic and cook slowly until soft. Return beef to casserole.

- Add the green pepper and paprika. Cover and cook slowly about 30 minutes. Add tomato sauce and water or stock and salt and pepper. Bring to a boil, cover, reduce heat and cook slowly for about 1½ hours or until meat is tender. Add more water, if necessary. May be cooked to this point in advance and refrigerated or frozen. Reheat before serving in 325 degree oven for about 30 to 45 minutes.

- Cook noodles according to package directions and drain. Arrange noodles on a dish, ladle goulash on top and sprinkle with parsley. Serve at once.

Texas Pot Roast

Possibly the best braised beef dish you'll ever put on a buffet or picnic table.

- Serves 6

3 to 4 pounds brisket of beef

1 tablespoon vegetable oil

Salt to taste

Freshly ground pepper

Garlic powder

2 6-ounce cans tomato paste

1 teaspoon Worcestershire sauce

1 tablespoon dried oregano

1 tablespoon dried thyme

2 4-ounce cans whole green chilies (mild or hot, according to taste preference)

1 10-ounce package frozen peas, defrosted

- Heat Dutch oven or heavy casserole until hot. Add oil and sear meat quickly on each side. Turn off heat.

- With the tip of a small sharp knife, make 8 little incisions on each side of the meat. Sprinkle both sides with salt, pepper and garlic powder.

- Mix tomato paste, Worcestershire sauce, oregano and thyme together and set aside.

- Rinse and split chilies and place over meat. Spread on tomato mixture. Cook, covered, over very low heat for about 2 to 2½ hours, adding a small amount of water, if needed, and baste frequently with the sauce. One hour before meat is finished, add peas and continue cooking until meat is tender. May be prepared up to 48 hours in advance. Heat slowly before serving.

- To serve, slice meat thinly on the diagonal. Spoon sauce over meat and place chilies on top. Pass remaining sauce. Accompany with cornbread and a mixed green salad.

Variation: Chuck roast can be substituted for brisket and cooked for 4 hours. Brisket may be cooked in 325 degree oven for 2 hours; chuck for 3 hours. Two thinly sliced onions and 1 minced garlic clove can be added. Sauté until soft after searing meat.

157

Georgia Beef Barbecue

When the crowd gets together for Sunday supper, this is the dish to serve. Keep it bubbling on the stove and let your guests help themselves.

- Serves 26 to 30

  10 pounds brisket of beef

  1 cup liquid smoke

  4 cups diced onion

  2 tablespoons minced garlic

  2 12-ounce cans tomato paste

  5 to 6 cups beer

  1 28-ounce can plum tomatoes with liquid

  1 cup dark brown sugar, firmly packed

  ⅔ cup red wine vinegar

  ½ cup Worcestershire sauce

  3 to 4 tablespoons chili powder

  2 tablespoons molasses

  4 teaspoons ground cumin

  2 teaspoons salt

  ¼ teaspoon ground cloves

- Preheat oven to 325 degrees.

- Set rack in bottom of roasting pan. Arrange meat in single layer on rack. Add liquid smoke to pan (meat should not touch liquid). Cover and bake, turning once, until meat is tender, 4 to 5 hours. Set meat aside. Reserve ¼ cup fat from surface and all pan liquid. Cool and refrigerate meat and fat overnight.

- To finish, melt fat in large heavy covered casserole over low heat. Add onion and garlic, cover and cook until soft, about 10 minutes, stirring occasionally. Mix in tomato paste.

- Measure reserved pan liquid and enough beer to make 5 ½ cups liquid, total. Blend into onion mixture. Stir in all remaining ingredients except meat and bring to boil. Reduce to low and simmer sauce for at least 30 minutes.

- Shred meat and add to sauce. Cover and simmer 1 hour. If sauce seems too thin, uncover pan, increase heat and boil to reduce. May be prepared up to 3 days in advance.

- To serve, spoon over split sesame buns. Accompany with coleslaw, sliced tomatoes and onion rings.

Classic Rib Roast of Beef

Traditional at Christmas, spectacular for any festive occasion

- 2 servings per rib

  1 2-rib to 4-rib roast of beef, short ribs removed, weighing 4½ to 12 pounds

  Flour for dredging

  Salt

  Freshly ground pepper

- Remove roast from refrigerator 2½ to 4 hours before cooking.

- Preheat oven to 500 degrees.

- Place roast in open, shallow roasting pan, fat side up. Sprinkle with a little flour and rub into fat lightly. Season with salt and pepper.

- Put roast in oven and roast according to the following chart, timing exactly. When cooking time is finished, turn off the oven. Do <u>not</u> open door at any time.

Ribs

Weight Without Short Ribs	Roast at 500 degrees
2	1½ to 5 pounds 25 to 30 minutes
3	8 to 9 pounds 40 to 45 minutes
4	11 to 12 pounds 55 to 60 minutes

This works out to be 15 minutes per rib or approximately 5 minutes cooking time per pound of ready-to-cook roast. This method should only be attempted with a well insulated oven.

• Allow roast to remain in oven until oven is lukewarm, or about 2 hours. Remove from oven, carve and serve.

Lamb Marrakech

The variety of accompaniments make this an entertaining entrée.

• Serves 12

7 pounds lean lamb, cut in 1½-inch cubes

1 cup peanut oil

4 large onions, finely chopped

8 cloves garlic, finely chopped

2 teaspoons salt (or to taste)

2 teaspoons crushed red chili pepper

½ teaspoon ground ginger

½ teaspoon ground cinnamon

2 teaspoons turmeric

9 or 10 large ripe tomatoes, peeled, seeded and chopped

2 cups white raisins, soaked in dry sherry

1½ cups toasted almonds

1½ cups toasted hazelnuts

Crisp fried onion rings

1 cup chopped fresh parsley

Couscous, cooked according to package instructions

• In a large pot, heat oil. Dry lamb cubes and brown lightly, a few at a time. Add onion and garlic and cook until translucent. Add salt, chili pepper, ginger, cinnamon, turmeric and tomatoes. Bring to a boil, adding a small amount of water, if necessary. Cover and simmer 1½ hours. May be prepared up to 24 hours in advance and refrigerated.

• At serving time, bring to a simmer and add raisins. Heat through. Present on a large, deep platter around a mound of couscous. Garnish with a sprinkle of toasted nuts, onion rings and parsley. Put remainder of garnishes in small bowls surrounding platter for guests to add more to taste.

159

Lamb with Mustard Crust

A grand presentation of a leg of lamb – the "crust" keeps it juicy and complements the flavor.

- Serves 6 to 8
2 to 3 cloves of garlic, peeled and cut into slivers
1 5-pound leg of lamb
Dry mustard
Water
2 to 3 teaspoons rosemary
Paprika
2 to 3 bunches watercress

- Preheat oven to 500 degrees.

- Make shallow incisions in lamb with tip of sharp knife and poke garlic slivers into incisions.

- Make a thick paste of mustard and water and coat outside of lamb. Sprinkle with rosemary and paprika while paste is still moist. Set lamb aside at room temperature.

- Put lamb on rack in a shallow roasting pan and roast for 15 to 20 minutes, or until golden brown. Reduce heat to 400 degrees and continue roasting for 40 minutes more, basting once. Internal temperature will be about 145 degrees for rare. For medium rare, continue roasting until meat thermometer registers 155 degrees. Remove from oven and let stand for 10 to 15 minutes. Garnish with bouquets of watercress and accompany with Cream Potato Gratin and Baked Fennel.

Lamb Orientale

This tangy roasted boneless leg of lamb is glazed with a pungent soy-based sauce.

- Serves 8
½ cup Dijon-style mustard
1½ tablespoons soy sauce
1 clove of garlic, minced
½-inch slice fresh ginger root, peeled and minced
1 teaspoon crushed, dried rosemary
¼ cup olive oil
1 6 to 7-pound leg of lamb, boned

- Combine mustard, soy sauce, garlic, ginger root and rosemary in a small bowl. Gradually whisk in oil to make a thick sauce. Brush thickly and evenly over lamb and let stand at room temperature for 2 to 3 hours.

- Preheat oven to 350 degrees.

- Place lamb on rack in a shallow roasting pan and roast for about 1 hour and 20 minutes (165 degrees on meat thermometer). Baste occasionally with any remaining sauce and pan drippings.

- To serve, remove lamb from pan and degrease pan drippings. Carve lamb into thin slices and drizzle lightly with drippings. Accompany with french-fried sweet potatoes and peas sauced in cream and butter.

Sweet and Sour Roast Leg of Lamb

The secret ingredient is grape jelly which makes the incredible sauce.

• **Serves 6 to 8**
  1 5 to 6-pound leg of lamb
  Salt
  Freshly ground pepper
  Flour
  1 cup grape jelly
  ¼ cup cider vinegar (more or less, according to taste)
  ½ teaspoon thyme
  1 clove of garlic, crushed
  2 teaspoons salt
  Freshly ground pepper
  1 pound purple grapes

• Preheat oven to 325 degrees.

• Rub salt and pepper on lamb and dust lightly with flour. Place lamb on rack in shallow roasting pan and roast until rare, 25 to 30 minutes per pound (about 150 degrees on meat thermometer). Remove roast from pan and tent loosely in foil while sauce is prepared.

• Drain off fat. Add jelly, vinegar, thyme, garlic, salt and pepper to pan drippings and mix thoroughly. Bring to a boil.

• Return lamb to pan. Spoon sauce over lamb and return to oven for an additional 15 minutes or until thermometer registers 165 degrees, basting frequently.

• To serve, strain sauce into a warm sauce boat. Place roast on a large platter and garnish with purple grape clusters.

Crown Roast of Pork

Remarkable and easy to prepare

• **Serves 6 to 8**
  Crown roast of pork, allowing 2 ribs per person (butcher will prepare)

Salt Marinade
  2 teaspoons sea salt
  ¾ teaspoon freshly ground pepper
  ½ teaspoon dried thyme
  ½ teaspoon dried sage
  ⅛ teaspoon allspice
  1 dried bay leaf, finely crumbled
  1 clove of garlic, mashed

• One day before serving, mix salt marinade ingredients thoroughly and rub into roast. Cover and refrigerate, turning occasionally.

• Five hours before serving, preheat oven to 450 degrees. Remove meat from refrigerator and rub off marinade. Pat dry with paper towels. Cover ends of ribs with small pieces of aluminum foil. Place roast in roasting pan. Place roast in oven and immediately reduce heat to 350 degrees. Roast for 30 minutes per pound (165 to 175 degrees on meat thermometer).

• To serve, remove aluminum foil tips. Paper "chop frills", cherry tomatoes or spiced apples may be used on each end. Center may be filled with wild rice.

161

West Indian Leg of Lamb

The exotic feature is the coffee-flavored sauce.

- **Serves 8**
  1 5-pound leg of lamb
  1 tablespoon salt
  2 cloves of garlic, thinly sliced
  2 cups very strong coffee
  ½ cup orange liqueur
  1 tablespoon molasses
  1 tablespoon dark brown sugar
  ½ teaspoon allspice
  ½ teaspoon cinnamon
  ¼ teaspoon mace or nutmeg
  Salt to taste
  1 tablespoon cornstarch

- Preheat oven to 325 degrees.

- Rub salt into lamb. Make incisions randomly over lamb surface with tip of small knife and insert garlic slivers.

- Combine coffee, ¼ cup orange liqueur, brown sugar, molasses and spices. Brush sauce on lamb. Place lamb on rack in shallow roasting pan and roast for 20 minutes per pound, basting frequently with sauce. Lamb should register 160 degrees on meat thermometer when finished. Remove lamb to serving platter and tent with foil to keep warm while making gravy.

- Pour pan drippings into a sauce pan. Mix cornstarch with a little cool water and whisk into gravy. Stir over low heat, adding more water, if necessary, until gravy lightly coats spoon and is clear.

- To serve, pour remaining ¼ cup of orange liqueur over lamb and ignite. When flames subside, carve and serve immediately with Mushroom Mousse.

Lemon Pork Chops

Lemon lovers, note this innovative entrée.

- **Serves 4**
  4 lean loin pork chops about 1 to 1½-inches thick
  Salt and pepper, if desired
  1 large lemon, sliced in rounds
  ½ cup catsup
  ½ cup water
  2 tablespoons brown sugar
  1 tablespoon fresh lemon juice

- Preheat oven to 350 degrees.

- Season chops with salt and pepper, if desired, and sear quickly on each side in a hot frying pan. Remove chops and arrange in baking dish. Put 1 slice of lemon on top of each chop.

- Mix catsup, water, brown sugar and lemon juice. Pour over chops. Bake, uncovered, for about 1 hour. Accompany with sautéed julienne of potatoes and zucchini and garnish with additional lemon slices.

Variation: Chicken thighs are a delicious alternative to pork. Reduce baking time to about 45 minutes.

Fruit-Stuffed Loin of Pork

Festive enough for your most important guests

- Serves 6 to 8

  4 pound boneless pork roast, prepared for stuffing

  1 cup pitted prunes

  1 cup dried apricots

  1 clove of garlic, cut in slivers

  Salt

  Freshly ground pepper

  ½ cup (4 ounces) unsalted butter, softened

  1 tablespoon dried thyme

  1 tablespoon molasses

  1 cup Madeira wine

  Watercress (garnish)

  Madeira Sauce (recipe follows)

- Preheat oven to 350 degrees.

- Using the handle of a wooden spoon, push dried fruits into pocket of roast, alternating prunes and apricots. With the tip of a small knife, make incisions in pork and insert garlic slivers. Tie roast with twine and rub surface with salt and pepper. May be prepared up to 6 hours prior to roasting. Bring to room temperature before continuing.

- Set roast in shallow pan and smear with butter. Sprinkle with thyme. Stir molasses into wine and pour over roast. Set pan on middle rack of oven and roast for 1½ hours (about 20 minutes per pound). Baste frequently. When roast is done (do not overcook), remove from oven and tent loosely with foil. Let stand 15 minutes.

- To serve, carve into ½ to ¾-inch slices, arrange on serving platter and spoon on pan juices. Garnish with watercress.

Variation: Prunes and apricots can be soaked overnight in water boiled with cinnamon, nutmeg, ground cloves and a little brown sugar. Add 1 tablespoon dark rum and 2 tablespoons Madeira.

Brown Sauce

3 tablespoons (1½ ounces) unsalted butter

¾ cup minced onion

½ cup diced carrots

4½ teaspoons all-purpose flour

2 cups beef stock

1 tablespoon minced shallots

2 medium cloves of garlic, minced

Bouquet garni

2 teaspoons tomato paste

¼ teaspoon black pepper

- In a small pan, melt butter and when hot, sauté onion and carrot. Cook for 5 minutes, stirring with a wooden spoon. Blend in flour, stirring constantly and cook for 10 minutes or until brown.

- Remove from heat, add beef stock and whisk until smooth. Add shallots, garlic, bouquet garni, tomato paste and pepper. Bring to boil, cover and simmer for 45 minutes. Strain through a fine sieve and then boil until reduced by ⅓.

Madeira Sauce

1 recipe Brown Sauce

2 tablespoons minced shallots

9 tablespoons Madeira

1 tablespoon cognac

- In a saucepan, cook shallots and 8 tablespoons of Madeira until mixture is reduced to 1 tablespoon. Do not burn. Whisk the strained brown sauce into the pan. Mix well and heat but do not boil. Remove from heat and add 1 tablespoon Madeira and cognac.

Nasi Goreng

An authentic Indonesian meat and rice mélange to tease the palates of your most sophisticated guests

- Serves 6 to 8

¼ cup vegetable oil

4 to 6 scallions, finely chopped

4 cloves of garlic, crushed

2 teaspoons (more or less, to taste) red chili peppers (dried or fresh, crushed or chopped)

2 teaspoons salt

6 cups cooked, cooled rice

1½ pounds diced roast pork, ham or cooked seafood (or a combination of all 3)

2 tablespoons (1 ounce) unsalted butter

8 eggs

¼ cup chopped scallions for garnish

- In a large frying pan or wok, heat vegetable oil. Add scallions, garlic, red pepper and salt and sauté until golden. Add rice, mixing well, and fry until golden and a little crusty, stirring often with a wooden spoon.

- Add meats and seafood and mix well, cooking for several minutes until heated through.

- In a frying pan, melt butter. Fry eggs or mix and sauté as an omelet.

- Serve Nasi Goreng in individual warm soup plates. Top each portion with a fried egg and a sprinkle of scallions or cut the omelet into strips and serve over the rice dish with a sprinkle of scallions. Traditional accompaniments are cold beer and a leafy salad with fresh fruit for dessert.

Pork Tenderloins with Madeira and Mushroom Sauce

A savory stuffing and a fragrant sauce

- Serves 8 to 10

4 whole pork tenderloins, split lengthwise (butterflied)

4 slices bacon, uncooked

Stuffing

3 cups fresh, soft bread crumbs

4 tablespoons (2 ounces) unsalted butter, melted

1 onion, finely chopped

¼ teaspoon each: dried savory, dried parsley, dried sage, dried rosemary or dried thyme

Salt and pepper to taste

- Preheat oven to 350 degrees.

- Combine stuffing ingredients thoroughly and set aside.

- Flatten tenderloins. Divide stuffing mixture among them and place 1 strip of bacon on each. Fold and tie both ends of each tenderloin. May be prepared in advance to this point.

- Place tenderloins in shallow roasting pan and roast, uncovered, about 1½ hours (165 to 175 degrees on meat thermometer).

Sauce

4 tablespoons (2 ounces) unsalted butter

2 tablespoons minced shallots or scallions

⅓ to ½ pound fresh mushrooms, thinly sliced

2 tablespoons all-purpose flour

1½ cups premium quality beef broth

½ cup Madeira

- Melt butter in medium-size sauce pan. When foam subsides, add shallots and sauté until translucent. Add mushrooms and sauté until lightly colored. Stir in flour and add broth gradually, whisking until smooth.

- Cook sauce until it thickens, stirring constantly. Lower heat and barely simmer for 10 minutes. May be prepared to this point up to 1 hour in advance. Cover and let stand prior to finishing.

- While sauce simmers, add Madeira and cook 5 more minutes. Season to taste with salt and pepper. Pour in heated sauce boat.

- To serve, carve each tenderloin into 1-inch thick slices. Arrange on platter, drizzle with Madeira and Mushroom Sauce and garnish with bouquets of watercress.

Speakeasy Pork Chops

Don't worry! The alcohol in the gin cooks out, leaving a distinctive flavor.

- **Serves 4**
  4 loin pork chops, 1½-inches thick
  Salt
  Freshly ground pepper
  Flour for dredging
  Vegetable oil
  1 clove of garlic, minced
  Grated rind from orange
  Juice of 1 large orange equal to ½ cup
  ½ cup gin
  ¼ cup chopped fresh parsley

- Sprinkle chops with salt and pepper. Dredge in flour. Coat bottom of frying pan with oil and sauté chops until brown on both sides.

- Sprinkle with garlic and grated orange rind. Pour on orange juice and gin. Cover pan and cook chops over low heat, turning them occasionally, until fork-tender (165 degrees on meat thermometer). Sauce will have thickened slightly. To serve, sprinkle chops with parsley and accompany with steamed rice and Maple Acorn Squash.

Tourtière

A famous French-Canadian minced pork pie – a delicious cold-weather "Sunday supper"

• **Serves 6**

1½ pounds minced fresh pork

1 small onion, diced

1 small clove of garlic, minced

½ teaspoon salt

½ teaspoon savory

¼ teaspoon freshly ground black pepper

½ teaspoon ground cloves

½ teaspoon ground cinnamon

½ cup water

2-crust pie pastry, unbaked

1 egg

• Preheat oven to 450 degrees.

• Combine pork, onion, clove of garlic, salt, savory, pepper, cloves, cinnamon and water in a heavy stove-top casserole. Bring to a boil. Reduce heat and cook, uncovered, for 30 minutes, stirring occasionally. Mixture should be damp, not watery. Refrigerate until chilled.

• Line 9-inch pie plate with pastry. Spoon in filling. Cover with remaining pastry and seal edges. Prick top with fork to release steam. Mix egg with a little water and brush lightly on top. Bake for 10 minutes; reduce heat to 350 degrees and bake 40 minutes longer until crust is light brown. May be cooled and frozen at this point. Reheat in 350 degree oven before serving. To serve, cut in wedges and accompany with a good chili sauce, if desired.

Bell Peppers Stuffed with Pork and Sausage

An uncommon stuffing for an all-time family favorite

• **Serves 4**

¼ to ½ cup chicken broth

¼ pound dry white French or Italian bread, crumbled

4 large yellow, red or green bell peppers

1 pound lean pork, freshly ground

½ pound hot sausage meat

1 medium onion, chopped

1 tablespoon freshly chopped parsley

1 cup cooked rice

3 cups fresh tomato sauce or Creole Tomato Sauce

¼ cup freshly grated Parmesan cheese

• Preheat oven to 350 degrees.

• Soak bread in small amount of broth, just enough to moisten. Meanwhile, slice off tops of peppers and hollow out ribs and seeds. Make sure peppers can stand up in baking dish.

• In a medium-size bowl, mix pork, sausage, onion, parsley and rice until well-blended but not "pasty". Stuff mixture into each pepper. Place in baking dish and cover with half of the tomato sauce. May be prepared to this point in advance. Cover and refrigerate.

• Bake peppers, uncovered, about 1 hour, basting halfway through with pan drippings. Meat mixture should not show any pink. To serve, heat remaining sauce. Make a "puddle" in the center of each plate and stand a pepper in the middle. Sprinkle cheese on top of each pepper. Pass remaining sauce.

Jambon en Saupiquet

Ham in a spicy wine sauce is an admirable presentation for left-over holiday ham.

- **Serves 6 to 8**
  4 tablespoons (2 ounces) unsalted butter
  3 shallots, minced
  ¼ cup vinegar
  1 tablespoon all-purpose flour
  Salt (optional)
  Freshly ground pepper
  ¼ cup dry white wine
  ¾ cup homemade or premium canned chicken stock
  8 juniper berries
  1 cup light cream
  8 slices of ham, about ½-inch thick
  ¼ cup chopped parsley for garnish

- Melt 1 tablespoon butter in frying pan. Add shallots and sauté until translucent. Add vinegar and simmer gently for 3 or 4 minutes. Sprinkle with flour, salt (if used) and pepper. Stir and cook gently until flour is well-incorporated. Whisk in wine and chicken stock. Add juniper berries and cream. Mix well and simmer very gently for about 30 minutes until sauce is thickened.

- Melt remaining butter in a large frying pan and sauté ham until lightly browned, about 5 minutes. Arrange ham on platter and spoon on some of the sauce. Sprinkle with parsley. Pass remaining sauce. Accompany with mashed potatoes.

Variation: Broil or grill ham slices, then drizzle with sauce.

Herbed Veal Stew

A bountiful buffet dish

- **Serves 8 to 10**
  3 pounds shoulder of veal, cut into 2-inch pieces
  3 tablespoons (1½ ounces) unsalted butter or oil
  1 cup thinly sliced onions
  2 cloves of garlic, minced
  1 teaspoon salt
  Freshly ground pepper
  ½ teaspoon dried thyme
  ½ teaspoon dried basil
  1 teaspoon chopped fresh parsley
  ¼ teaspoon grated orange zest
  2½ tablespoons all-purpose flour
  1¼ cups dry white wine or vermouth
  1 16-ounce can of tomatoes with liquid
  3 tablespoons tomato paste
  ½ pound fresh mushrooms, thinly sliced
  ½ package (5 ounces) frozen peas
  ¼ cup chopped fresh parsley
  1 orange, thinly sliced (garnish)

- Preheat oven to 350 degrees.

- In a large frying pan, heat butter or oil on medium-high heat. Add veal cubes, a few at a time, and brown. Add onions and garlic and sauté until golden. Drain off excess oil.

- Add salt, pepper, thyme, basil, parsley, orange zest and flour. Stir thoroughly but gently. Add wine, tomatoes and tomato paste, mixing carefully. Pour into a serving casserole, cover and bake for 1¼ hours, until veal is tender.

- Stir mushrooms and peas into the mixture and continue baking, covered, another 10 minutes. Garnish with chopped parsley and serve.

167

Italian Veal Stew

Hot Italian sausage is essential to this savory veal and wine casserole.

- Serves 6

1½ pounds boneless shoulder of veal, cut in 1½-inch
    cubes

¾ cup dry red wine

¼ cup all-purpose flour

2 tablespoons (1 ounce) unsalted butter

2 tablespoons olive oil

½ pound hot Italian sausage, cut in ½-inch slices

1 medium onion, chopped

1 clove of garlic, minced

1 16-ounce can tomatoes, or 5 peeled ripe tomatoes

1 cup good quality chicken stock

1 tablespoon fresh or 1 teaspoon dried basil

½ teaspoon dried rosemary, crushed

Salt to taste

Freshly ground pepper

1 tablespoon fresh lemon juice

1 large sweet red pepper, cut into ½-inch slices

1 large green bell pepper, cut into ½-inch slices

½ pound fresh mushrooms, thickly sliced

¼ cup chopped fresh parsley

1 teaspoon grated lemon rind

- Marinate veal in wine for 1½ hours. Drain, reserving marinade, and pat meat dry. Lightly dust meat with flour and set aside.

- Heat butter and oil in deep, heavy casserole and brown veal, a few cubes at a time, over medium heat until lightly brown. Remove veal and set aside. Brown sausage and reserve with veal. Sauté onions and garlic until lightly brown (don't let garlic burn).

Add reserved marinade, tomatoes, stock, basil and rosemary to pan, stirring and scraping up brown bits. Boil 5 minutes.

- Return veal and sausage to pan. Add salt, pepper and lemon juice. Reduce heat and simmer for 1 hour, covered. Degrease as needed. May be prepared 1 to 2 days ahead to this point, refrigerated or frozen. Reheat prior to serving time.

- Add peppers and mushrooms and simmer another 30 minutes or bake, covered, in a 350 degree oven for 30 minutes. To serve, sprinkle with lemon rind and parsley. Accompany with steamed potatoes or pasta.

Scallops of Veal Marsala

Sweet sherry is a fine substitute for Marsala wine.

- Serves 6

1½ pounds veal scallops, sliced thinly and pounded flat

1 teaspoon salt

Flour for dredging

½ cup olive oil

1 cup thinly sliced fresh mushrooms

½ cup finely chopped shallots

½ cup chopped celery

1 clove of garlic, minced

1 tablespoon chopped fresh parsley

1 cup good quality beef broth

1 cup Marsala wine

4 tablespoons (2 ounces) unsalted butter

¼ cup freshly grated Parmesan cheese

½ pound linguine

¼ cup chopped fresh parsley for garnish

- Cut meat in serving pieces. Sprinkle with salt and lightly dredge in flour. Set aside to dry.

- In a large frying pan, heat 2 tablespoons of olive oil and add mushrooms. Cook gently for about 5 minutes. Remove with a slotted spoon and set aside. Add remaining oil to pan and heat. Over high heat, brown pieces of veal, a few at a time, for about 1 minute on each side. Remove meat and keep warm on a platter under a tent of foil. (Add more oil if needed.)

- Reduce heat and pour off excess oil, leaving a little in pan. Add shallots, celery, garlic and parsley and sauté quickly until golden. Add broth and simmer 15 minutes. Add wine and simmer an additional 15 minutes. Stir in butter and cheese. Add veal and mushrooms and heat through.

- Cook linguine according to package instructions. Drain and arrange on a large platter. Place veal over noodles and pour on sauce. Garnish with chopped parsley and serve at once. Accompany with sautéed strips of red and green sweet peppers.

Veal au Gratin

A light sauce laced with wine and a glaze of cheese are the highlights of this superb dish.

- Serves 4

4 tablespoons (2 ounces) unsalted butter, melted

2 small to medium onions, minced

2 tablespoons finely chopped parsley

2 tablespoons finely chopped green pepper (optional)

1½ pounds veal scallops, thinly sliced and pounded flat

Salt

Freshly ground pepper

1 cup dry white wine

2 slices bread, crumbled

4 tablespoons freshly grated Parmesan or Gruyère cheese

- Preheat oven to 300 degrees.

- Pour half of the butter in a shallow baking dish large enough to take the veal in one layer. Sprinkle onion, parsley and green pepper (if used) over butter.

- Sprinkle veal scallops with salt and pepper and place over vegetables. Pour wine over veal.

- Mix fresh bread crumbs with cheese and spread over veal. Drizzle remaining 2 tablespoons butter over crumbs. Cover casserole with aluminum foil and bake for about 45 minutes. Heat broiler. Remove foil and place casserole under broiler until cheese and crumb mixture browns lightly. Serve at once accompanied by parslied new potatoes.

Veal Normandy

Apple brandy and apples are sublime with veal.

- Serves 4
  1 pound veal scallops, thinly cut and pounded flat
  Salt
  Freshly ground pepper
  Flour
  3 tablespoons (1½ ounces) unsalted butter
  2 Granny Smith apples, peeled, cored and thinly sliced
  ¼ cup apple brandy
  1 cup heavy cream
  1 to 2 tablespoons fresh lemon juice
  1 Granny Smith apple, unpeeled, cored and sliced into 4 rings
  2 cups steamed white rice

- Sprinkle veal scallops with salt and pepper and lightly dust with flour. Allow to dry.

- In a large frying pan, melt butter until bubbly and sauté veal until white (about one minute). Don't brown. Remove from pan to platter and keep warm under a foil tent.

- Add apple slices to pan and sauté until soft but not mushy. Add apple brandy and light with match. Shake pan until flame subsides. Add cream. Bring to boil and reduce until thick enough to coat spoon. Add lemon juice, salt and pepper to taste. Return veal to pan and heat until warm.

- Ring serving platter with rice and place veal in center. Garnish with apple rings and serve at once along with Peas with Proscuitto.

Veal Sevilla

Oranges and olives give a Spanish flavor.

- Serves 4 to 6
  1½ pounds veal scallops, thinly cut and pounded flat
  ½ teaspoon salt
  ½ teaspoon freshly ground black pepper
  1 11-ounce can Mandarin orange segments
  2 tablespoons olive oil
  2 tablespoons (1 ounce) unsalted butter
  ½ cup good quality beef consommé
  8 pitted green olives, thinly sliced
  2 tablespoons chopped fresh parsley

- Cut veal scallops into pieces about 3-inches square. Sprinkle with salt and pepper. Drain Mandarin oranges, reserving juice.

- In a large heavy frying pan over high heat, heat oil and butter. Quickly brown veal scallops, a few at a time, about 1 or 2 minutes on each side. Remove with a slotted spoon to a heated platter.

- Pour consommé and juice from oranges into frying pan, stirring to scrape up all brown bits from pan. Add sliced olives and orange sections, heat quickly, and pour over veal. Sprinkle with chopped parsley and serve at once. Steamed rice garnished with a sprinkle of grated orange peel is an excellent accompaniment.

Vitello Medaglione Asparagi

A triumphant dish reminiscent of Northern Italy

- Serves 8 to 10
  18 medium-size fresh asparagus spears, cleaned and peeled
  18 medallions of veal, trimmed and pounded thin
  Dijon-style mustard
  Salt
  Freshly ground pepper
  Freshly grated nutmeg
  Allspice (optional)
  1 teaspoon minced fresh garlic
  4 tablespoons (2 ounces) unsalted butter
  ¼ cup olive oil
  18 mushrooms, sliced
  2 tablespoons bacon fat
  ¼ medium onion, sliced
  2 tablespoons flour
  ½ cup white wine
  ¾ cup chicken stock (homemade or premium canned)
  1 tomato, peeled, seeded, and sliced in thin strips

- Preheat oven to 375 degrees.

- Blanch asparagus in boiling water until al dente (about 2 to 3 minutes). Drain and set aside on paper towels to cool.

- Place pounded slices of veal on flat surface and spread with a thin coating of mustard. Season with a pinch each of salt, pepper, nutmeg, allspice and garlic. Place 1 asparagus spear at end of each medallion and wrap, securing with toothpick. Repeat until all medallions of veal are filled with the asparagus.

- In a large frying pan, melt butter, oil and bacon fat. Lightly dust each veal roll with flour and brown quickly. (Oils should be hot but not smoking.) Remove veal rolls from pan and arrange neatly in a large, shallow casserole.

- Sauté onion and mushrooms in remaining oil until brown. Add 2 tablespoons flour, stirring until blended. Add wine, chicken stock and tomato strips. Simmer for 5 minutes. Pour over veal rolls. Bake for 20 to 25 minutes until veal is tender. May be prepared to this point an hour in advance and kept warm in low oven. Garnish with rice mixed with butter and freshly grated Parmesan cheese. Decorate with minced parsley. Serve with Belgian endive salad tossed with Vinaigrette Dijonnaise.

171

Veal in Vermouth Cream Sauce

Fragrant, flavorful and fancy

• Serves 4

1½ pounds veal scallops, thinly cut and pounded flat

Salt

Freshly ground pepper

Flour

1 tablespoon unsalted butter

1 tablespoon olive oil

¾ to 1 cup vermouth

1 cup sliced fresh mushrooms

½ cup heavy cream

½ pound cooked egg noodles

1 tablespoon grated lemon peel

• Sprinkle veal with salt and pepper and lightly dust with flour.

• In a large frying pan, melt butter and oil. Brown veal on each side until golden brown, about 1 minute per side.

• Add mushrooms and vermouth and simmer about 5 minutes. Add cream and heat through. Serve immediately over noodles and garnish with grated lemon rind. Accompany with steamed, buttered zucchini.

Variation: Boneless chicken or turkey breast, pounded thin, are excellent substitutes for the veal.

Veal Veritas

Infallible

• Serves 4

4 tablespoons (2 ounces) butter, melted

2 medium onions, minced

2 tablespoons parsley, chopped

1 pound veal cutlets or veal tenders

Salt and pepper

1 cup dry white wine

2 slices bread, crumbled

4 tablespoons Swiss cheese, grated

• Preheat oven to 300 degrees.

• Pour half of butter into shallow baking dish and cover with onion and parsley. Lay veal on this and season with salt and pepper.

• Cover with wine and set aside.

• Mix bread and cheese with last half of butter. Sprinkle over veal. Cover with lid or aluminum foil.

• Bake 1 hour.

Beef Stew Mexican Style

Olé!

- Serves 8 to 10

3 pounds boneless beef chuck, cut in 1-inch cubes

3 tablespoons salad oil

3 tablespoons (1½ ounces) unsalted butter

4 medium onions, chopped

½ teaspoon dried thyme

¼ teaspoon cinnamon

⅛ teaspoon cloves

2 tablespoons flour

1 tablespoon catsup

1 bay leaf

2 teaspoons salt

½ teaspoon pepper

1 teaspoon grated lemon peel

1½ cups dry white wine

1 29-ounce can pear halves

6 sweet potatoes

3 tablespoons seedless raisins

Chopped parsley (garnish)

- Wipe beef with damp paper towels.

- In 6-quart Dutch oven, brown beef cubes in oil and butter, turning with tongs to brown on all sides. Do not crowd. Remove meat from pan.

- Add chopped onions, thyme, cinnamon and cloves to drippings. Sauté, stirring, 5 minutes or until tender.

- Remove from heat. Stir in flour, catsup, bay leaf, salt, pepper and lemon peel. Gradually stir in wine.

- Drain pears and set aside, reserving 1 cup syrup. Add syrup and browned beef to mixture in Dutch oven.

- Place large sheet of waxed paper over top and place lid on top of paper.

- Bring to boil; reduce heat and gently simmer, covered, about 1 hour and 20 minutes, or until meat is tender.

- Gently cook sweet potatoes in boiling water 30 minutes, or until tender. Drain and cool

- Peel sweet potatoes and halve lengthwise.

- When meat is tender, add sweet potatoes, reserved pears and raisins. Cook uncovered for 10 minutes or until heated through and liquid is slightly thickened.

- Garnish with chopped parsley.

$\mathscr{P}$OULTRY

Robert Rauschenberg (American, born 1925), *Flush*, 1964, oil and silkscreen inks on canvas, 95 3/16 x 71 5/16". Centennial gift of the Woodward Foundation

Rauschenberg has used silkscreen transfers to create the kaleidoscopic effect of this painting. With this technique all of the images could exist on a single surface, which allowed for illusions of transparency and depth. The artist then fused the various elements into an integrated whole with his vigorous brushstrokes. Some of the subjects were taken from photographs of New York that Rauschenberg made from his loft window. Others, such as the birds, are standards in his iconography.

Apricot Brandied Chicken

Pretty presentation to multiply for a party

- Serves 4

  4 large whole chicken breasts, split, skinned and boned

  ¼ cup all-purpose flour

  Garlic powder to taste

  6 tablespoons (3 ounces) unsalted butter

  2 tablespoons olive oil

  ⅔ cup apricot jam

  Grated peel from 2 lemons

  ⅔ cup brandy

  1 chicken bouillon cube

  4 tablespoons chopped fresh parsley

  1 tablespoon cornstarch, dissolved in 2 tablespoons lemon juice

  ⅔ cup fresh Bing cherries with stems left on

- Preheat oven to 275 degrees.

- Flour chicken lightly. Sprinkle with garlic powder.

- In a large frying pan, combine butter and olive oil. Add chicken and sauté over medium-high heat until lightly browned.

- While chicken is browning, combine apricot jam, lemon peel, brandy, chicken bouillon cube, chopped parsley and cornstarch mixture in a small saucepan. Simmer over medium heat, stirring occasionally until thickened.

- Remove sautéed chicken with slotted spoon and place in a shallow, ovenproof casserole. Pour marinade over chicken and bake for 1 hour, basting occasionally. May be prepared to this point 24 hours in advance. Cover and refrigerate. Bring to room temperature, reheat and proceed as directed.

- Remove from oven. Scatter cherries over chicken and place under broiler just long enough to warm the cherries (about 2½ minutes).

- Serve with puréed broccoli and wild or brown rice.

  Variation: Substitute 4 small whole Cornish hens for chicken. Increase baking time to 1 hour and 15 minutes.

Chicken with Almond-Mustard Sauce en Papillote

Savory sauced chicken cooks in individual "envelopes".

- Serves 6

  3 tablespoons (1½ ounces) unsalted butter

  18 green onions, white part only, quartered lengthwise

  9 small carrots, peeled and julienned

  6 medium turnips, peeled and julienned

  ½ teaspoon salt, or to taste

  Freshly ground pepper

  6 tablespoons dry vermouth

  3 ounces slivered almonds

  Additional 3 tablespoons (1½ ounces) unsalted butter

  8 medium shallots

  6 tablespoons dry vermouth

  2 cups unsalted chicken stock

  ¼ cup heavy cream

2 tablespoons Dijon-style mustard

6 boneless chicken breast halves, skinned and cut
   diagonally into large pieces

Baker's parchment paper or aluminum foil

- Preheat oven to 475 degrees.

- In a large frying pan, heat 3 tablespoons butter over high heat. Add onion, carrots, turnips and stir until lightly browned. Season with salt and pepper. Blend in 6 tablespoons vermouth and simmer until liquid is nearly evaporated. Remove vegetables from pan with slotted spoon. Sprinkle with almonds and set aside.

- In same frying pan, heat additional 3 tablespoons butter over medium heat. Add shallots and sauté until golden. Add 6 tablespoons vermouth and stir, scraping up any brown bits. Cook until reduced to a thin glaze. Blend in stock and reduce to about ½ cup. Stir in cream and mustard and boil 30 seconds. Remove from heat.

- Cut 6 pieces of "baker's parchment paper" or aluminum foil and brush lightly with vegetable oil or cooking spray. Divide vegetables among the 6 pieces of parchment and arrange 3 to 4 pieces of chicken on top. Spoon some sauce over chicken. Fold parchment into package, leaving some room for expansion. May be prepared to this point up to 6 hours in advance. Refrigerate. Remove from refrigerator 1 hour prior to baking.

- Arrange packages on baking sheets, folded sides down, on rack in upper third of oven. Bake for 20 minutes.

- To serve, place papillotes on individual plates and accompany with sliced potatoes which have been sautéed in a mixture of butter and oil and seasoned with salt and paprika.

Chicken Bombay

Fun to serve with condiments à l'Indienne as garnishes

- Serves 6

1 small onion, chopped

1 small apple, cored, peeled and chopped

1 tablespoon unsalted butter

1 10¾-ounce can condensed cream of chicken soup

Salt to taste (optional)

2 teaspoons curry powder

2 cups cooked chicken, cubed

3 ripe avocados

3 cups cooked rice

Pimiento strips for garnish

Condiments: raisins, chutney, kumquats, crumbled crisp
   bacon, chopped peanuts, green pepper slices, toasted
   coconut, pineapple chunks

- In a 2-quart saucepan, sauté chopped onion together with chopped apple. Stir in undiluted chicken soup, salt and curry powder.

- Heat over low flame until smooth, stirring frequently. Add chicken.

- Peel and halve the avocados. Place avocados on a bed of rice and fill with curry mixture. Garnish with strips of pimiento. Serve accompanied by bowls of the condiments.

Variation: Instead of 2 cups cooked chicken, use 2 cups cooked and peeled shrimp.

177

Chicken Breasts Argenteuil

An elegant presentation

• **Serves 8**
4 whole chicken breasts, halved, skinned and boned
4 tablespoons (2 ounces) butter or margarine, melted
¾ teaspoon dried tarragon
Salt and freshly ground pepper to taste
24 fresh asparagus spears, blanched
Hollandaise sauce (see Sauces and Marinades)
Paprika (garnish)

• Preheat oven to 375 degrees.

• Pound chicken breasts between 2 pieces of waxed paper until flattened.

• Brush inside of breast halves with melted butter. Sprinkle lightly with tarragon, salt and pepper.

• Place 3 asparagus spears, crosswise, in center of each breast and fold ends over. Fasten with toothpicks.

• Place folded side down in a greased shallow casserole. May be prepared to this point 8 hours in advance. Cover and refrigerate. Return to room temperature before continuing. Brush chicken and asparagus with butter. Bake for 45 minutes.

• Remove from oven. Spoon warm Hollandaise over chicken and sprinkle with paprika. Accompany with sautéed potato balls and haricots verts.

Chicken Breasts in Green Peppercorn Sauce

Sautéed chicken breasts glazed with a piquant sauce can be a dramatic centerpiece for a dinner party.

• **Serves 4**
4 large chicken breasts, halved, skinned and boned
6 tablespoons (3 ounces) unsalted butter
3 tablespoons minced onion
⅓ cup dry white wine
½ cup heavy cream
3 teaspoons green peppercorns (drained – chop 2 teaspoons)
¼ teaspoon dried tarragon
Salt and pepper to taste
Sprigs of watercress (garnish)

• Brown chicken over medium-high heat in 4 tablespoons of the butter. Reduce heat, add onion and brown slowly until onions are translucent and chicken is tender, adding more butter if necessary. Remove chicken and onions from pan and set aside on a warm platter.

• Add wine to pan and bring to a boil. Reduce heat and cook until liquid is reduced to 2 tablespoons. Stir in heavy cream, chopped peppercorns and tarragon. Continue cooking until sauce is reduced and thickened.

• Add tarragon, salt and pepper to taste and 1 teaspoon whole green peppercorns. Remove from heat. Spoon sauce over chicken and serve at once, garnished with watercress sprigs. Accompany with a garland of sautéed cherry tomatoes and mushroom caps.

Chicken with Ginger Sauce

A South Sea touch for your chicken repertoire

- **Serves 4**

  2 large whole chicken breasts, halved, skinned and boned

  Salt

  Freshly ground pepper to taste

  2 tablespoons (1 ounce) unsalted butter

  1½-inches fresh ginger root, peeled and finely chopped

  2 teaspoons chopped shallots

  1 clove of garlic, minced

  1½ teaspoons cornstarch

  ½ cup water

  2 tablespoons soy sauce

  2 tablespoons brandy

  1 teaspoon dried thyme

  1 teaspoon dried rosemary

- Preheat oven to 350 degrees.

- Lightly grease a shallow ovenproof casserole just large enough to hold chicken pieces. Sprinkle chicken with salt and pepper and place in casserole.

- Prepare sauce by melting butter in a small saucepan. Lightly sauté ginger, shallots and garlic. Dissolve cornstarch in water and combine with ginger mixture. Add soy sauce and brandy. Continue to heat, stirring constantly until mixture bubbles. Add thyme and rosemary. Stir and simmer 5 minutes. Sauce may be prepared to this point 24 hours in advance. Cover and refrigerate. Bring to room temperature before continuing.

- Brush chicken with sauce. Place in oven and bake 30 minutes, removing after each 10 minute period to brush with additional sauce. Pour remaining sauce over chicken and bake an additional 5 minutes.

- Serve in center of platter on a bed of watercress. Top each chicken breast with a large grilled mushroom cap. Surround with a variety of fresh vegetables.

Variation: Substitute pork tenderloin for chicken. Increase baking time by 15 minutes.

Chicken a l'Orange

Chicken with a pungent citrus sauce

- **Serves 8**

  4 large whole chicken breasts, halved and boned

  ½ cup all-purpose flour

  1 teaspoon salt, or to taste

  ½ teaspoon paprika

  ½ cup (4 ounces) unsalted butter

  2 tablespoons vegetable oil

  1 teaspoon grated lemon rind

  1 teaspoon grated orange rind

  1 6-ounce can frozen orange juice concentrate, undiluted

  ¼ cup Madeira or sherry

  ½ cup toasted almonds

  1 navel orange, unpeeled and sliced (garnish)

- Dust chicken lightly with mixture of flour, salt and paprika.

- In a large frying pan, heat butter and oil over medium-high heat. Add chicken pieces and sauté until golden brown. May be prepared to this point 6 hours in advance. Cover and refrigerate. Bring to room temperature before continuing.

- Add orange rind, lemon rind and orange juice concentrate. Cover and simmer 15 minutes. Remove lid and cook, stirring until sauce is thickened. Add Madeira or sherry, cook 2 to 3 minutes and serve garnished with toasted almonds and orange slices. Accompany with parslied rice and steamed, buttered sugar snap peas.

Chicken Piquant

A quick version of Coq au Vin

- **Serves 4**

  3½ pound chicken, cut into serving pieces

  1 pound fresh mushrooms, sliced

  ¾ cup red wine

  ¼ cup soy sauce

  ⅛ cup olive oil

  2 tablespoons brown sugar

  4 tablespoons water, mixed with 2 tablespoons cornstarch

  1 clove of garlic, crushed

  ¼ teaspoon dried oregano

  Parsley for garnish

- Place mushrooms in bottom of casserole and top with chicken pieces.

- Mix all other ingredients. Pour over the chicken.

- Bake, uncovered, at 350 degrees for 1½ hours.

- Sprinkle with parsley and serve with steamed new potatoes or buttered egg noodles.

Chicken Saltimbocca

This is a spectacular "company" dish which should be assembled in advance and requires little attention before serving.

- **Serves 6**

Chicken

3 large whole chicken breasts, halved, skinned and boned

¼ pound Prosciutto, thinly sliced

6 thin slices Mozzarella cheese

Pesto

1 cup olive oil

1 small clove of garlic, chopped

½ cup pine nuts

1½ cups fresh basil leaves

½ cup freshly grated Parmesan cheese

- Preheat oven to 325 degrees.

- Pound chicken cutlets between two pieces of waxed paper until thin.

- Prepare pesto by combining olive oil and garlic in food processor. Blend until oil is beige in color and garlic is minced (10 seconds). Add pine nuts, basil leaves and Parmesan cheese. Use off-on motion until ingredients are well blended. Pesto will be coarse and grainy.

- On each piece of chicken place 1 slice of prosciutto, 1 slice of cheese and spread with 2 tablespoons pesto. Roll each cutlet. Secure with a toothpick.

- Place in a shallow oven-proof baking dish. May be prepared to this point 8 hours in advance. Cover and refrigerate. Bring to room temperature before continuing.

- Bake for 40 minutes, basting occasionally. If desired, place under broiler for the last 3 minutes to brown. Do not overcook.

- Garnish with sprigs of fresh basil. Serve on a nest of linguine with Zucchini-Tomato Fans.

Variation: Substitute Fontina cheese for Mozzarella cheese.

Chinese Chicken

The chicken is marinated for extra flavor, then baked in a crumb crust for crunch.

- **Serves 8 to 10**
  3 chicken breasts, split and boned
  6 chicken drumsticks
  6 chicken thighs
  6 chicken wings (optional)
  2 cups dark soy sauce
  3 cloves garlic, crushed
  4 tablespoons curry powder or to taste
  2 cups dry bread crumbs
  8 to 10 preserved kumquats (optional)

- Preheat oven to 350 degrees.

- Place chicken parts, skin side down, in a large shallow glass baking dish just large enough to hold chicken in a single layer.

- In a small bowl, combine soy sauce, crushed garlic and curry powder. Mix thoroughly and pour over chicken. Marinate in refrigerator 8 to 12 hours, turning occasionally.

- Remove from refrigerator, shake off excess marinade and sprinkle lightly with crumbs.

- Place chicken parts on a rack and bake for 45 minutes. (It is not necessary to turn or baste.) Serve hot or at room temperature. Accompany with steamed brown rice and stir-fried broccoli. Garnish chicken with preserved kumquats.

Curried Chicken Breasts with Zucchini

Interesting combination of colors and flavors sets this chicken dish apart.

- **Serves 8**
  4 large whole chicken breasts, halved, skinned and boned
  2 tablespoons olive oil
  Salt to taste
  Freshly ground pepper to taste
  1 8-ounce zucchini, ends trimmed, cut into ¼-inch rounds
  2 teaspoons curry powder, or to taste
  1 tablespoon unsalted butter
  2 tablespoons finely chopped shallots
  1½ cups chicken stock or canned chicken broth
  6 tablespoons heavy cream
  Sprigs of Italian parsley (garnish)

- Place chicken breasts in a bowl. Add 1 tablespoon of the olive oil, salt and pepper to taste. Add zucchini. Sprinkle curry powder over all. Mix to coat pieces evenly.

- In a large heavy frying pan, heat the remaining tablespoon of olive oil. Place chicken pieces in a single layer, alternating with zucchini rounds. Cook over moderately-high heat until chicken and zucchini pieces are browned. May be prepared to this point 6 hours in advance. Cover and refrigerate. Bring to room temperature before continuing. Transfer to a warm platter.

- Pour off excess fat from frying pan. Add butter and shallots then cook, stirring, for 30 seconds. Add broth and continue cooking until mixture is reduced to 1¼ cups. Add cream and bring to boil, stirring constantly.

- Return chicken and zucchini to frying pan and turn until well coated with sauce. Cook 2 minutes. Garnish with sprigs of Italian parsley. Serve around a mound of white rice and peas. Pass spicy mango chutney.

Mediterranean Chicken Rolls

Stuffed breasts of chicken are glazed with a fruity Moroccan-inspired sauce.

- **Serves 6**

Chicken

3 large whole chicken breasts, split, skinned and boned

2 cups soft bread cubes

1½ cups seedless grapes, halved, plus a few bunches for garnish

¼ cup sliced or slivered almonds

¼ teaspoon salt or to taste

⅛ teaspoon freshly ground pepper

¼ teaspoon ground coriander

½ cup (4 ounces) unsalted butter or margarine, melted

1 egg, beaten

1 tablespoon water

¼ cup all-purpose flour

½ cup fine bread crumbs

- Preheat oven to 350 degrees.

- Pound each chicken breast between 2 pieces of waxed paper to make a 5 ½-inch square.

- Combine bread cubes, ½ cup of the grapes, almonds, salt, freshly ground pepper, coriander and ¼ cup of the butter. Mix gently.

- Spoon approximately ¼ cup of the mixture onto each piece of chicken. Roll, tucking in sides and fasten with toothpicks.

- Combine beaten egg with water. Roll chicken in flour, then egg mixture, then bread crumbs. Cover and chill at least 1 hour or overnight.

- In a large frying pan, brown chicken rolls over medium-high heat in remaining ¼ cup melted butter. Transfer to an ovenproof baking dish. May be prepared 8 hours in advance to this point. Cover and refrigerate. Bring to room temperature before continuing. Bake for 30 minutes.

Sauce

2 tablespoons butter or margarine

¼ cup raisins

2 teaspoons granulated sugar

⅛ teaspoon allspice

¾ cup chicken stock or canned chicken broth

¼ cup dry sherry

1 tablespoon cornstarch

2 tablespoons water

- Melt butter in small saucepan. Stir in raisins, sugar, allspice, chicken broth and sherry.

- Combine cornstarch with cold water. Add to raisin mixture. Cook, stirring until thickened and bubbly. Add remaining 1 cup of grapes. Cook until grapes are heated, about 2 minutes.

- To serve, arrange chicken breasts vertically down center of an oval platter. Pour a few spoonfuls of sauce on each roll. Flank the chicken rolls on one side with a julienne of steamed carrots and on the other side with steamed couscous. Then garnish with fresh grape clusters.

Tandoori Chicken

The name of this dish refers to a jar-shaped clay oven used in India. It's a colorful, flavorful assemblage.

- Serves 8

2 2½ pound chickens

3 tablespoons fresh lemon or lime juice

1 teaspoon salt

1 cup plain yogurt

3 cloves of garlic, minced

2 tablespoons fresh ginger root, finely chopped, or 2
  teaspoons ground ginger

2 teaspoons ground cumin

2 teaspoons ground coriander

1 teaspoon paprika

½ teaspoon cayenne pepper

½ teaspoon red food coloring (optional)

2 tablespoons (1 ounce) unsalted butter or margarine,
  melted

- Remove skin from chicken. With paper toweling, pat cavities and outside surfaces dry. Cut deep slits in chicken.

- Combine lemon juice and salt, rub all over chicken, pressing mixture into slits.

- Combine yogurt, garlic, ginger root, cumin, coriander, paprika, cayenne pepper and food coloring.

- Place chicken in mixing bowl. Using half of marinade, rub well into each chicken. Pour remaining marinade over chicken. Cover and marinate 24 hours in refrigerator.

- Preheat oven to 400 degrees.

- Place chickens on rack in shallow roasting pan.

Brush with melted butter. Roast uncovered 15 minutes. Reduce temperature to 350 degrees and roast until tender, about 45 minutes. Serve with Basmati rice, chutney and a colorful assortment of miniature cooked vegetables. (Basmati rice is available in most fine supermarkets.)

Note: The addition of red food coloring to the marinade produces the high red color that is typical of this dish as served in India.

Vermouth Chicken

Sautéed chicken breasts are finished in the oven in a bath of vermouth and onions.

- Serves 4

2 large whole chicken breasts, split, skinned and boned

½ cup (4 ounces) unsalted butter or margarine

½ cup diced onions or shallots

6 large mushroom caps, sliced vertically

¼ cup vegetable oil

½ cup all-purpose flour

Freshly ground black pepper

Salt to taste

¾ cup dry vermouth

¼ cup water

½ cup slivered almonds, toasted

- Preheat oven to 350 degrees.

- Pound chicken breasts to flatten evenly; cut away ragged edges. Cut each breast in half on the diagonal.

- In a large frying pan, melt butter or margarine.

Add onions and mushrooms. Cook over moderately high heat about 10 minutes or until onions are translucent and mushrooms begin to brown. Remove from pan and set aside.

- Dip chicken pieces in flour and season with salt and pepper to taste.

- Add vegetable oil to frying pan. When hot, quickly sauté chicken until golden brown. Remove from pan and place in casserole large enough to hold chicken in one layer.

- Add vermouth and water to frying pan. Bring to a boil, scraping pan to deglaze. Lower heat and cook until sauce is reduced to a rich brown syrup. Add mushrooms and onions, mix, then pour over chicken. May be prepared to this point 8 hours in advance. Cover and refrigerate. Bring to room temperature before continuing.

- Cover casserole with foil and bake for 15 to 20 minutes. Remove from oven, sprinkle with toasted almonds and serve. Accompany with rice cooked in chicken broth and stir-fried snow peas.

Chicken Livers with Apples

A piquant fruited sauce offsets the richness of the livers.

- **Serves 6 to 8**
  4 tablespoons (2 ounces) unsalted butter
  6 tart apples, peeled, cored and sliced into sixths
  ¼ cup brown sugar
  1½ pounds chicken livers, cleaned and drained
  Salt to taste
  Freshly ground pepper

1 to 2 tablespoons undiluted canned bouillon or ½ bouillon cube
1½ tablespoons cornstarch .
2 tablespoons apple or orange juice
¾ cup apple or orange juice
1 tablespoon fresh lemon juice
2 tablespoons currant or apple jelly
1 8-ounce package medium green or white noodles, cooked

- In a large frying pan, melt 2 tablespoons butter and add apples and brown sugar. Cook over low heat about 10 minutes or until apples are soft but not mushy. Remove from pan and set aside.

- In the same pan, melt remaining 2 tablespoons of butter and add livers. Sauté for 5 minutes. Season with salt, pepper and bouillon. Cook 3 minutes over medium heat. Do not overcook.

- Combine cornstarch with 2 tablespoons apple or orange juice to form smooth paste. Add ¾ cup apple or orange juice, lemon juice and jelly. Blend well and add to livers, stirring over medium heat until sauce thickens. Serve on top of green or white noodles surrounded with the apple slices.

Variation: For brunch, try the livers over sliced toasted brioche. A dash of apply brandy is a flavorful addition to the sauce.

Roast Cornish Hens with Brandied Fruit Sauce

A grand presentation for little birds

- **Serves 8**

  8 1-pound Cornish game hens (giblets removed)

  2 teaspoons salt or to taste

  ¼ teaspoon freshly ground pepper

  1 cup (8 ounces) unsalted butter, melted

  ½ cup water

- Preheat oven to 425 degrees.

- Pat hens dry. Fold wings across backs so that tips touch; tie legs together. Rub each hen with salt and pepper. Brush each with 1 tablespoon melted butter.

- Arrange breast side up on rack in shallow roasting pan. Add ½ cup water to pan. Bake hens until juices run clear when pierced in thickest part of thigh. Baste every 15 minutes with remaining butter (about 45 to 50 minutes). May be prepared to this point 24 hours in advance. Cover and refrigerate. Reheat at serving time. Transfer hens to platter, discarding strings; tent with foil. Reserve ¼ cup drippings for sauce.

  Sauce

  1 36-ounce jar brandied peaches, drained (reserve syrup), halved and pitted

  1 pint fresh strawberries, hulled

  2 tablespoons granulated sugar

  2 tablespoons cornstarch

  ¼ cup peach preserves

  1 2-inch cinnamon stick

  4 whole cloves

  ¼ cup brandy or Armagnac

- Measure 2 cups peach syrup; sprinkle berries with sugar; dissolve cornstarch in ¼ cup of the peach syrup. Bring reserved ¼ cup drippings to simmer in heavy large frying pan. Mix in cornstarch; stir until thick (about 30 seconds). Slowly whisk in remaining peach syrup; add preserves, cinnamon and cloves. Simmer until thick, whisking constantly, about 2 minutes. Add peaches, increase heat and boil 1 minute. Add berries and cook just until heated. Spoon over hens, discarding spices.

- Sprinkle brandy over hens. Serve immediately on large platter garnished with watercress and flanked by green beans almondine and pecan rice.

Variation: Substitute duck breasts for Cornish hens.

Braised Duck with Potatoes

Interesting and flavorful duck dish from Peru needs only a basket of warmed tortillas to complete the presentation.

- **Serves 3 to 4**

  4 cups water

  1 4½ to 5-pound raw duck, cut into serving pieces

  2 tablespoons distilled vinegar

  1 teaspoon salt

  1 28-ounce can crushed tomatoes

  1 cup chicken stock, canned or homemade

  1 large onion, sliced

  6 cloves of garlic, sliced

  6 bay leaves

  1½ teaspoons dried thyme

¾ teaspoon dried oregano

Salt to taste

Freshly ground pepper to taste

3 cups peeled, ½-inch potato cubes

½ cup long grain rice

1 bouillon cube

1 cup water

Corn tortillas

- In heavy large saucepan, combine water, duck, vinegar and 1 teaspoon salt. Bring to boil, skimming surface. Reduce heat and simmer 15 minutes. Drain. Discard excess skin and easily-removed bones. Return meat to saucepan.

- Purée tomatoes with stock, onion and garlic in food processor. Add to duck. Stir in bay leaves, thyme and oregano. Season with salt and pepper. Bring mixture to boil. Reduce heat and simmer 1 hour, turning duck occasionally.

- Add potatoes. Cover and cook until duck and potatoes are tender (about 15 minutes). Can be prepared to this point 24 hours in advance. Cover and refrigerate. Reheat at serving time.

- Cook rice, along with bouillon cube in 1 cup water for about 20 minutes or until rice is tender and water is absorbed. Serve duck on rice garnished with the 6 bay leaves and surrounded by the potatoes.

Variation: Place partially cooked duck on serving casserole. Add sauce and bake for 1 hour at 350 degrees. Add potatoes and bake an additional 15 minutes.

Honey Citrus Turkey

Boneless filets of turkey breast have the character to stand up to this bright sauce.

- **Serves 4**

2 pounds turkey breast filets

⅓ cup honey

2 teaspoons grated lemon peel

2 teaspoons grated orange peel

¼ cup lemon juice

1½ teaspoons Dijon-style mustard

½ teaspoon curry powder

½ teaspoon ground ginger

2 large navel oranges, unpeeled

- Preheat oven to 375 degrees.

- Place turkey in a 10 x 15 x 2-inch baking dish.

- Combine honey, lemon peel, orange peel, lemon juice, mustard, curry and ginger. Brush half of mixture over turkey pieces.

- Cut 1 orange in half, lengthwise, then into ¼-inch slices. (Reserve 1 orange for garnish.) Tuck orange slices around turkey.

- Bake, uncovered, for 10 minutes, basting occasionally. Turn turkey filets over and brush with remaining sauce. Bake 15 minutes longer, basting occasionally or until turkey is tender when pierced with a fork. May be prepared to this point 6 hours in advance. Reheat at serving time. Garnish with fresh orange slices and accompany with steamed rice and steamed sugar snap peas.

$\mathcal{V}$EGETABLES AND ACCOMPANIMENTS

Tree carpet, Persian, sixteenth–seventeenth century, wool and cotton, 17'4" x 11'9". The Joseph Lees Williams Memorial Collection

This stately carpet is one of the best-known examples of the classic era of Persian carpet weaving. No surviving tree carpet can parallel its field pattern, thickly planted with flowering trees and cypresses, and its rich, lively border of intersecting bands of contrasting colors has few rivals.

Beets in Orange Sauce

Pretty and piquant

- Serves 6

  3 cups large beets

  1 tablespoon (½ ounce) unsalted butter

  1 tablespoon all-purpose flour

  ¼ cup water

  ½ cup corn syrup

  ½ cup orange juice

  1 tablespoon lemon juice

  ⅛ teaspoon salt, or to taste

  ¼ teaspoon grated orange peel

- Peel, slice and cook beets until tender.

- Melt butter, add flour and blend until smooth.

- Add water, corn syrup, orange juice, lemon juice and salt. Cook over low heat, stirring constantly until mixture has thickened. Add beets and grated orange peel.

French Baked Beets with Lemon Cream

May also be served as a delicious and unusual first course.

- Serves 4

  8 small beets, about 1½ inches in diameter

- Preheat oven to 325 degrees.

- Rinse beets. Trim roots and tops leaving beets whole with skin intact. Place beets in a gratin dish or other small shallow baking dish. Cover tightly with foil and bake 1½ hours, or until beets are tender when pierced with a fork.

Lemon Cream

1 tablespoon (½ ounce) unsalted butter

1 shallot, minced

¼ cup dry white wine

1 cup heavy cream

4 teaspoons grated lemon peel

2½ teaspoons fresh lemon juice, strained

⅓ teaspoon salt, or to taste

⅛ teaspoon white pepper

Pinch sugar

A few thin strips of lemon peel (garnish)

Lemon Cream

- In a small saucepan, melt butter over low heat. Add minced shallot and cook 2 minutes. Stir in wine and cook until liquid is reduced to about 2 tablespoons.

- Stir in cream, bring to a boil and cook, stirring over medium heat until sauce is thick enough to coat a spoon.

- Just before serving, add grated lemon peel, lemon juice, salt, pepper and sugar.

- Peel beets, spoon on lemon cream. May be prepared to this point 24 hours in advance. Cover and refrigerate. If serving cold, serve immediately upon removal from refrigerator. To serve as a hot vegetable, remove from refrigerator and bring to room temperature. Reheat and sprinkle with lemon peel to garnish.

Variation: Substitute Brussels sprouts for beets. Serve hot.

Baked Carrots and Apples

Color, texture and taste combined

- **Serves 6**

  2 cups carrots, peeled and coarsely shredded

  4 medium apples, peeled and grated

  1 cup shredded coconut

  ⅔ cup honey

  3 tablespoons (1½ ounces) unsalted butter, melted

  Salt to taste

  1½ teaspoons cinnamon

  2 teaspoons lemon juice

  1 slice of canned pineapple, drained (garnish)

- Preheat oven to 350 degrees.

- Combine all ingredients and spoon into a lightly oiled 1-quart casserole. May be prepared to this point 24 hours in advance. Cover and refrigerate. Bring to room temperature before continuing.

- Bake 35 minutes. Garnish with pineapple.

Cheddar Carrot Gratin

Brilliant when you need a splash of color

- **Serves 8 to 10**

  3 pounds fresh carrots, peeled and sliced into 1-inch pieces

  1 cup sharp Cheddar cheese, grated

  1 small green pepper, finely chopped

  1 medium onion, finely chopped

  2 tablespoons (1 ounce) unsalted butter, melted

  Salt and freshly ground pepper to taste

  4 tablespoons toasted, buttered bread crumbs (optional)

- Preheat oven to 350 degrees.

- Cook carrots until fork-tender. Drain. Coarsely chop with a food processor or egg chopper.

- Add cheese, chopped green pepper and onion. Combine with melted butter, salt and pepper.

- Place in a buttered 2-quart casserole. Top with bread crumbs, if desired. May be prepared to this point 24 hours in advance. Cover and refrigerate. Bring to room temperature before continuing. Bake for ½ hour or until crumbs begin to brown.

Carrot Soufflé

An ordinary vegetable becomes special!

- Serves 6
  1½ pounds carrots, coarsely grated
  ½ cup (4 ounces) unsalted butter or margarine, softened
  2 tablespoons sugar
  ½ teaspoon salt
  1 teaspoon ground ginger, nutmeg or curry to taste
  3 tablespoons all-purpose flour
  3 whole eggs, lightly beaten
  1 teaspoon baking powder

- Preheat oven to 350 degrees. Lightly oil or butter 6 ½-cup custard cups and set into baking dish.

- Steam carrots until tender (about 5 minutes). Drain and combine with butter or margarine, sugar, salt and spices.

  OR

- Combine carrots, butter or margarine, sugar, salt and spices in a microwave dish and cover with plastic wrap. Microwave on HI for 3 minutes. Turn dish ¼-turn and finish cooking for an additional 3 minutes.

- In food processor, purée ⅔ of the carrot mixture along with flour, eggs and baking powder. Combine puréed mixture with remainder of grated carrots and pour into the prepared custard cups. May be prepared to this point 24 hours in advance. Cover and refrigerate. Bring to room temperature before continuing.

- Place custard cups into baking dish. Place baking dish in oven; fill ½ full with hot water. Bake for 25 minutes or until tester comes out clean.

- Serve in custard cups or unmolded.

  Family Variation: Combine mixture in food processor. Pour into oiled 1-quart soufflé dish. Bake at 400 degrees for 15 minutes, reduce oven to 350 degrees for 30 to 35 minutes. Serve.

Cauliflower au Gratin

The cauliflower is mashed in this unusual version.

- Serves 10 to 12
  1 head cauliflower, cleaned and quartered
  6 tablespoons (3 ounces) unsalted butter or margarine
  ¾ cup grated American cheese
  ¾ cup grated Swiss cheese
  1½ cups milk
  Salt and freshly ground pepper to taste
  ¼ cup grated Swiss cheese
  ¼ cup bread crumbs
  Paprika

- Preheat oven to 350 degrees.

- Cook cauliflower until tender in a large saucepan filled with water to cover.

- Drain well. Mash coarsely with 4 tablespoons of the butter.

- Combine the cheese. Add to the cauliflower along with the milk, salt and freshly ground pepper.

- Place in a buttered 2-quart casserole. Dot with remaining butter. Sprinkle with rest of cheese, then bread crumbs, then paprika.

- Bake 1 hour. Serve immediately.

Corn Pudding

Best with the fresh corn of summer

- Serves 4 to 6
  2 cups uncooked corn kernels (4 large ears) or 1 17-ounce can, drained
  ½ cup grated Cheddar cheese
  3 large eggs, plus 1 extra egg white
  4 tablespoons (2 ounces) unsalted butter, melted
  ½ cup light cream
  1 teaspoon sugar
  ½ teaspoon salt
  Pinch of cayenne
  2 jalapeño peppers, seeded and finely chopped

- Preheat oven to 325 degrees. Generously butter a 2-quart baking dish.

- Place corn and cheese in a large mixing bowl and toss to combine.

- Separate eggs and set whites aside. Whisk together the egg yolk, melted butter, cream, sugar, salt and cayenne. Stir in the chopped jalapeño peppers. Combine with corn mixture.

- Whisk egg whites until soft peaks form. Fold into corn mixture.

- Transfer to prepared baking dish. Bake approximately 50 minutes or until center is set.

Variation: Serve in tomato shells (½ tomato per person) or scooped out, parboiled green pepper halves. Shorten baking time to 30 minutes.

Eggplant Patties

Especially delicious when served as a base for creamed spinach

- Serves 4 to 5
  1 medium eggplant, about 2 pounds
  3 tablespoons all-purpose flour
  1 egg
  1 teaspoon sugar
  1½ teaspoons baking powder
  Salt and pepper to taste
  2 tablespoons peanut oil

- Peel eggplant and cut into 1½-inch cubes. Cook in boiling, salted water (enough to cover pieces) until soft. Drain well, then chop.

- Combine flour, egg, sugar, baking powder, salt and pepper. Blend until smooth.

- Mix well-drained eggplant into flour mixture. When mixture is completely blended, form into patties and refrigerate for 30 minutes. May be prepared to this point 4 hours in advance. Cover and refrigerate. Remove from refrigerator and proceed as directed.

- Heat oil in a large frying pan until it begins to smoke. Sauté patties over medium-high heat until brown. Serve.

Mexican Eggplant

An unusual presentation for eggplant which combines layers of cheese and a cumin-spiced sauce.

• **Serves 6 to 8**

1 large eggplant, peeled and sliced

¼ cup olive oil

1 28-ounce can tomato sauce

1 4-ounce can green chilies

1 cup sliced green onions

3 cloves of garlic, minced

½ teaspoon cumin

1 cup pitted black olives, sliced

1½ cups shredded Cheddar cheese

½ cup commercial sour cream

8 sprigs fresh cilantro or parsley (garnish)

• Preheat oven to 450 degrees.

• Grease baking sheet. Place slices of eggplant close together on sheet and brush with olive oil.

• Bake 10 to 12 minutes until soft. Remove from oven and lower oven temperature to 350 degrees.

• In a large saucepan combine tomato sauce, green chilies, onions, minced garlic and cumin. Simmer 10 minutes. Stir in sliced olives.

• Grease a shallow 9 x 11 x 2-inch baking dish. Layer eggplant, sauce and cheese, ending with cheese. May be prepared to this point 8 hours in advance. Cover and refrigerate. Bring to room temperature before continuing.

• Bake, uncovered at 350 degrees for 25 minutes or until cheese melts and mixture is bubbling. Serve hot topped with a dollop of sour cream and a sprig of cilantro or parsley on each plate.

Note: Excellent as part of a buffet or on its own as a light supper dish with corn chips and a salad of mixed greens, avocado and grapefruit, dressed with a light vinaigrette.

Fennel Provençal

Serve this delicious Mediterranean-style dish with lamb.

• **Serves 4**

4 bulbs of fennel, trimmed and cut in half, lengthwise

½ cup olive oil

1 medium onion, peeled and thinly sliced

3 cloves garlic, chopped

1 12-ounce can Italian tomatoes, drained and chopped

Salt and pepper, to taste

½ cup bread crumbs

½ cup grated Parmesan cheese

1 teaspoon lemon peel, grated

1 clove garlic, finely minced

• Preheat oven to 350 degrees.

• Cut fennel halves into julienne strips.

• In a large frying pan, sauté onion and garlic in oil for 2 minutes. Add fennel and stir-fry until fennel begins to brown.

• Add tomatoes, salt and pepper. Lower heat and cook gently 5 minutes.

- Transfer mixture to a heavy, shallow gratin dish. May be prepared to this point 8 hours in advance. Cover and refrigerate. Allow to return to room temperature before continuing.

- Prepare topping by combining bread crumbs, Parmesan cheese, grated lemon peel and finely minced garlic cloves.

- Sprinkle over fennel. Bake 15 minutes or until topping is brown and crisp.

Baked Fennel

A crunchy winter vegetable with a subtle anise flavor

- **Serves 6**
  7 firm fennel bulbs
  ½ cup olive oil
  Juice of 1 lemon
  Salt and pepper (optional and to taste)
  ¼ cup Parmesan cheese, freshly grated

- Preheat oven to 400 degrees.
- Cut the stems from the fennel bulbs and trim the bottoms. Cut into halves, leaving the center core.
- Blanch the fennel in boiling water for 10 minutes or until almost tender. Drain and cool.
- Cut away the tough core leaving just enough to hold the layers of fennel together.
- Place fennel halves into baking dish which has been greased with a little of the oil. Sprinkle with remaining oil, lemon juice, salt and pepper.

- Sprinkle with Parmesan cheese. Bake in 400 degree oven for 20 minutes.

Leeks au Gratin

This makes splendor of the lowly leek.

- **Serves 6**
  8 small leeks (3 pounds)
  2 tablespoons (1 ounce) unsalted butter
  Salt and freshly ground pepper to taste
  ⅛ teaspoon freshly grated nutmeg
  1 cup heavy cream
  ½ cup freshly grated Parmesan cheese

- Trim stem of each leek. Cut off enough of the green section to leave a main section of about 7 inches. Split leeks in half, lengthwise. Cut the split leeks crosswise into 1½-inch lengths. Rinse well in cold water. Drain.

- Melt butter in a large, heavy frying pan. Add leeks, salt, pepper and nutmeg. Cook, stirring, about 1 minute. Add cream; bring to a simmer. Cover and cook 15 minutes. Uncover and reduce excess liquid over high heat.

- Spoon hot leeks into a large buttered gratin dish. Sprinkle the top with Parmesan cheese and place under the broiler until nicely glazed, about 5 minutes. May be prepared 24 hours in advance. Cover and refrigerate. Place in 350 degree oven for 20 minutes to reheat.

195

Baked Lettuce

In Brazil this is a "company dish" to accompany seafood and roasted meats.

- Serves 6 to 8
  2 firm heads iceberg lettuce, washed, left whole
  3 quarts water combined with 1 tablespoon salt
  1½ cups plain yogurt or commercial sour cream
  ½ teaspoon salt
  Few grains of freshly ground pepper
  1 tablespoon (½ ounce) unsalted butter, melted
  2 tablespoons finely grated onion
  16 to 20 slices peeled cucumber
  1 egg yolk
  1 teaspoon melted butter
  4 tablespoons fresh bread crumbs
  Cucumber curls (garnish)

- Preheat oven to 400 degrees.

- In an 8-quart kettle, bring salted water to a boil. Add lettuce and boil vigorously for 10 minutes. Drain and plunge into cold water for 3 or 4 minutes. Drain again.

- Quarter and core lettuce. Gather leaves together and shred thinly with a sharp knife. Place in a buttered casserole.

- Mix yogurt with salt, pepper, 1 tablespoon melted butter and grated onion. Spoon over lettuce.

- Arrange cucumber slices over yogurt. Mix egg yolk with melted butter. Brush cucumber slices with egg yolk mixture. Sprinkle bread crumbs over all. Bake 15 to 20 minutes or until brown. May be prepared 2 hours in advance and reheated 5 to 10 minutes prior to serving. Garnish with cucumber curls and serve.

Mushroom Mousse

- Serves 12 to 16
  2 pounds mushrooms, chopped
  5 tablespoons plus 4 tablespoons unsalted butter
  4 tablespoons all-purpose flour
  1 cup light cream or milk
  3 eggs, separated
  Salt and pepper to taste
  ¼ cup sliced, sautéed mushrooms (garnish)

- Preheat oven to 325 degrees.

- In a large frying pan, heat 5 tablespoons of the butter. Sauté chopped mushrooms until tender (about 5 minutes). Remove from heat and drain well, reserving liquid. Place mushrooms in a large mixing bowl.

- Melt remaining 4 tablespoons of butter; add flour, and cook, stirring constantly for 3 minutes. Add cream slowly, mixing well. Add 1 cup of the mushroom liquid and stir well to combine.

- Add 1 cup of the mushroom-cream sauce to the reserved mushrooms. Season well with salt and pepper to taste. May be prepared 2 hours in advance. Cover and refrigerate. Bring to room temperature before continuing.

- Beat egg yolks until fluffy; stir into the mushroom mixture. Beat egg whites until stiff. Fold into the mushroom mixture and pour into a 2-quart oven-proof soufflé dish.

- Place soufflé dish in a slightly larger pan filled with ¼ inch of warm water. Bake 40 to 50 minutes or until set. Serve immediately, garnished with sliced sautéed mushrooms. The remainder of the sauce may be served as an accompaniment at the table.

Puréed Parsnips

An old fashioned vegetable which beautifully compliments poultry.

- Serves 4

  2 pounds parsnips, peeled and cut into 1-inch pieces

  1 teaspoon lemon juice

  Salt and freshly ground pepper, to taste

  ⅓ cup heavy cream

- Place parsnips in a 1½-quart saucepan. Fill pan with water until the parsnips are half covered. Place lid on pot and cook over medium-high heat for 10 minutes or until parsnips are tender and water has evaporated. Watch carefully so that the parsnips do not burn.

- Mash parsnips well or purée in food processor. Return to saucepan.

- Add lemon juice, salt and pepper to taste, and heavy cream. Mix well. May be prepared to this point 24 hours in advance. Cover and refrigerate. Reheat at serving time adding 2 tablespoons heavy cream before heating. Serve hot.

Variation: Substitute 1½ tablespoons butter or margarine for the heavy cream when reheating.

Puréed Peas

The color and texture of this variation makes it most versatile.

- Serves 4

  2½ cups chicken stock

  2 10-ounce boxes frozen peas

  1 cup watercress, leaves only (about ½ bunch)

  1 tablespoon unsalted butter, melted

  Salt and pepper to taste

- Preheat oven to 350 degrees.

- In large saucepan, bring 2 cups of the chicken stock to a boil. Add peas and watercress and cook 4 to 5 minutes, until barely tender. Remove from heat and cool. Drain liquid and reserve.

- In a food processor, purée peas and watercress, adding 2 or 3 tablespoons of the chicken stock as each batch is puréed. (This process usually requires 2 batches). Place in a 1-quart buttered casserole or soufflé dish. May be prepared to this point 24 hours in advance. Cover and refrigerate. Bring to room temperature before continuing.

- Add butter, salt and pepper. Heat in oven for 20 to 25 minutes.

Peas with Prosciutto

An Italian-inspired vegetable accompaniment

- Serves 6
  ½ cup finely chopped scallions
  ½ cup (4 ounces) unsalted butter
  4 cups fresh green peas or 2 packages frozen peas
  2 cups Boston lettuce, shredded
  1 teaspoon dried basil
  ¼ cup water
  1 cup julienne strips of prosciutto
  ½ teaspoon salt, or to taste
  ¼ teaspoon pepper
  3 tablespoons freshly grated Parmesan cheese (optional)

- In a large frying pan, sauté scallions in 6 tablespoons of butter until soft. Stir in peas, shredded lettuce, basil and water. Cover pan and cook over low heat about 15 minutes or until peas are barely tender.

- In a small frying pan, sauté prosciutto strips in remaining 2 tablespoons butter until heated through.

- Combine prosciutto with peas. Add salt and pepper to taste. Stir Parmesan cheese into mixture, if desired.

Cheddar Squash

An elegant accompaniment to pork

- Serves 8 to 10
  2 pounds yellow squash or zucchini
  2 eggs, separated
  1 cup commercial sour cream
  2 tablespoons all-purpose flour
  1½ cups shredded Cheddar cheese
  ½ cup dry bread crumbs
  1 tablespoon butter or margarine
  4 slices bacon, cooked until crisp, drained and crumbled
  2 tablespoons chopped fresh parsley (garnish)

- Preheat oven to 350 degrees.

- Trim ends of squash but do not peel. In a large saucepan, cook squash whole in water to cover until barely tender (about 15 to 20 minutes). Drain.

- Cut squash into ¼-inch slices. Reserve a few slices for garnish.

- In a 2-quart bowl, mix egg yolks, sour cream and flour until well blended.

- Beat egg whites until stiff. Combine beaten egg whites with yolk mixture. Gently combine with squash slices.

- Layer ½ of the squash in a greased 2-quart shallow casserole. Cover with ½ of the shredded Cheddar cheese. Repeat.

- Combine bread crumbs with butter or margarine. Sprinkle around inside edge of the casserole. Sprinkle bacon over all.

- Bake 20 to 25 minutes. Garnish and serve.

Maple Acorn Squash

Wonderful flavor combination

- Serves 4
  2 acorn squash, halved, seeds removed
  2 tablespoons (1 ounce) unsalted butter, melted
  ½ cup heavy cream
  ½ cup maple syrup

- Preheat oven to 350 degrees.

- Place squash, cut side up, into a shallow, buttered baking dish. Brush inside of each half with melted butter.

- Mix equal amounts of heavy cream and maple syrup. Fill each cavity ½ full with the mixture. May be prepared 6 hours in advance. Cover and refrigerate. Bring to room temperature before continuing.

- Bake, uncovered for 1 to 1½ hours. (Filling should be thick, not watery).

Baked Tomatoes Provençal

The best summer tomatoes are essential to this sauté.

- Serves 6
  4 tablespoons olive oil
  3 medium beefsteak or Jersey tomatoes, sliced
  Salt and freshly ground pepper to taste
  2 medium cloves garlic, peeled and minced
  2 tablespoons chopped fresh parsley

- Heat olive oil in a large, heavy frying pan. Add tomato slices to hot oil.

- Sprinkle with salt and pepper to taste; then sprinkle evenly with minced garlic.

- Reduce heat and cook slowly until bottom of tomatoes are almost brown. Turn and cook reverse side until almost brown. Remove from heat, sprinkle with chopped fresh parsley and serve. Great with beef or lamb accompanied by crusty French bread.

Broiled Deviled Tomatoes

Serve along with a steak or scrambled eggs.

- **Serves 6**

  3 large, ripe tomatoes, halved

  6 tablespoons (3 ounces) unsalted butter, room temperature

  5 teaspoons Worcestershire sauce

  ½ teaspoon hot pepper sauce

  1 teaspoon dry mustard

  1 teaspoon grated onion

  Salt to taste

  1 teaspoon minced parsley (garnish)

- Arrange tomato halves closely together in a buttered gratin dish.

- Cream together butter, Worcestershire sauce and hot pepper sauce. Add dry mustard, grated onion and salt to taste.

- Spread butter mixture on tomato halves. May be prepared 8 hours in advance up to this point. Cover and refrigerate. Bring to room temperature before continuing.

- Broil under a preheated broiler, about 4 inches from the heat, basting frequently for 8 to 10 minutes or until tomatoes are soft and tops are brown.

- Serve immediately, garnished with minced parsley.

Zucchini with Pesto

Instead of pesto on pasta, try it on julienne of zucchini – a delicious, lower-calorie alternative.

- **Serves 4**

  ⅓ cup tightly packed fresh basil

  4 tablespoons olive oil

  2 tablespoons pine nuts or walnuts

  1 egg

  2 tablespoons freshly grated Parmesan cheese

  2 cloves garlic, minced

  1¼ pounds zucchini

  1 teaspoon salt, or to taste

  ⅛ teaspoon pepper

  Additional 1 tablespoon olive oil

- Place basil, olive oil, pine nuts or walnuts, egg, cheese and garlic into food processor bowl. Using off-on motion, process until mixture is coarsely chopped. May be prepared to this point 24 hours in advance. Refrigerate or freeze. Bring to room temperature.

- Cut zucchini into 2x¼x¼-inch strips.

- In a medium frying pan, heat 1 tablespoon olive oil and stir-fry zucchini over medium-high heat for 3 minutes. Stir in pesto, salt and pepper. Serve immediately.

Tian of Zucchini, Potato and Tomato

A "tian" is a clay baking dish used in Morrocan cooking, but you can use any attractive shallow casserole for this vegetable side dish.

• **Serves 4**

2 large zucchini, ends removed

3 medium tomatoes, stem ends removed

2 medium baking potatoes, peeled

¼ cup olive oil

Salt and freshly ground pepper

2 tablespoons fresh basil, chopped (garnish)

• Preheat oven to 400 degrees.

• Thinly slice zucchini, tomatoes, and potatoes.

• Arrange vegetables in a 9-inch by 11-inch shallow baking dish, alternating slices of each vegetable. Coat with olive oil and place in oven for approximately 40 minutes or until vegetables are slightly crisp.

• Sprinkle with salt and freshly ground pepper to taste. May be prepared to this point 24 hours in advance. Cover and refrigerate. Bring to room temperature before continuing and reheat. Garnish with chopped basil and serve.

Zucchini Flan

A marvelous main dish as well as a side dish or appetizer

• **Serves 8 to 10**

3 cups zucchini, unpeeled, diced into ¼-inch cubes

1 small onion, finely chopped

1 cup biscuit mix

4 eggs

½ cup vegetable oil

½ cup Parmesan cheese, grated

½ teaspoon dried marjoram

¼ cup chopped fresh parsley

¼ teaspoon salt

Freshly ground pepper

2 tablespoons chopped parsley (garnish)

• Preheat oven to 350 degrees.

• In a bowl, combine zucchini and onion. Fold in biscuit mix until vegetables are coated.

• Beat eggs slightly and stir into zucchini mixture.

• Add oil, cheese, marjoram, parsley, salt and pepper, stirring well after each addition.

• Pour into well-buttered 10-inch pie plate and bake for 30 to 40 minutes or until tester inserted in center comes out clean.

• Serve hot or at room temperature garnished with a sprinkle of chopped parsley.

201

Missoni Vegetables

Named in honor of the Italian designer known for her multi-hued fabrics

- **Serves 12 to 14**

  4 tablespoons olive oil

  3 tablespoons bread crumbs

  1½ Bermuda onions, peeled and thinly sliced

  4 medium potatoes, peeled and thinly sliced

  Salt and freshly ground pepper, to taste

  1 medium zucchini, quartered lengthwise, seeded and cut into ⅛-inch strips

  1 eggplant, quartered lengthwise, seeded and cut into ⅛-inch strips

  1 yellow squash, quartered lengthwise, seeded and cut into ⅛-inch strips

  1 red bell pepper, seeded and cut into ⅛-inch strips

  1 green pepper, seeded and cut into ⅛-inch strips

  1 yellow pepper, seeded and cut into ⅛-inch strips (optional)

  ¼ to ⅓ cup Greek-style olives, pitted and halved

  ¼ teaspoon dried thyme

- Preheat oven to 400 degrees.

- Oil the bottom of a large gratin or lasagna pan. Lightly sprinkle bread crumbs over oil.

- Layer onion slices over bottom of the pan; then layer potato slices over onions. Generously sprinkle with salt and pepper.

- Beginning in center of pan, alternate contrasting rows of vegetables in a colorful awning-stripe pattern, i.e. alternate rows of eggplant, yellow squash, red pepper, zucchini, etc.

- Push some of the pitted olive halves into vegetable design between rows. Repeat layering of vegetables until pan is full. Push remaining olive halves into design.

- Drizzle olive oil over all; add salt and pepper to taste; sprinkle with thyme. May be prepared to this point 24 hours in advance. Cover and refrigerate. Bring to room temperature before continuing.

- Cover tightly with aluminum foil. Bake for 1½ hours.

Barley and Pine Nut Casserole

Unusual and tasty accompaniment to pot roast

- **Serves 4**

  6 tablespoons (3 ounces) unsalted butter

  ½ cup pine nuts

  1 cup barley

  1 medium onion, peeled and chopped

  ¼ cup minced parsley

  ¼ cup minced chives or green onion, including tops

  ¼ teaspoon salt or to taste

  Freshly ground black pepper to taste

  2 14-ounce cans beef or chicken broth

- Preheat oven to 350 degrees.

- In a large frying pan, melt 2 tablespoons of the butter. Add pine nuts and sauté over medium-high heat, stirring constantly until lightly toasted. Remove nuts and set aside.

- Add remaining 4 tablespoons butter, barley and chopped onion. Cook, stirring occasionally over medium-high heat until lightly browned.

- Remove from heat and stir in toasted pine nuts, parsley, chives, salt and pepper.

- Heat beef or chicken broth to boiling and add to barley mixture, stirring well. Transfer to a buttered 1-quart casserole.

- Bake, uncovered, 1¼ hours or until barley is tender and liquid is absorbed. May be prepared to this point 24 hours in advance. Cover and refrigerate. Bring to room temperature and reheat at serving time in 350 degree oven for 20 to 25 minutes.

Variations: Add ¼ cup sliced mushrooms along with the barley and chopped onion. Slivered almonds may be substituted for the pine nuts.

Risotto Gorgonzola

Make just before serving to maintain its creamy texture.

- Serves 6
  ¼ teaspoon powdered saffron
  3¼ cups chicken stock
  2½ tablespoons (5 ounces) unsalted butter or margarine
  1½ tablespoons minced onion
  1 cup rice, preferably Arborio (available in gourmet shops)
  6 tablespoons dry white wine
  ½ cup crumbled Gorgonzola cheese
  Freshly ground black pepper, to taste

- Preheat oven to 400 degrees.

- Combine saffron with ½ cup of the stock. Set aside.

- Melt butter or margarine in a 2-quart saucepan. Add onion and cook over medium-high heat until soft. Add rice and stir quickly. Combine with wine and saffron mixture. Mix well. Pour in 1½ cups of the stock and cook over medium-high heat, stirring and adding stock as needed until all liquid is absorbed.

- Stir in ¼ cup of the cheese.

- Melt remaining butter and combine with rice. Top with freshly ground black pepper and remaining ¼ cup of cheese.

- Bake 15 to 20 minutes or until cheese is melted and rice is thoroughly heated.

Variation: Substitute Roquefort or Stilton for the Gorgonzola.

Rice with Mandarin Oranges

An excellent accompaniment to poultry

- Serves 8

  2 cups long grain rice

  4 cups water

  3 chicken bouillon cubes

  Curry powder to taste

  ½ teaspoon white pepper

  Juice of 1 lemon

  ⅓ cup golden raisins

  1 13-ounce can mandarin oranges, drained

  2 tablespoons chopped fresh parsley

- Cook rice in water according to package directions, adding bouillon cubes, curry powder, white pepper, lemon juice and raisins.

- When rice is fully cooked, stir in mandarin oranges and parsley. Serve hot.

  Variation: Substitute brown rice or a combination of long grain and wild rice.

Bucatini Amatriciana

Serve as an entrée or a continental first course

- Serves 6 to 8

  8 ounces pancetta (Italian bacon), cut into small cubes (smoked bacon may be substituted)

  5 tablespoons olive oil

  1 tablespoon chopped red bell pepper

  1 tablespoon finely chopped onion

  15 medium-size fresh plum tomatoes, peeled and finely chopped or one 1-pound 12-ounce can Italian plum tomatoes

  10 large, fresh basil leaves, chopped

  ¼ cup grated Parmesan cheese

  Salt and freshly ground black pepper, to taste

  Pinch of sugar

  1 pound bucatini pasta (or any thick pasta such as rigatoni, ziti, penne or rotini)

- Heat oil in a large frying pan. Add pancetta and cook over medium heat, stirring occasionaly for 5 minutes.

- Stir in chopped red pepper and chopped onion. Cook over high heat until pepper softens (about 3 to 4 minutes).

- Add chopped tomatoes. Reduce heat to medium and cook for 1 to 2 minutes.

- Add chopped basil and stir until well blended. Add grated cheese, salt and pepper to taste and a pinch of sugar if the flavor is too acidic.

- Continue cooking for 5 minutes, stirring sauce and mashing tomatoes to blend well. May be prepared to this point three days in advance. Cover and refrigerate. Reheat and serve as directed. May be frozen. To serve, defrost and heat until bubbly.

- In a large kettle, cook pasta al dente. Drain and quickly toss with two-thirds of the sauce. Serve immediately. Pass additional sauce in a small bowl.

Linguine with Artichoke Sauce

Most of the ingredients can be "on the shelf" for an elegant last-minute supper.

- Serves 4

¼ cup virgin olive oil

4 tablespoons (2 ounces) unsalted butter

2 tablespoons all-purpose flour

1 cup chicken stock

2 cloves garlic, minced

2 teaspoons lemon juice

1 to 2 teaspoons parsley, chopped

1 14-ounce can artichoke hearts, drained, rinsed and chopped

3 tablespoons Parmesan cheese, freshly grated

1 to 2 teaspoons capers, drained

½ pound linguine

2 tablespoons (1 ounce) unsalted butter

1 tablespoon virgin olive oil

- In a large frying pan, heat ¼ cup olive oil and 4 tablespoons butter until melted.

- Add flour and cook, stirring, for 3 minutes.

- Stir in chicken stock, garlic, lemon juice and parsley. Cook over moderate heat 5 minutes.

- Add artichoke hearts, Parmesan cheese and capers. Cook 8 minutes.

- Cook pasta al dente. Drain and toss with additional 2 tablespoons butter, 1 tablespoon olive oil and remaining 1 tablespoon cheese.

- Add sauce, toss and serve.

Variation: Instead of 1 14-ounce can artichoke hearts, use ½ can artichokes, 2 chopped, fresh tomatoes and ¼ cup chopped fresh basil.

Fettucine Pagliafieno

A wonderful entrée or an appealing first course

- Serves 6 to 8

¾ pound sliced prosciutto, chopped in ½-inch squares

½ pound sliced bacon, cut in ½-inch squares

12 ounces plain egg fettucine

12 ounces spinach fettucine

1 10-ounce package frozen peas

2 egg yolks

2 pints (32 ounces) heavy cream

Freshly ground pepper

¼ pound freshly grated Parmesan cheese

- Brown bacon and prosciutto in frying pan; drain off excess fat.

- Cook fettucine according to package directions; drain and keep warm.

- Cook peas according to package directions; drain.

- Mix egg yolks and cream; add to meat, and heat but do not boil. Add peas.

- Arrange fettucine in serving bowl or on a platter. Pour on cream mixture and toss. Season with a few grinds of pepper. Serve at once with freshly grated Parmesan cheese.

Pasta with Parmesan and Asparagus

The crunch of asparagus combined with the smoky flavor of bacon

- **Serves 6 to 8**

½ pound fresh asparagus (tips only)

¼ pound bacon

6 small to medium mushrooms, sliced

3 garlic cloves, minced

1 cup heavy cream

½ cup grated fresh Parmesan cheese

1½ pounds fettucine

1 medium tomato, peeled, seeded and diced

Salt to taste

Freshly ground pepper to taste

Chopped fresh parsley (garnish)

Paprika (garnish)

- In a large frying pan, cook bacon until brown, drain and reserve.

- Sauté mushrooms and asparagus tips in bacon drippings 6 or 7 minutes until tender. Pat dry and reserve.

- Sauté tomato until soft. Reserve with asparagus and mushrooms.

- Discard grease in pan. Add cream, garlic and cheese to pan. Stir until smooth and heated through.

- Cook pasta in boiling salted water until al dente. Drain well and return to pot.

- When ready to serve, add cream sauce to pasta and toss. Stir in crumbled bacon and vegetables.

- Sprinkle with chopped fresh parsley and paprika.

Springtime Spaghetti

Blanching the vegetables in a microwave speeds the preparation of this bountiful dish.

- **Serves 8 to 10**

4 cups broccoli florets (1 large head)

2 small zucchini, trimmed, quartered lengthwise and cut into 1-inch lengths

4 asparagus spears, trimmed and cut into 1-inch lengths

½ pound fresh green beans, trimmed and cut crosswise into 1-inch sections

½ cup peas, fresh or frozen

7 tablespoons virgin olive oil

6 ounces fresh mushrooms, thinly sliced

¼ teaspoon dried red pepper flakes (or to taste)

1 teaspoon salt (or to taste)

Freshly ground black pepper

¼ cup finely chopped parsley

1 teaspoon finely chopped fresh garlic

1¼ pounds fresh ripe tomatoes, cubed and drained (or 1 box cherry tomatoes, halved)

¼ cup fresh basil, finely chopped (or 2 teaspoons dried)

4 tablespoons (2 ounces) unsalted butter

2 tablespoons chicken broth, homemade or canned

½ to ¾ cup heavy cream

⅔ to 1 cup freshly grated Parmesan cheese

1 pound spaghetti

⅓ cup pine nuts, lightly toasted

- Bring a large pot of water to a boil and separately blanch broccoli, zucchini, asparagus, green beans and peas. Set aside in a large bowl.

• In a frying pan, heat 1 tablespoon olive oil. Add mushrooms and sauté for about 2 minutes. Stir in salt, pepper, red pepper flakes and parsley. Remove and add to vegetables.

• Heat 3 tablespoons olive oil. Add ½ teaspoon garlic and the tomatoes. Reduce heat and cook 5 minutes. Stir in basil, remainder of olive oil, garlic and the vegetable mixture. Cook until just heated through.

• Cook spaghetti al dente. Drain and return to pot. Toss with butter, chicken broth, ½ cup cream and Parmesan cheese. Add ½ of reserved vegetables and toss. Turn out onto serving platter. Add remaining vegetable mixture, arranging tomatoes on top. Add additional cream if desired. May be prepared to this point 1 hour in advance and kept warm, covered, in a 150 to 200 degree oven. Sprinkle with pine nuts. Serve with additional Parmesan cheese.

Parmesan Potato Sticks

The whole family will fight over these!

• Serves 6 to 8
  3 large Idaho potatoes
  ½ cup (4 ounces) unsalted butter, melted
  ½ cup Parmesan cheese
  ½ cup bread crumbs
  3 tablespoons sesame seeds
  Paprika

• Preheat oven to 400 degrees.

• Cut potatoes into eighths, lengthwise. (Do not remove skin).

• Dip potatoes into melted butter. Coat all sides well.

• Combine Parmesan cheese, bread crumbs and sesame seeds. Coat each potato stick well.

• Place on a greased cookie sheet. Sprinkle with paprika. May be prepared to this point 24 hours in advance. Cover and refrigerate. Bring to room temperature before continuing.

• Bake for 45 to 50 minutes or until crisp.

Variation: Instead of Parmesan cheese, use an additional ½ cup of sesame seeds. Do not sprinkle with paprika.

Potato Gratin

Worth the calories!

- **Serves 6 to 8**

  1 large clove garlic

  2 tablespoons (1 ounce) unsalted butter, softened to room temperature

  6 medium Idaho or Maine potatoes, peeled and thinly sliced

  Salt and freshly ground pepper to taste

  ½ teaspoon freshly grated nutmeg

  2 cups heavy cream, lightly salted

- Preheat oven to 325 degrees.

- Crush garlic clove and rub onto the interior of a 1½-quart baking dish. Remove any garlic pieces that adhere to the dish.

- Butter dish heavily, using the entire 2 tablespoons of butter.

- Place potatoes into a large bowl. Mix well with salt, pepper and nutmeg.

- Transfer ⅓ of the potatoes into the baking dish; pour ⅓ of the cream over them; repeat with another ⅓ of potatoes and cream; then repeat one more time.

- Shake the baking dish well. May be prepared to this point 3 to 4 hours in advance. Cover and refrigerate. Bring to room temperature before continuing. Place in the oven and bake 30 minutes. Remove from oven and break the crust of the cream.

- Bake another 15 minutes. Break the newly-formed crust again. Finish baking until the surface of the potatoes is deep golden in color.

Note: Keeps for hours in a 190 degree oven.

Roesti Potatoes

A European version of "home fries" is served pancake-style and cut into wedges.

- **Serves 6 to 8**

  6 large baking potatoes

  ½ cup (4 ounces) unsalted butter

  2 tablespoons vegetable oil

  2 teaspoons salt

  ½ teaspoon pepper

  6 tablespoons (3 ounces) unsalted butter, melted

- Boil unpeeled potatoes in water to cover for 10 minutes. Remove from heat, drain and peel. Coarsely grate in food processor.

- In a large heavy frying pan, heat ½ cup butter with vegetable oil over high heat until foaming subsides.

- Spoon ½ of the potatoes into the frying pan. Press down with a spatula. Sprinkle with 1 teaspoon of the salt and ¼ teaspoon of the pepper. Drizzle with 4 tablespoons of the melted butter.

- Add remaining potatoes, salt, pepper and butter. Shake pan so that potatoes do not stick. Cook over high heat 5 minutes, pressing hard with the spatula.

- Cover with lid slightly smaller than the frying pan.

- Reduce heat to medium and cook covered for 15 to 20 minutes. Shake pan a few times so that potatoes do not stick. May be prepared to this point 3 hours in advance. Keep warm in frying pan in a 190 degree oven until serving time.

- Unmold by placing a round serving plate over the pan, then invert potatoes onto the plate, crusty side up. Delicious with steaks, chops or venison. Serve with creamed spinach for a hearty winter repast.

Praline Sweet Potatoes

Perfect with turkey for Thanksgiving or ham for Easter

- Serves 8

  4 cups sweet potatoes, peeled, cooked and mashed

  3 tablespoons (1½ ounces) unsalted butter, melted

  ¼ cup firmly packed brown sugar

  ⅓ cup orange juice

  2 teaspoons brandy

  1 teaspoon salt

  ⅛ teaspoon pepper

  1 teaspoon grated orange peel

  ½ teaspoon ginger

  ½ teaspoon cinnamon

  ¼ teaspoon allspice

- Preheat oven to 350 degrees.
- Combine all ingredients except praline topping. Mix well. Spoon into a buttered, 2-quart shallow baking dish.

  Praline Topping

  ⅓ cup firmly packed brown sugar

  ½ cup chopped pecans

  ¼ cup unsalted butter, melted

  ½ teaspoon cinnamon

- In a 1-quart mixing bowl, make praline topping by combining brown sugar, pecans, butter and cinnamon. Spread over potato mixture. May be prepared to this point 48 hours in advance. Cover and refrigerate. Bring to room temperature before continuing. Bake 30 minutes in oven.

Chestnut Compote

Serve in a silver or crystal bowl as a side-dish for roast duck or turkey.

- Serves 6 to 8

  1 pound dried, peeled chestnuts or 1 can water-packed chestnuts, drained

  ¾ cup raisins

  2 tablespoons vinegar

  ½ cup brown sugar

  1½ tablespoons butter

- Cook chestnuts (if dried) and raisins in a 2-quart saucepan with water to cover, about 1 hour or until chestnuts are tender. (If using water-packed chestnuts combine with raisins, which have been plumped in boiling water for 10 minutes).

- Add vinegar, sugar and butter. Cook over low flame, stirring occasionally until mixture thickens slightly. May be prepared to this point several months in advance. Cover and refrigerate or freeze. Reheat at serving time.

Variation: Cook ¾ cup pitted prunes and/or dried apples along with the chestnuts and raisins.

Spiced Fruit

An accompaniment to ham or roast duckling

- **Serves 6 to 8**
  5 ounces dried apples
  6 ounces dried apricots
  5 ounces pitted prunes
  2 navel oranges, peeled and sliced
  1 cup raisins
  ½ cup mango chutney
  ¼ cup sugar
  1 teaspoon cinnamon
  3 whole cloves

- In a 4-quart saucepan, combine all ingredients with 8 cups of water. Cook over high heat, stirring occasionally, for 1 hour.

- Lower heat and allow mixture to simmer for 1 additional hour. Stir 3 or 4 times while simmering to prevent burning.

- Remove from heat. Discard cloves. Spoon into a serving bowl and serve hot.

Variation: Serve cold as a dessert in a crystal compote. This dessert is especially delicious served over slices of toasted pound cake.

Pineapple Bake

An unusual accompaniment to game, poultry or ham

- **Serves 4 to 6**
  8 tablespoons (4 ounces) unsalted butter
  ½ cup sugar
  3 eggs, beaten
  1 20-ounce can crushed pineapple, undrained
  4 slices fresh white bread, crumbled

- Preheat oven to 425 degrees.

- In small saucepan, melt butter over low heat. Remove from heat, add sugar and mix well.

- In a 2-quart bowl, combine undrained pineapple with butter mixture, beaten eggs and crumbled white bread. Mix well and pour into a 2-quart baking dish. May be prepared to this point 4 to 6 hours in advance. Cover and refrigerate. Bring to room temperature before continuing.

- Bake for 25 minutes. Serve hot.

Brown and Wild Rice Mélange

Excellent served with chicken, ham or beef

- **Serves 6 to 8**

  ½ cup (4 ounces) unsalted butter

  1 cup brown rice

  1 cup wild rice

  1 cup chopped onion

  1 cup celery, sliced ⅛-inch thick crosswise

  1 pound fresh mushrooms, sliced ¼-inch thick crosswise

  3½ cups chicken broth

  ¼ teaspoon dried thyme

  ¼ cup fresh chopped parsley

  ½ teaspoon salt (or to taste)

  Freshly ground black pepper

- Melt butter in a 2-quart saucepan. Add brown rice, wild rice, chopped onion, sliced celery and mushrooms. Sauté over medium-high heat stirring frequently for about 5 minutes.

- Add chicken broth, thyme, parsley, salt and pepper.

- Cover pan and cook over low heat for 1 hour, stirring occasionally, or until all broth is absorbed and rice is tender.

  Variation: Add ⅓ cup toasted chopped pecans just before serving.

Rice and Artichokes

A delicious accent for poultry or veal

- **Serves 4 to 6**

  4 tablespoons (2 ounces) unsalted butter

  ¼ cup chopped onions

  1 clove garlic, minced

  1 14-ounce can artichoke hearts, drained

  2½ cups boiling chicken stock

  1 cup long grain uncooked rice

  ½ cup Parmesan cheese, shredded

  1 to 2 tablespoons Parmesan cheese, grated

  2 tablespoons minced parsley

- Preheat oven to 350 degrees.

- Melt butter in a 12-inch frying pan. Add onions and garlic and sauté over medium-high heat until limp.

- Thoroughly blend in artichokes, chicken stock, rice and shredded Parmesan cheese. Transfer to a 1½-quart casserole. Top with grated Parmesan cheese.

- Bake for 40 to 45 minutes or until rice has cooked and the Parmesan cheese has browned slightly.

- Sprinkle with parsley and serve immediately.

_S_auces and Marinades

213

Mandarin square, Chinese, 1670–1700, embroidered silk and gold, 14 3/4 x 13 3/4". Purchased: John T. Morris Fund

The Chinese court costumes of the Ch'ing Dynasty (1644–1912) are rich in symbolism and splendid in material and technique. Their interest lies in the fine weaving and exquisite embroidery of the elaborate patterns as well as in the ideas that the designs were meant to convey. This example, known as a mandarin square, was one of the badges of rank worn by nobles and officials and their families.

Poppy Seed Dressing

Slightly sweet, slightly tart dressing for mixed greens

- **Makes about 2 cups**
  ¼ to ½ cup granulated sugar (depending on how sweet you wish it)
  1 teaspoon dry mustard
  1 teaspoon paprika
  1 teaspoon salt
  ⅓ cup honey
  1 cup vegetable oil
  1 tablespoon poppy seeds

- In a blender or glass jar, thoroughly mix all of the ingredients in the order presented. Refrigerate for up to 2 weeks. Bring to room temperature and mix well before serving.

- Pour on a salad of mixed greens, toss gently and garnish with grated carrots and thinly sliced poached or canned pears. A sprinkle of Parmesan cheese makes a tangy final touch.

Creamy Dressing

A rich, tangy sauce for crisp greens

- **Makes 2½ cups**
  1 pint commercial sour cream
  1 cup premium mayonnaise
  ¾ tablespoon fresh lemon juice
  ¾ tablespoon white wine vinegar
  ¾ tablespoon vegetable oil
  2 teaspoons mustard seeds
  ¾ tablespoon steak sauce
  ½ teaspoon garlic powder
  1 large head iceberg lettuce
  Radish roses, black olives, parsley sprigs

- Combine sour cream, mayonnaise, lemon juice, vinegar and oil and whisk until smooth. Add mustard seeds, sauce and garlic powder and stir until blended. Cover and refrigerate until well chilled. May be prepared to this point up to 48 hours in advance.

- At serving time, cut lettuce into 6 wedges and place in individual chilled salad bowls. Pour dressing over each wedge and decorate with radish roses, black olives and parsley sprigs.

Variation: Pour dressing over spinach leaves torn in bite-size pieces. Garnish with sliced fresh mushrooms and crumbled bacon bits.

Homemade Food-Processor Mayonnaise

Easy, fast and foolproof

- **Makes 2 cups**
  2 large egg yolks, room temperature
  2 teaspoons white wine vinegar
  1 teaspoon Dijon-style mustard
  ¼ teaspoon salt, or to taste
  Freshly ground white pepper to taste
  1½ cups vegetable oil (or a mixture of olive oil and vegetable oil)
  Juice of ½ fresh lemon
  Milk or cream

- In a bowl of food-processor (or blender) combine yolks, 1 teaspoon vinegar, mustard, salt and pepper and blend until combined.

- With processor or blender running, slowly drip in ½ cup oil. Add remaining 1 teaspoon vinegar, remaining 1 cup oil and lemon juice in a steady stream. Use milk or cream to thin mayonnaise, if desired.

Variation: Add 1 or 2 crushed garlic cloves before adding oil. Perfect with cold, boiled lobster or shrimp.

Microwave Hollandaise Sauce

A never-fail version of an old favorite

- **Makes ⅔ cup**
  4 tablespoons (2 ounces) unsalted butter
  2 egg yolks, well-beaten
  1 tablespoon fresh lemon juice
  ¼ cup light cream
  ½ teaspoon dry mustard
  ¼ teaspoon salt

- In a 2-cup liquid measure, melt the butter on HI for 45 seconds to 1 minute.

- Using a wire whisk, beat in all the other ingredients in the order listed. Cook on HI for 1½ to 2 minutes or until thick, whisking every 15 seconds.

- This sauce can be refrigerated and reheated on MEDIUM-LOW until hot, whisking every 15 seconds.

Creole Tomato Sauce

Microwave magic sauce for spaghetti, rice, vegetables, fish or eggs

- **Makes 3 cups**
  2 tablespoons bacon fat or oil
  2 tablespoons all-purpose flour
  1 large onion, chopped
  2 cloves garlic, minced or pressed
  ¾ cup chopped green pepper (½ large pepper)
  1 1-pound 12-ounce can whole tomatoes, cut up
  1 tablespoon minced fresh parsley
  1 teaspoon Worcestershire sauce
  1 teaspoon salt
  ½ teaspoon sugar
  Dash cayenne pepper

- In a 2-quart casserole, heat fat or oil on HI 1 minute.

- Add flour and cook on HI for 1 to 1½ minutes.

- Add onion, garlic, green pepper and cook on HI for 5 to 7 minutes or until onions are tender.

- Add remaining ingredients and cook on HI for 5 minutes, then on SIMMER for 25 minutes, stirring once. This sauce freezes well and can be refrigerated for up to 5 days.

Variation: Can be prepared on conventional range.

215

Fiery Barbecue Sauce

*Outstanding on pork spare ribs,
chops, chicken or burgers*

- **Makes 2½ cups**
- ½ cup minced fresh onion
- 3 cloves garlic, minced
- 3 tablespoons (1½ ounces) unsalted butter
- 3 tablespoons firmly packed dark brown sugar
- 2 tablespoons cider vinegar
- 1 cup catsup
- 2 beef bouillon cubes
- 1 cup water
- 1 tablespoon Worcestershire sauce
- 2 teaspoons Dijon-style mustard
- 1 tablespoon hot pepper sauce
- Salt
- Pepper
- Dash cayenne pepper
- 1 tablespoon fresh lemon juice

- In large stainless steel saucepan, cook onion and garlic in butter over medium heat until translucent.

- Add sugar and vinegar and cook until sugar dissolves.

- Add all other ingredients except lemon juice, adjust seasonings to taste and bring mixture to a boil.

- Stir and let boil for 25 minutes. Add lemon juice. Refrigerate until needed.

Hawaiian Beef Marinade

*Some ideas for this oriental-style
marinade: steak; London broil; beef
short ribs; flank steak*

- **Makes 2 cups**
- ½ teaspoon curry powder
- ½ cup soy sauce
- ½ cup pineapple juice
- ½ cup sherry
- 2 tablespoons powdered ginger
- 1 garlic clove, crushed
- 2 teaspoons dry mustard
- 1 tablespoon olive oil

- Combine all ingredients thoroughly.

- Pour over meat and refrigerate overnight or all day.

- Remove meat from marinade and pat dry with paper towels. Grill or bake until done. Baste occasionally with reserved marinade.

Hoisin Marinade

*Wonderful on grilled butterflied leg of
lamb, chicken or ribs!*

- **Makes 1 cup**
- ¾ cup Chinese Hoisin sauce
- 9 tablespoons medium dry sherry
- 6 tablespoons minced scallions
- 6 tablespoons soy sauce

6 tablespoons mashed garlic cloves

6 teaspoons brown sugar

3 teaspoons peeled, chopped fresh ginger

- Combine all of the ingredients thoroughly.

- Pour over meat of your choice and refrigerate overnight.

- Grill or roast meat until done, basting with marinade.

Mixed Herb Mustard Sauce

The subtle sweetness combined with the tang of the mustard makes this a delicious accompaniment to ham, cold meat or sandwiches.

- Makes 1½ cups

1 cup smooth Dijon-style mustard

1½ teaspoons mixed herbs using equal amounts of dried tarragon, dried basil and dried thyme

1 tablespoon light brown sugar

1 teaspoon chopped chives

1 teaspoon fresh lemon juice

1 teaspoon chopped parsley

- Mix all ingredients together and refrigerate. Will keep for several weeks.

Cucumber Sauce

Delicious with salmon mousse and other fish dishes

- Makes about 2½ cups

2 large cucumbers, peeled and seeded

1 cup Homemade Food-Processor Mayonnaise

1 cup commercial sour cream

1 tablespoon Dijon-style mustard

1 tablespoon lemon juice

½ teaspoon coarse salt

¼ teaspoon pepper

½ cup snipped fresh dill

¼ cup fresh chives, finely chopped

- Grate cucumbers into bowl.

- Combine cucumbers with other ingredients, mixing well.

- Refrigerate several hours

Desserts

Attributed to Lodewyck van der Helst (Dutch, 1642–c. 1684), *Portrait of a Man and a Woman Seated Outdoors*, c. 1670, oil on canvas, 62 1/2 x 46 1/2". Purchased for the W. P. Wilstach Collection

By the middle of the seventeenth century a taste for elegance and luxury dominated the portrait market. The costly fabrics and ornaments worn by this Dutch couple advertise their economic well-being. The man looks prosperous in his red velvet coat, and the woman is splendid with her baroque earrings and pearl Juliet cap. Their tenderly clasped hands have long been symbolic of marriage, and the small dog (Fido) at the man's feet reinforces the concept of fidelity.

Brown Edge Vanilla Wafers

A versatile cookie favorite

- **Makes about 3 dozen**
  1 cup (8 ounces) unsalted butter
  1 cup granulated sugar
  2 eggs
  2 teaspoons vanilla extract
  1½ cups sifted all-purpose flour
  Pinch of salt

- Preheat oven to 350 degrees.

- In a bowl, cream butter and sugar until light and fluffy. Add eggs, one at a time, and incorporate well. Add vanilla, flour and salt. Mix thoroughly.

- Drop dough by half-teaspoonful at least 2 inches apart, onto lightly greased cookie sheets. Bake 10 to 12 minutes in oven or until edges start to brown (watch carefully). Remove from pan at once with a spatula and cool on racks. Store in air-tight container.

Variations: Add ½ to 1 teaspoon grated orange or lemon peel to batter; glaze cooled cookies with your favorite icing; sprinkle colored sugar on warm cookies; sandwich 2 cookies together with jam or butter cream filling; shave semi-sweet chocolate on warm cookies.

Mocha Almond Crunch

A delightful accompaniment to after-dinner coffee

- **Makes 20 to 24 pieces**
  1 cup (8 ounces) unsalted butter
  2 tablespoons instant coffee powder
  ½ teaspoon salt
  ½ teaspoon almond extract
  1 teaspoon vanilla extract
  1 cup granulated sugar
  2 cups sifted all-purpose flour
  2 cups semi-sweet chocolate morsels
  1 cup blanched almond slivers

- Preheat oven to 375 degrees.

- In a large bowl, mix butter, coffee, salt, almond and vanilla extracts. Beat in sugar, then gradually add flour until mixture is well-blended. Fold in chocolate morsels.

- Spread mixture in an ungreased 15 x 10 x 1-inch (jelly roll) pan. Press almonds on top. Bake for 20 to 22 minutes. Remove from oven. Cool on rack. Cut or break into irregular pieces. Store in air-tight container or freeze.

Blueberry Sour Cream Torte

A festive dessert at summer parties garnish with strawberries for a sparkling Independence Day finale.

- **Serves 10 to 12**

Crust

12 tablespoons (6 ounces) unsalted butter, softened

¼ cup granulated sugar

2 egg yolks

2 cups all-purpose flour

1 teaspoon baking powder

½ teaspoon salt

- Preheat oven to 400 degrees.

- Cream butter with sugar. Add egg yolks and beat until fluffy. Stir in flour, baking powder and salt.

- Press ⅔ of crust mixture on bottom of 9-inch springform pan. Bake for 10 minutes. Cool. Reduce oven temperature to 350 degrees.

- Press remaining crust mixture 1½ inches up side of pan.

Filling

3½ cups fresh blueberries

¾ cup granulated sugar

¼ cup quick-cooking tapioca

½ teaspoon finely shredded lemon peel

½ teaspoon ground cinnamon

⅛ teaspoon grated nutmeg

- In a large saucepan, combine berries, sugar, tapioca, lemon peel and spices. Let stand 15 minutes. Cook over moderate heat, stirring, until bubbly. Turn into crust.

Topping

2 egg yolks, lightly beaten

2 cups commercial sour cream

½ cup granulated sugar

1 teaspoon vanilla extract

Garnish

½ cup heavy cream, whipped

½ cup blueberries

- Blend egg yolks with sour cream, sugar and vanilla. Spoon over berries.

- Bake in 350 degree oven 45 minutes, cool, then chill. Decorate with whipped cream and remaining berries.

Blueberry Cake with Two Sauces

Traditional cake goes glamorous when served with two sauces, one orange flavored, the other, blueberry

• **Serves 8 to 10**

Cake

¼ **cup (2 ounces) unsalted butter**

¾ **cup granulated sugar**

2 **large eggs, lightly mixed**

1 **cup all-purpose flour**

1 **teaspoon baking powder**

½ **teaspoon salt**

1 **teaspoon ground cinnamon**

1 **teaspoon ground allspice**

1 **pint blueberries, washed and cleaned**

• Preheat oven to 375 degrees.

• Cream butter and sugar together. Add eggs, flour, baking powder, salt, cinnamon and allspice. Fold in berries.

• Bake in greased and floured 9 x 9-inch square pan for 30 to 40 minutes, until lightly browned and cake tester comes out clean. Cool to room temperature.

Buttered Orange Sauce

¼ **cup (2 ounces) unsalted butter**

½ **cup granulated sugar**

1 **tablespoon all-purpose flour**

¼ **cup boiling water**

2 **tablespoons orange-flavored liqueur**

• In a saucepan, cream butter and sugar. Add flour and mix well. Pour boiling water over mixture and bring to a boil. Remove from heat, stir in liqueur. Serve warm with cake.

Blueberry Sauce

1 **pint blueberries**

1 **cup granulated sugar**

¼ **cup water**

1 **tablespoon corn starch**

2 **tablespoons water**

• In a saucepan, mix berries with sugar and water. Bring to a boil. Dissolve corn starch in 2 tablespoons water and add to berries. Cook until thickened. Serve warm with cake.

Peanut Butter Chocolate Chip Cheesecake

Possibly the most unusual cheesecake ever

• **Serves 16**

Crust

1 **12-ounce box vanilla wafers**

½ **cup granulated sugar**

2 **teaspoons unsalted butter, melted**

• Preheat oven to 350 degrees.

• Make crust by combining wafers and sugar in processor to make uniform crumbs. Add butter and mix well. Press into bottom and halfway up sides of 9-inch springform pan. Set aside.

Filling

1 pound cream cheese, softened

1½ cups granulated sugar

1 6-ounce jar creamy peanut butter

5 large eggs

½ cup commercial sour cream

2 teaspoons fresh lemon juice

¾ cup chocolate chips

- Combine cream cheese, sugar, peanut butter, eggs, sour cream and lemon juice in processor and blend until smooth. Add chips and process for 10 seconds with on-off motion.

- Pour filling carefully into crust. Bake 70 to 80 minutes until center is firm. Remove from oven but leave oven on, and let stand for 15 minutes before adding topping.

Topping

1 cup commercial sour cream

¾ cup chocolate chips, melted

¼ cup granulated sugar

- Blend sour cream, melted chocolate and sugar and spread over cake. Bake for an additional 10 minutes. Let cool, and chill for at least 3 hours or overnight. Unmold carefully and serve in thin wedges.

Chocolate Orange Cheesecake

Equally good is the "Blond" variation that follows.

- **Serves 12 to 14**

  1¾ cups chocolate wafer cookie crumbs

  4 tablespoons (2 ounces) unsalted butter, melted

  3 8-ounce packages cream cheese, softened

  1 cup granulated sugar

  4 large eggs, room temperature

  2 tablespoons orange liqueur

  Zest of 1 large orange

  Cocoa powder

- Preheat oven to 325 degrees.

- Mix cookie crumbs with butter and press into bottom of 8-inch springform pan. Chill in freezer for at least ½ hour.

- In the large bowl of an electric mixer, beat cream cheese, sugar, eggs, liqueur and orange zest at medium speed until very smooth, about 20 minutes. Pour into crust and level batter by quickly rotating pan in one direction, then the other.

- Bake about 1 hour or until top feels nearly dry. Filling will move slightly when pan is shaken gently. Cool cake on a rack, then refrigerate at least 5 or 6 hours.

- To serve, unmold and dust top of cake with cocoa.

Variation: For Blond Cheesecake, substitute 1¾ cups shortbread cookie crumbs for chocolate wafers; use 1 teaspoon vanilla extract instead of liqueur and zest. Dust finished cake with powdered shortbread cookie crumbs.

223

Gâteau de Marrons au Chocolat

Chocolate and chestnuts combine for richness in this make-ahead party dessert.

• Serves 10

1 1-pound 5-ounce can unsweetened whole chestnuts, drained

¾ cup granulated sugar

½ cup (4 ounces) unsalted butter, melted and cooled

8 ounces sweetened chocolate, melted and cooled

½ pint whipping cream, whipped until stiff

10 candied chestnuts

• Purée chestnuts in food processor. Add sugar and butter and mix well. Pour in chocolate, with blade running, and blend until mixture is smooth and thoroughly incorporated.

• Pour into 1-quart mold and chill until firm, at least 4 hours, and up to 2 days prior to serving.

• Invert onto serving plate using cloth, wrung out in hot water, to loosen bottom and sides. Decorate with rosettes of whipped cream garnished with whole candied chestnuts. Slice thinly as this is very rich.

Mocha Fudge Cake

A tall, dark and handsome cake to thrill any chocolate cake afficionado

• Serves 12 to 14

Cake

1 cup (8 ounces) unsalted butter, softened

1 pound dark brown sugar

3 cold eggs

2 ounces unsweetened baking chocolate, melted and cooled

1 teaspoon vanilla extract

2 cups cake flour

1 teaspoon baking soda

1 cup ice water

• Preheat oven to 350 degrees.

• In a large mixing bowl, cream butter. Add sugar, eggs, cooled chocolate and vanilla extract. Cream well.

• In a small bowl, mix flour and baking soda. Add to butter mixture alternately with ice water, ending with flour.

• Pour into a greased and floured 10-inch tube pan.

• Bake for 50 minutes or until tester comes out clean. Cool for 15 minutes before removing from pan.

Mocha Icing

1 3-ounce package cream cheese, softened

1 pound confectioners sugar

1 ounce unsweetened chocolate, melted

2 tablespoons strong liquid coffee, cooled

1 tablespoon vanilla extract

1 cup chopped walnuts (optional)

- Cream all ingredients well. Mixture should be thick enough to spread. Add more coffee if needed.

- Frost cake. Press walnuts around outside of cake.

Peanut Brittle Sundaes with Whiskey Sauce

An ice cream dessert for grown-ups

- **Serves 8 to 10**
  ½ gallon quality coffee ice cream
  1 8-ounce package peanut brittle
  2 eggs
  1 cup granulated sugar
  ½ pint heavy cream, whipped
  1 tablespoon rum
  2 ounces whiskey

- Scoop out ice cream and roll into 8 to 10 balls. Refreeze immediately on a cookie sheet.

- Pulverize peanut brittle until powdery. Roll each ice cream ball in brittle crumbs and refreeze. If not serving at once, place frozen balls in heavy duty plastic bag and keep up to 2 days.

- One hour before serving, beat eggs until lemon-colored. Gradually incorporate sugar. Fold in whipped cream, rum and whiskey.

- To serve, place each ice cream ball in a sundae dish or compote dish and spoon on sauce. Serve at once.

Pennsylvania Dutch Apple Cake

Cinnamon and sugar glaze this authentic "kuchen".

- **Serves 6 to 8**
  1 rounded tablespoon butter or margarine, softened
  ¾ cup granulated sugar
  1 whole egg
  2 tablespoons boiling water
  1 cup all-purpose flour
  1 teaspoon baking powder
  ¼ teaspoon salt
  3 medium to large firm tart apples, pared, cored and sliced into thin wedges
  3 tablespoons granulated sugar
  1 teaspoon cinnamon

- Preheat oven to 350 degrees.

- In a mixing bowl, cream butter and sugar. Beat in egg. Slowly add boiling water. Stir in flour, baking powder and salt. (Batter will be stiff.)

- Lightly grease an 8 or 9-inch loose-bottom cake pan or pie tin. Press dough into pan.

- Cover dough with sliced apples arranged in concentric circles. Push apples into dough slightly. Sprinkle with sugar and cinnamon and bake for 50 to 60 minutes. Serve warm with whipped cream or vanilla ice cream. (This cake should be served on the same day it is baked as it does not "stand" well.)

Variations: Substitute fresh peaches, skinned and sliced; blueberries, washed and dried; or purple prune plums, split and stoned but with skins, for the apples.

225

Pineapple Carrot Cake

A glamorous presentation

- Serves 12 to 16

Cake

2 cups all-purpose flour

2 teaspoons baking soda

2 teaspoons cinnamon

½ teaspoon salt

3 eggs at room temperature

¾ cup almond oil or vegetable oil

¾ cup buttermilk

2 cups granulated sugar

2 teaspoons vanilla extract

1 8 to 10-ounce can crushed pineapple, drained (reserve juice for frosting)

2 cups grated carrots

2 ounces shredded coconut

1 cup chopped walnuts, pecans or almonds

- Preheat oven to 350 degrees.

- Sift dry ingredients together. Beat eggs; add oil, buttermilk, sugar and vanilla. Mix well. Add to dry ingredients, blending well. Mix in pineapple, carrots, coconut and nuts.

- Grease 2 9-inch or 3 8-inch cake pans. Pour in batter and bake for approximately 55 minutes.

Glaze

¾ cup granulated sugar

½ teaspoon baking soda

½ cup buttermilk

½ cup (4 ounces) unsalted butter

1 tablespoon maple syrup

1 teaspoon vanilla extract

- In medium-large saucepan, combine sugar, baking soda, buttermilk, butter and syrup. Simmer over low heat. Remove from heat and stir in vanilla. Pour over warm cakes in pans.

Frosting

8 ounces cream cheese, softened

½ cup (4 ounces) unsalted butter, softened

1½ to 2 cups confectioners sugar

3 to 6 tablespoons pineapple juice (reserved from cake)

Decorations

1 cup grated coconut

12 to 16 walnut halves, toasted almonds or pecan halves

- Beat together cream cheese and butter. Slowly add sugar. Mix in enough juice to make frosting spreadable.

- After glazed cakes cool, remove from pans. Spread frosting on top of each layer; put together and frost sides. Pat coconut onto sides and arrange nut pieces decoratively on top. Any remaining frosting can be piped on as rosettes.

Chocolate Mousse

Quick, easy and decadent

- **Serves 4**

  6 ounces semi-sweet chocolate or 4 ounces semi-
  sweet and 2 ounces bittersweet chocolate

  2 tablespoons orange liqueur

  1 tablespoon fresh orange juice

  2 egg yolks

  2 whole eggs

  1 teaspoon vanilla extract

  ¼ cup granulated sugar

  1½ cups heavy cream

  Candied orange peel (garnish)

- In a heavy saucepan over low heat, melt chocolate in orange liqueur and juice. Set aside.

- In a food processor, mix egg yolks, eggs, vanilla and sugar. Blend for 2 minutes. Add 1 cup heavy cream and blend for an additional 30 seconds. Add chocolate mixture and blend until smooth. Pour into 4 individual ramekins or stemmed crystal goblets. Chill at least 4 hours.

- To serve, whip remaining ½ cup cream until stiff and spoon or pipe onto each serving. Garnish with a twist of orange peel.

Variation: Replace orange liqueur with coffee liqueur and the orange juice with strong coffee. Garnish with chocolate coffee beans.

Coffee Sponge

Try serving this delicate custard in demi-tasse topped with a dab of whipped cream and a chocolate coffee bean.

- **Serves 4 to 8**

  1½ cups strong brewed coffee

  ½ cup granulated sugar

  ⅛ teaspoon salt

  1½ envelopes unflavored gelatin

  ½ cup milk

  2 egg yolks, beaten

  1 teaspoon vanilla extract

  2 egg whites

  ½ pint heavy cream, whipped

  Chocolate coffee beans (garnish)

- In a double boiler over boiling water, mix coffee, sugar and salt. Soften gelatin in milk and add to coffee mixture. Stir until well blended. Add egg yolks and stir until thick, about 5 minutes. Cool. Add vanilla.

- Beat egg whites until stiff but not dry. Carefully fold into coffee mixture. Pour into 4 stemmed glasses, a 6 ½-inch ring mold or 8 demi-tasse. Chill for several hours until firm. Decorate with whipped cream and chocolate coffee beans.

Russian Crème

Raspberries, whipped cream and rum – what could be better?

- **Serves 8**

  32 whole lady fingers, split

  8 to 10 tablespoons medium-dark rum

  ¼ to ½ cup seedless raspberry preserves

  2 cups heavy cream

  2 egg yolks

  1 cup granulated sugar

  Fresh raspberries or candied violets

  ½ cup heavy cream, whipped

- Sprinkle each half of lady fingers with 5 tablespoons of rum. Then spread each half with raspberry preserves. Press halves together, sandwich-fashion.

- Arrange lady finger sandwiches vertically in concentric circles, beginning at the outside of the dish and working toward center. Cover and refrigerate.

- In a mixing bowl, whip cream until quite stiff. In a larger bowl, beat egg yolks for 2 to 3 minutes until light and lemon-colored. Gradually add sugar and beat for several minutes. Add remaining 3 tablespoons of rum and beat to incorporate thoroughly.

- Pour ¼ of the whipped cream into the egg mixture to lighten it, then fold it back into the remaining whipped cream and mix only until just blended.

- Pour mixture over lady fingers making sure all cracks and crevices are filled. Refrigerate for at least 3 hours or until thoroughly chilled.

- Before serving, pipe rosettes of whipped cream on top and decorate with fresh raspberries, if available, or candied violets.

228

Variation: Place lady fingers in springform pan and proceed as above. To serve, unmold and decorate as suggested. Tie a pink ribbon around it for a truly gala touch.

Syllabub

This delightful English dessert is rich and sweet – a heady combination of brandy, wine, cream and spices.

- **Serves 8**

  1 medium lemon

  ⅜ cup white wine

  2 tablespoons brandy

  ¼ cup granulated sugar

  8 ounces heavy cream

  ¼ teaspoon grated nutmeg

- One day prior to serving, peel lemon carefully to avoid the bitter white pith. Put peel in small glass bowl or jar, along with juice of the lemon, wine and brandy. Allow to macerate overnight.

- On the day of serving, strain wine mixture into a larger bowl, reserving lemon peel. Add sugar and stir until dissolved. Add cream and nutmeg and whip briskly until soft peaks form. Do not overbeat.

- To serve, spoon into small stemmed glasses, such as sherry glasses. Refrigerate until serving time. Present with a garnish of slivered lemon peel and demi-tasse spoons.

Flan Flambé

The pyrotechnics which make this custard favorite so splendid upon presentation are easy when you follow the directions below.

- Serves 6 to 8
  1 cup granulated sugar
  3 whole eggs
  8 egg yolks
  2 12-ounce cans evaporated milk
  ¾ cup additional granulated sugar
  2 teaspoons vanilla extract
  ½ cup cognac

- Preheat oven to 350 degrees.

- In a large heavy pan, melt 1 cup sugar over a low flame, stirring, until sugar turns an amber color. Do not allow to get too dark. Pour into 6 to 8-cup mold and rotate mold until entirely coated with caramelized sugar. Set aside to cool.

- In a large bowl, mix whole eggs, yolks, milk, sugar and vanilla. Strain into mold. Place mold in a larger pan filled with hot water reaching halfway up mold. Bake 1 hour or until knife inserted in center comes out clean.

- Cool slightly and turn onto a large platter with a lip to hold liquid caramelized sugar and cognac. Refrigerate until well-chilled.

- At serving time, gently warm cognac in a small pan but do not boil. Pour warm brandy over flan and ignite at the table. When flames subside, serve in dessert bowls spooning caramel sauce on each portion.

Soufflé aux Pruneaux

You won't believe how truly divine the wrinkled prune can become until you try this elegant froth.

- Serves 8
  6 egg whites, room temperature
  ¼ cup granulated sugar
  1 cup puréed prunes (about 1 pound)
  ½ cup heavy cream, whipped
  8 prunes, pitted and softened in warm water
  8 whole toasted almonds
  ¼ cup Armagnac
  ¼ cup granulated sugar

- Beat egg whites until stiff. Gradually incorporate sugar.

- Using a large spatula, gently but quickly fold in prune purée.

- Butter a 3-quart double-boiler and lid and sprinkle with granulated sugar. Pour in prune mixture. Cover and set over boiling water for 1 hour. Make sure water doesn't boil away.

- Immediately turn out onto serving platter. Serve at once, garnishing each plate with a dollop of whipped cream and a stuffed Armagnac prune.

Armagnac Prunes
- Insert an almond in center of each prune.

- In a small saucepan, poach prunes in Armagnac mixed with sugar until lightly glazed, about 5 minutes. May be prepared in advance.

Champagne Fruit Dessert Soup

To capture all the syrup in this dessert, serve it in shallow bowls.

• **Serves 4 to 6**

½ cup granulated sugar

Zest of 1 lemon

Zest of 1 orange

Zest of 1 lime

1 vanilla bean, split lengthwise

3 cups cold water

1 cup champagne

2 sprigs fresh mint plus 12 to 14 fresh mint leaves

1 ripe peach

1 ripe nectarine

1 ripe mango

1 ripe kiwi

6 ounces of at least 3 kinds of fresh berries, such as raspberries, blackberries, blueberries or small strawberries

• In a 2-quart non-aluminum saucepan, combine sugar, citrus zests, vanilla bean and two sprigs of mint with 2 cups of the water. Bring to a boil, remove from heat and set aside for 3 to 4 hours. Strain and chill.

• Rinse and peel all of fruit (except berries). Discard pits. Cut each fruit into paper-thin slices. Add them to the chilled syrup. Refrigerate 2 to 3 hours or overnight.

• To serve, chill shallow soup bowls. Add remaining water and champagne to fruit mixture. Divide among bowls being certain each bowl has ¾ cup liquid. Divide assorted berries equally among bowls.

• Stack the mint leaves and cut into thin slivers.

Scatter over soup and garnish with mint sprigs. Keep chilled until serving time.

Variation: Halved and pitted Bing cherries, small unpeeled purple plums, papaya and fresh pineapple can be included. Slice paper-thin.

Crustless Apple Pie

An up-to-date variation of an old-fashioned cobbler

• **Serves 8**

5 large crisp cooking apples

½ cup (4 ounces) unsalted butter, softened

1 cup light brown sugar

1 cup all-purpose flour

Nutmeg

• Preheat oven to 425 degrees.

• Quarter, core and peel apples. Cut into lengthwise slices ½-inch thick, and arrange in 9-inch pie plate.

• Cream butter and sugar. Blend in flour. Mixture will be thick. Pat into a "dough" and place over apples. Sprinkle with nutmeg.

• Bake for 10 minutes. Reduce heat to 350 degrees and bake 20 minutes longer. Serve hot or cold with vanilla ice cream.

Figs with Mascarpone

Mascarpone, an Italian cream cheese available in gourmet stores, makes a divine sauce for this irresistible fruit finale.

- Serves 12
  4 cups dry red wine
  ½ cup granulated sugar
  2 pounds dried figs
  1 tablespoon fresh lemon juice
  ¾ pound Mascarpone, room temperature
  3 tablespoons light brown sugar
  1½ cups commercial sour cream
  8 navel oranges, peeled, pith cut away and sliced ⅛-inch thick

- In a large non-aluminum saucepan, combine wine and sugar. Bring to a boil, stirring until sugar is dissolved. Add figs and simmer, covered, 35 minutes or until figs are very tender. Add lemon juice and transfer figs with a slotted spoon to a bowl.

- Turn up heat under wine mixture and boil until syrupy. Pour over figs and cool to room temperature. May be prepared up to one week in advance and refrigerated until serving time.

- Make sauce by beating Mascarpone with brown sugar until fluffy. Whisk in sour cream.

- To present: Arrange orange slices around edge of a large platter. Mound figs in center. Pour syrup over figs but not on oranges. Pour Mascarpone mixture into sauce boat. To serve, place an orange slice or two on plate, top with several figs and pass sauce.

Oranges Orientale

A glamorous dessert when you want a very special fruit finale

- Serves 8 to 10
  8 large navel oranges
  2 cups granulated sugar
  2 cups water
  ¼ teaspoon cream of tartar
  ½ cup orange liqueur
  1 teaspoon grenadine
  8 crystallized violets (garnish)

- Peel oranges thinly, taking only the skin and no white pith. Cut peels into long skinny slivers and place in saucepan with sugar, water and cream of tartar and bring to a boil. Reduce heat to a simmer and cook until thick and syrupy, about 25 to 30 minutes. Remove from heat and stir in liqueur and enough grenadine to reach a pretty orange color. Allow to cool but do not refrigerate.

- Peel all the white off the oranges. Slice oranges. Arrange attractively in large glass bowl. Refrigerate at least 2 hours.

- To serve, spoon cooled syrup over orange slices and arrange peel decoratively. Garnish with candied violets, or put 1 orange back together and set in center of bowl. Place remaining slices around the "whole" orange and proceed as above with syrup, peel and violets.

231

Grapes Juanita

A truly unusual way to serve grapes

- **Serves 8 to 10**

  2 pounds seedless green grapes, stems removed

  1 cup commercial sour cream

  ½ cup light brown sugar

  2 teaspoons grated orange rind

- Place grapes in large bowl. Mix sugar with sour cream and pour over grapes. Chill at least 2 hours.

- To serve, spoon into stemmed glasses and sprinkle with orange rind. Accompany with 2 Brown Edge Wafers per serving.

Pears Baked in Red Wine

Spiced wine perks up the pears.

- **Serves 6**

  6 unripened pears

  1 cup light brown sugar

  ¼ teaspoon cinnamon

  ½ teaspoon grated lemon rind

  ¼ cup red wine

  Crème frâiche or commercial sour cream (garnish)

- Preheat oven to 275 degrees.
- Peel pears, trying to leave stems intact. Place in baking dish.

- Mix brown sugar, cinnamon and lemon rind. Sprinkle over pears. Add wine. Cover and bake for 2 hours, basting occasionally. Uncover and continue baking for 1 hour, basting occasionally.

- To serve, place slightly warm pears in individual dessert dishes and spoon on sauce. Garnish with a dollop of crème frâiche or sour cream.

Pennsylvania German Strawberry Shortcake

To many, the only true strawberry shortcake is with a biscuit cake.

- **Serves 6 to 8**

  Biscuit

  3 cups sifted all-purpose flour

  4½ teaspoons baking powder

  1½ teaspoons salt

  5 tablespoons granulated sugar

  ¾ cup unsalted butter

  2 large eggs, lightly mixed

  ½ cup milk

  2 tablespoons butter, melted

- Preheat oven to 450 degrees.

- In a large bowl, sift together baking powder, flour, salt and sugar.

- Cut in butter until mixture is crumbly like cornmeal. Combine eggs with milk and stir quickly into dry ingredients.

- Turn out on floured board and gather into a soft ball. Roll out to ¾-inch thickness. Do not overwork dough. Using a cookie cutter or a water glass, cut out rounds. Place on ungreased cookie sheet, brush with melted butter and bake 15 minutes or until golden brown. Remove from oven and cool.

Filling and topping

3 pints strawberries

1 cup granulated sugar

½ pint whipping cream

1 teaspoon orange-flavored liqueur (optional)

- Pick over berries, hull and reserve prettiest berries for garnish. Slice remainder, mix with sugar and cook over low heat only until juice flows. Remove from heat and chill.

- Whip cream until stiff and flavor with liqueur, if desired. Chill.

- To serve, split each biscuit horizontally. Spoon strawberry mixture over bottom half; spread on a layer of whipped cream. Place other half of biscuit on top. Swirl on more cream and top with a beautiful berry. Pass remaining strawberry sauce.

Note: Although all the parts of this delicacy can be prepared in advance, it is best to assemble as close to serving time as possible so biscuits do not become soggy.

Variations: Instead of individual biscuits, dough can be baked in a 9-inch round cake pan. Split cooled "cake" and assemble as above. Try fresh peaches instead of strawberries for another summer treat.

Fresh Blueberry Pie

Although deceptively simple, the true taste of the fresh berries sparkles.

- Serves 8

1½ quarts fresh blueberries, picked over

1 cup water

2½ tablespoons cornstarch

1 cup granulated sugar

Dash of salt

Dash of cinnamon

1 9-inch pastry shell, baked and cooled

Whipped cream or vanilla ice cream

- In a non-aluminum saucepan, mix 1 pint of blueberries with 1 cup of water and cook down to produce 1 cup of "blueberry juice". Add sugar, salt, cinnamon and cornstarch which has been diluted with 2 tablespoons cool water. Cook mixture gently until thickened.

- Fill pie shell with ½ quart of berries. Pour hot mixture over fruit. Add remaining berries. Cool and serve with whipped cream or vanilla ice cream. A strawberry garnish will turn this glorious pie into a dessert for the glorious Fourth.

Tulips with Raspberries

A little bit of patience pays off with one of the most beautiful desserts in our collection.

- **Serves 6**

  6 tablespoons (3 ounces) unsalted butter, room temperature

  ¼ cup granulated sugar

  ½ cup sifted all-purpose flour

  ½ teaspoon vanilla extract

  3 large egg whites, room temperature

  2 pints fresh raspberries (or other fresh fruit)

  ½ pint heavy cream, whipped (garnish)

- Preheat oven to 425 degrees.

- Cut 6 7-inch rounds of baking parchment paper and butter lightly.

- In a bowl, cream butter with sugar until light and fluffy. Gradually add flour and vanilla and mix well.

- In a bowl, whip egg whites with salt until they hold peaks. Fold ¾ of the egg whites into butter mixture; discard remaining egg whites.

- Spread about 2 tablespoons of batter in an even layer on each paper round leaving ¼-inch border around edge. Place on baking sheets and bake 4 to 6 minutes or until edges are golden.

- Immediately invert each cookie, with the parchment attached, over a small bowl approximately 4 to 5 inches in diameter. Remove paper and pinch in sides to form a "flower". Let cool for 5 minutes and transfer to a rack. Store in an air-tight tin or freeze until needed.

- To serve, place "tulip" on a lace doily-covered dessert plate. Fill cup with berries or fruit and top with a swirl of whipped cream.

Apple Pie with Coconut Crumb Topping

Although good cold, this is splendid when served warm with vanilla ice cream.

- **Serves 6 to 8**

  Pie

  1½ tablespoons instant tapioca

  ½ cup granulated sugar

  ⅛ teaspoon salt

  ¾ teaspoon ground cinnamon

  ¼ teaspoon grated nutmeg

  5 cups Granny Smith apples, pared, cored and thinly sliced

  1 tablespoon fresh lemon juice

  1 9-inch unbaked pie shell

- Preheat oven to 400 degrees.

- In a large bowl, mix tapioca, sugar, salt, spices, apples and lemon juice. Turn into pie shell. Bake 35 minutes.

  Topping

  ⅓ cup dark brown sugar, packed

  ⅓ cup graham cracker crumbs

  4 tablespoons (2 ounces) unsalted butter, chilled and cut into bits

  ½ cup coconut flakes

- Mix sugar, crumbs, butter bits and coconut flakes to make a streusel topping. Spread over just-baked pie and return to oven. Bake 10 minutes longer.

French Raspberry Pie

Crisp pastry filled with a rich vanilla custard and topped with sweet-tart raspberries

- Serves 8

2 cups milk

1 vanilla bean

⅓ cup all-purpose flour

½ cup granulated sugar

¼ teaspoon salt

4 egg yolks

1 whole egg

¼ cup heavy cream, whipped

1 baked deep 9-inch pie shell

1½ pints fresh raspberries

1 6-ounce jar red currant jelly

- In a double boiler, scald the milk with the vanilla bean. Remove bean.

- In a bowl, mix flour, sugar and salt. Add a little of the scalded milk, stirring until smooth. Add to the remaining milk in the double boiler and cook, stirring, until thickened.

- In a bowl, beat together the egg yolks and egg. Add a little of the hot mixture, and stir until smooth. Add this to the remaining sauce and cook over simmering water, stirring constantly, until the

mixture has thickened. Strain the mixture into a large bowl. Cool. Carefully, but completely, fold in whipped cream. Turn into baked pie shell and cover with raspberries.

- Melt the jelly over very low heat, stirring, and spoon evenly over raspberries. Chill pie thoroughly before serving.

Fresh Coconut Pie

An unbelievably sensuous pie

- Serves 10 to 12

1 fresh coconut

¾ pound miniature marshmallows (12-ounce package)

3 cups heavy cream, whipped until thick

1 10-inch baked pie shell

- Puncture hole in soft spot at end of coconut. Strain milk into 3-quart pot. Put coconut in 325 degree oven for 15 minutes. Wrap in towel and crack outside shell with a hammer to release coconut meat. Peel brown skin from meat and wash and pat dry. Grate coarsely in a food processor. Measure out 2 cups and refrigerate remainder for another use.

- Add marshmallows to coconut milk and cook over low heat until marshmallows melt. Cool and refrigerate until mixture starts to jell (about 1 hour).

- With an electric mixer, beat jellied mixture well until light and frothy. Fold in whipped cream. Fold in 1 cup of coconut. Pile into pie shell and cover entire top of pie with the remaining cup of coconut. Refrigerate at least 6 hours before serving.

Kentucky Pecan Pie

The splash of bourbon enhances the Southern accent.

- Serves 8

1 9-inch unbaked pie shell

4 eggs, lightly beaten

1 cup granulated sugar

1 cup dark corn syrup

1 tablespoon all-purpose flour

½ teaspoon salt

3 tablespoons (1½ ounces) unsalted melted butter

1 cup pecans plus 8 pecan halves for decoration

1 teaspoon vanilla extract

1 teaspoon bourbon

1 tablespoon fresh lemon juice

½ pint heavy cream whipped with 2 tablespoons bourbon and 2 tablespoons sugar

- Preheat oven to 375 degrees.

- In a deep bowl, combine eggs, sugar, syrup, flour, salt, butter, vanilla, bourbon and pecans. Mix well. Add lemon juice and mix well.

- Pour mixture into pie shell and decorate with reserved pecan halves. Place on baking sheet and bake for 55 minutes or until knife inserted in center comes out clean. Remove from oven and chill before serving. Present each wedge with a dollop of "bourbon cream".

Pumpkin Mousse Pie

The light texture makes this an appropriate closing to a holiday meal.

• **Serves 8**

Crust
1½ cups graham cracker crumbs
⅓ cup unsalted butter, melted
2 tablespoons granulated sugar
½ teaspoon cinnamon
½ teaspoon ground ginger

• Preheat oven to 425 degrees.

• Combine all ingredients thoroughly and press into 10-inch pie pan.

• Bake for 10 minutes. Allow to cool.

Filling
½ cup granulated sugar
½ cup dark brown sugar
10 ounces cream cheese
2 extra large eggs
1 teaspoon vanilla extract
½ teaspoon fresh lemon juice
1 teaspoon grated orange rind
2 tablespoons amber rum
2 tablespoons light cream
1 teaspoon ground cinnamon
½ teaspoon ground ginger
½ teaspoon allspice
1 16-ounce can pumpkin purée
1 cup whipped cream flavored with rum (garnish)

• Preheat oven to 300 degrees.

• In a large bowl of an electric mixer, cream sugars and cream cheese. Add eggs and blend thoroughly. Incorporate vanilla, lemon juice, orange rind, rum, cream, spices and purée.

• Pour into pie shell and bake for approximately 1 hour. Center will be slightly soft when tested and will firm as it cools. Serve warm or cool with a dollop of whipped cream flavored with rum.

Chocolate Butternut Sauce

This sauce hardens and makes a crackling glaze on ice cream.

• **Makes about 2 cups**
1 cup (8 ounces) unsalted butter
12 ounces semi-sweet chocolate bits
1 teaspoon vanilla extract
1 cup coarsely chopped pecans or walnuts
1 quart vanilla ice cream

• In the top of a double boiler over low heat, melt butter and chocolate. Remove from heat and stir in vanilla and nuts.

• Serve while warm over ice cream.

Raspberry Bavarian Tart

Crunchy crust—sweet filling

- **Serves 10 to 12**

Pastry

6 tablespoons (3 ounces) unsalted butter

2½ tablespoons granulated sugar

⅓ teaspoon salt

1 egg yolk

1 cup all-purpose flour

⅓ cup finely chopped almonds

- Preheat oven to 400 degrees.
- Cream butter, sugar and salt until fluffy. Add egg yolk and beat thoroughly. Mix in flour and almonds.
- Press into a 10-inch tart pan with removable sides. Bake 12 minutes. Cool, then chill.

Filling

1 10-ounce package frozen raspberries, partially thawed and drained

2 egg whites

1 cup granulated sugar

1 tablespoon fresh lemon juice

¼ teaspoon vanilla extract

¼ teaspoon almond extract

⅛ teaspoon salt

1 cup heavy cream

Fresh raspberries for garnish

- In a large bowl of an electric mixer, beat raspberries, egg whites, sugar, lemon juice, vanilla and

almond extracts and salt until it thickens and expands in volume, up to 15 minutes.

- Whip cream until stiff and carefully fold into raspberry mixture. Pile into pastry and freeze at least 8 hours. To serve, remove pan sides and slide onto serving platter. Surround with fresh raspberries.

Tangy Lemon Custard Tart

Bake this in a tart tin and serve in wedges or use a 9-inch square pan and you have everyone's favorite lemon squares.

- **Serves 6 to 8**

Crust

½ cup (4 ounces) unsalted butter

½ cup confectioners sugar

1 cup plus 1 tablespoon all-purpose flour

- Preheat oven to 350 degrees.
- Cream together butter and confectioners sugar. Cut in all but 2 tablespoons of flour (reserve the 2 tablespoons for filling). Make soft dough and press into 9-inch round loose-bottom cake tin. Bake for 20 minutes or until lightly browned.

Filling

2 eggs

1 cup granulated sugar

Reserved 2 tablespoons all-purpose flour

½ teaspoon baking soda

Dash of salt

1 tablespoon grated lemon rind

4 tablespoons fresh lemon juice

Confectioners sugar

Candied lemon peel for garnish

- Beat 2 eggs with granulated sugar until creamy. Mix in flour, soda, salt, rind and lemon juice. (If custard is not tart enough, add a little more juice and rind.)

- Pour custard into crust and return to oven for 20 to 25 minutes until filling is golden brown. While still warm, sprinkle a thick "crust" of confectioners sugar over custard, then cut into wedges. Serve at room temperature. (If baking in square pan, proceed as above and cut into squares.)

Butter Crunch

Sprinkle on ice cream for super sundaes – or eat it like candy.

- Serves 8 to 10

1 cup (8 ounces) unsalted butter

1 cup granulated sugar

2 tablespoons water

1 tablespoon light corn syrup

¾ cup chopped pecans or walnuts

4 ounces semi-sweet chocolate bits

1 quart vanilla ice cream

- In a 3-quart enamel or non-stick saucepan, melt butter over low heat. Remove from heat and stir in sugar with a wooden spoon until well-blended. Return to low heat. Stir rapidly until it begins to bubble.

- Add water and corn syrup and mix well. Place candy thermometer into the mixture. Stir frequently over low heat until thermometer registers 300 degrees (hard crack). May take 25 to 30 minutes. Remove from heat at once and sprinkle nuts over surface and quickly mix in.

- Pour mixture onto lightly buttered cookie sheet and spread ¼-inch thick with a spatula. Cool to room temperature.

- Melt chocolate and spread half of it over crunch. Refrigerate until firm. Turn out of pan onto wax paper and spread reverse side with chocolate. When firm, chop or break into pieces and store in a tightly covered container in a cool place. Serve over ice cream or as a candy.

Chocolate Krinkle Cookie

A great addition to a holiday cookie tray

- Makes 50 to 60

  ½ cup corn oil

  4 squares unsweetened chocolate, melted

  2 cups sugar

  4 eggs

  2 teaspoons vanilla

  ½ teaspoon salt

  2 cups flour

  2 teaspoons baking powder

  1 cup confectioners sugar

- Preheat oven to 350 degrees.

- Mix together corn oil and melted chocolate. To this mixture add the sugar, eggs (one at a time), vanilla, salt, flour, and baking powder. Chill until hard.

- Roll into balls, the size of a quarter, or smaller. Roll balls in confectioners sugar.

- Bake on greased cookie sheet 10 to 15 minutes.

Grasshopper Finale

So easy — so good

- Serves 6

  6 large scoops rich vanilla ice cream

  1 ounce green crème de menthe

  1 ounce crème de cocao

- Combine all ingredients in blender or food processor, just until blended.

- Serve in chilled parfait glasses.

Thomas Eakins (American, 1844–1916), *Actress (Portrait of Suzanne Santje)*, 1903, oil on canvas, 79 3/4 x 59 7/8". Gift of Mrs. Thomas Eakins and Miss Mary Adeline Williams

Eakins's portraits of women reflect nothing of the conventional ideals of female beauty nor of the fashion of the day. His genius as a portraitist lies rather in his ability to perceive and then reveal the psychology of an individual. Here the large slashing strokes of red, orange, and light pink define the dress of the actress but suggest little of the form underneath. Her face is broadly painted in separate color areas with little attempt at detailing.

$\mathcal{A}$CKNOWLEDGMENTS

The Women's Committee of the Philadelphia Museum of Art is pleased to have sponsored *The Philadelphia Museum of Art Presents the Fine Art of Cooking*, a collection of favorite recipes. This book was made possible through the efforts of many people, all of whom deserve our special thanks. These volunteers, whose names appear on the following pages, graciously contributed and tested more than one thousand recipes and gave generously of their time and energy to produce and distribute this publication.

We are also particularly grateful to George H. Marcus, Conna Clark, and James A. Scott of the Museum's staff, who expertly guided the project from start to finish, and to Alice B. Lonsdorf and Mary H. Schnabel and their committee, who have enthusiastically marketed the book.

Finally, we sincerely thank those who purchase this cookbook, for all proceeds from its sale will be used to help support the Philadelphia Museum of Art, one of the area's outstanding cultural institutions. We hope you enjoy using this book as much as we have enjoyed preparing it.

Ann T. Hines, 1985 - 88

Martha H. Morris, 1988 -

Presidents

The Women's Committee of the

Philadelphia Museum of Art

Elizabeth T. Harbison

Beverly M. McLarnon

Chairmen

Cookbook Steering Committee

- Frances Abramson
Jane Acton
John Alberici
Sandy Alberici
Charlotte Ann Albertson
Mrs. Robert C. Allen
Maggie Alofsin
Elizabeth Anderson
Walter H. Annenberg
E. Ann Armour
Jean Athan
Agnes R. Baberick
Cheryl Ervin Baldi
Mrs. C. Wanton Balis
Jo Ballangee
Mrs. David M. Barclay
Mimi Barefield
Marylynn Bates
Nancy D. Baxter
Mrs. Thomas E. Beach
Joanne L. Beck
Julie Collins Berger
Marty Lou Berglund
- Mrs. William G. Berlinger, Jr.
Edna S. Beron
Louise Binswanger
Mrs. Harold E. Birr
Rita Bonaccorsi Bocher
Ingrid E. Bogel
Mrs. David M. Bogle
Mrs. Richard Boje
Mrs. John A. Bolz
Mrs. Richard C. Bond
Mrs. Willard S. Boothby, Jr.
Frances D. Borie
Betty Bradley
Suzanne S. Bralow
Emilie R. Brégy
Dotty Breskman
Diane Brigham
Edie Bristol
Alene G. Brodie
Doss Brown
- Elizabeth S. Browne
Stanhope S. Browne
Mrs. Johathan Brownell
Elizabeth S. Browning
Mrs. W. W. Keen Butcher
Noel Butcher-Pratt
Krista Butvydas
Gregory T. Campbell
Mrs. Richard R. Carr
Corinne Ceglia
Mrs. Henry M. Chance

Jane Perkins Claney
Margaret Strawbridge Clews
- Patricia S. Clutz
Mrs. Charles L. Coltman, III
Mrs. Tristram C. Colket, Jr.
Mrs. James D. Compton, III
Mrs. Robert W. Connor
Mrs. Randall E. Copeland
Marjorie Matthews Corr
Bernard Cowdery
Victoria Cox
Jacquelin W. Crebbs
Ruth C. Cross
Julie Dannenbaum
Joyce and Arleen Dascola
Betty Dashwood
Eileen Davis
Mrs. Thomas G. Davis
Maude de Schauensee
Mrs. Meyer de Schauensee
Mrs. Russell R. DeAlvarez
Charlotte Diamond
Martha Stott Diener
Eda Diskant
Edith R. Dixon
Alison Longstreth Dodge
Mrs. Douglas A. Donald
Cynthia W. Drayton
Mrs. Richard Drayton
- Diane Hirsch Drutt
William Drutt
Ira Dubner
Mrs. G. Martin Dudley
Mrs. Jonathan Dyer
Mrs. Antony Edgar
Marilyn Entwisle
Gina B. Erdreich
Adrienne M. Erickson
Marybeth G. Ervin
Mrs. John S. Estey
Benny Evans
Robert W. Failing
Mrs. F. W. E. Farr
Mrs. John J. Fawley
Harriet Coblentz Feinberg
Jill L. Feldman
Ruth Ferber
Pamela M. Fernley
Priscilla Ferrater-Mora
Eleanor Fitzsimmons
Patricia S. Flammer
Phyllys B. Fleming
Elainne Fox
- Alyne Freed

- Mrs. Jack M. Friedland
- Eleanore H. Gadsden
Mary E. Genovese
Mrs. Geyelin
Mary Gibbons
John P. Golaschevsky
Mrs. Warren P. Goldburgh
Mrs. Seymour Golden
Peppe Goldstein
Nancy Goldy
Mrs. James R. Gordon
Charlotte Graham
Robin Gray
Eleanor H. Gribbel
Estelle Gross
Judy Gushner
Dr. F. Otto Haas
Mrs. Francis J. Haines
Mrs. Frederick Halbach-Merz
George Hanagan
Mrs. Allen N. Hansen
Martha Ann Hanson
- Elizabeth T. Harbison
Renata K. Harbison
Robert J. Harbison, III
Beverly May Harding
Elisabeth W. Harpham
Bobbits Harrington
John A. Harrington
Rosanna C. Harris
Steve Haughney
Susie Hauser
Jean Ballard Hebard
Mrs. Benjamin H. Heckscher
Betty Heimark
Mrs. Harriet Heller
Eleanor Helm
Marjorie D. Helmetag
Irene Pauletta Hembarsky
Mrs. J. Welles Henderson
Benjamin A. Hewitt
Pat Hillerman
- Mrs. Robert S. Hines
Sean Hogan
Jane A. Holben
Mary W. Holben
- Cynthia Holstad
Diane V. Horn
Marilyn L. Horner
Ellen Gonchar Horowitz
Sandra Horrocks
Mrs. William S. Hyland
Mary Marshall Hynson
Anne Vilar Iskrant

Ellen S. Jacobowitz
Suzanne C. Jacobs
Mrs. Marylyn S. Jeffers
Mrs. Keith Jennings
- Mrs. Hugh Johnson
Mrs. Morgan R. Jones
Barbara Jordan
Suzanne Kalkstein
Virginia S. Kaufman
Jeannette Kean
Elnora Keiper
Mrs. James B. Kelley, 3rd
Jeanne Kemp
Debby Kendall
June Kerrick
Sara J. Ketcham
Allan Ketterer
Nancy G. Klavans
Helen Klein
Bette Jane Kleinbard
Norma Klorfine
Eugénie Knight
Theodore P. Koehle
Lucille Kolson
Jane Korman
Tamara Kraig
Bette Krieger
Charles A. Krieger
L'Auberge
La Collina
- Mrs. C. Marshall Lamason
Mrs. Robert C. Landon
Mrs. Isabel Lapayowker
Barbara J. G. Larmon
Ellen Lawrence
Virginia Leach
Mrs. John B. Leake
Thana C. Leary
- Mrs. H. Fairfax Leary, Jr.
Le Bec Fin
Le Bernardin
Eleanor L. Lemonick
Michelle D. Leonard
Joan L. LePard
Mrs. Stephen E. Levin
Mrs. Arnold Levine
Mrs. D. Christopher Le Vine
Mrs. Daniel C. Lewis
Lydia P. Lewis
Marilyn Lifson
Roslyn Littman
- Alice B. Lonsdorf
Mrs. Frank P. Louchheim
Mrs. Edward S. Madara, Jr.

243

Mandana
• Celeste Manley
Frances J. Markle
Virginia M. Marks
• Mrs. Charles N. Marshall
Mrs. E. Wellford Mason
Cynthia Rugart Matza
Melissa Mayer
Susan Mayer
Eleanor Mazer
Anne Elizabeth McCollum
Barbara McCray-Jackson
Cynthia M. McKeown
• Beverly M. McLarnon
W. Brian McLarnon
Helen L. McLean
Mona McLean
Nancy M. McNeil
Lawrie H. Merz
Diana Meskill
Joe and Lynne Mikuliak
Marianne T. Miller
Barbara A. Moll
• Mrs. Set Momjian
Karen Monaksy
Monte Carlo Living Room
Mrs. Edward A. Montgomery,
    Jr.
Ann Moore
Nancy Morris
• Mrs. I. Wistar Morris, III
Anne T. and W. R. Morton
Renée Moss
Sandra Moss
Melissa Moyer
Sandra Kittner Myers
Mrs. Ramon R. Naus
Mrs. Frank L. Newburger, III
Mrs. Francis B. Nimick, Jr.
Mary R. Norris
• Sallie Norris
Mrs. Bertram L. O'Neill
Jeanne C. O'Neill
Alma Oberst
Mrs. Marvin Orleans
Marjorie Orr
Osteria Romana
Mrs. William B. K. Parry
Ann Percy
Alberta C. Pew
Alice A. Pitt
Sandi Polillo
Mrs. Hobart D. Pollard
• Mrs. Harold W. Pote

Phyllis H. Powell
Mrs. Alfred W. Putnam
Alfred W. Putnam, Jr.
Mrs. Alfred W. Putnam, Jr.
Joan Putney
Charles A. Ragusa
Hannah Sullivan Randolph
Marie Louise Reese
Katharine Steele Renninger
Irene Resnick
Josephine Reus
Mary Jane Rhodes
Polly W. Riggs
Mrs. A. Addison Roberts
Mrs. Brooke Roberts
Mrs. Norman Robinson
Tara Glass Robinson
Suzanne Root
Mrs. Stanley W. Root, Jr.
Gail Rosenberg
Bernice Rosenbluth
Bernice Rosenfeld
Laura and Mark Rosenthal
Marguerite M. Rosner
Louise F. Rossmassler
Michael Roth
Mrs. Stephen Roth
Terry Hoff Roth
Marion M. Rothman
Mrs. Mark E. Rubenstein
Barbara K. Ryan
S. P. Q. R. Ristorante
Sally Sablosky
Jane Sanderson
Wilhelm L. Sandvik
• Mrs. Stuart T. Saunders, Jr.
Susan Scharf
Mrs. Victor Schlesinger
• Mary H. Schnabel
Neda Schwab
Gay Scott
Mrs. Isadore M. Scott
Peggy Lee Scott
Robert Montgomery Scott
Ruth Radbill Scott
Joanne Sebring
Mrs. Donald A. Semisch
Roger Sevy
Mrs. Warren Sewall
Darrel Sewell
Mitzi Shalit
Dr. Marion Shapiro
Mrs. Willoughby Sharp
Kathleen C. Sherrerd

Marla K. Shoemaker
Frann Sue Shore
Idell Shore
Mrs. Edward Sickles
Ellen Simon
Mrs. John Skinner, Jr.
Margaret Slack
Carole Smith
Mrs. G. Morrow Smith
Mrs. Estelle C. Snellenburg
Ruth E. Snyder
Mrs. Lewis S. Somers, 3rd
Thora Jacobson Sorgini
Louanne B. Spielman
Gail D. Sprout
Robin Koslo Stahl
Sally Stanley
Suzanne W. F. Steigerwalt
Mrs. Burton K. Stein
• Mimi Stein
Susannah Baker Story
Mark Stout
Mrs. George Strawbridge
Carl Brandon Strehlke
Sandra Sudofsky
Phyllis Sullivan
Mrs. William H. L. Sullivan
Cecelia Segawa Tannenbaum
Mrs. William Tasman
Helen Taws
Evelyn Taylor
Pleasants Tinkler
Emelie Tolley
Amy C. Torrey
Tony Umile
Mrs. J. Randolph Updyke
Mrs. A. Whitten Vogel
Helene Voron
Trudy Wagner
Mrs. E. Perot Walker
Pam Walker
Jan Wall
Anthony T. Wallace
Mrs. Elva Walsh
Mrs. Silas L. Warner
Jane Watkins
Christine Grove Weidmann
Catherine Weidner
Bernice Weinstock
Ilsa West
Anna Lamberton Whelpley
Frances White
Mrs. Harvey E. White
Mrs. Thomas R. White, Jr.

Mrs. Peter G. Wilds
Mrs. G. Price Wilson
Lisa M. Witomski
Mrs. Elias Wolf
Mary S. Wright
Anne W. Yarnall
Margaret Knight Yarnall
Charlotte Yudis
Mrs. Harry C. Zug

• Cookbook Committee

244

$\mathcal{I}$NDEX

W

Y

Z

The Philadelphia Museum of Art
presents *The Fine Art of Cooking*
When ordering, please use attached
forms and send $21.95 plus $3.00 for
shipping and handling per copy,
payable to: "Women's Committee —
PMA Cookbook," and mail to:

Cookbook
Philadelphia Museum of Art
P. O. Box 7646
Philadelphia, PA 19101-7646

(Pennsylvania residents add $1.32
sales tax, per copy)

Order One for a Friend!

Proceeds from the sale of the cookbook will
benefit the Philadelphia Museum of Art.

The Fine Art of Cooking

Philadelphia Museum of Art, P. O. Box 7646, Philadelphia, PA 19101-7646

Please send _____ copies of *The Fine Art of Cooking* at $21.95 per copy, plus $3.00 shipping and handling per copy. (Pennsylvania residents add $1.32 sales tax, per copy.)

Or, charge to: ____Visa ____ MasterCard Account Number _____

Expiration date: _____ Signature of Cardholder: _____

Enclosed is a check for $ _____ payable to: "Women's Committee — PMA Cookbook"

Name _____

Address _____

City/State/Zip _____

Proceeds from the sale of this cookbook will benefit the Philadelphia Museum of Art.

The Fine Art of Cooking

Philadelphia Museum of Art, P. O. Box 7646, Philadelphia, PA 19101-7646

Please send_____ copies of *The Fine Art of Cooking* at $21.95 per copy, plus $3.00 shipping and handling per copy. (Pennsylvania residents add $1.32 sales tax, per copy.)

Or, charge to: ____Visa _____ MasterCard Account Number _____

Expiration date: _____ Signature of Cardholder: _____

Enclosed is a check for $ _____ payable to: "Women's Committee — PMA Cookbook"

Name _____

Address _____

City/State/Zip _____

Proceeds from the sale of this cookbook will benefit the Philadelphia Museum of Art.

GUEST PASS
One free general admission
Philadelphia Museum of Art
The Fine Art of Cooking

Name _____

Address _____

City _____ State _____ Zip _____

GUEST PASS
One free general admission
Philadelphia Museum of Art
The Fine Art of Cooking

Name _____

Address _____

City _____ State _____ Zip _____